"LAST WORDS"
WARNING!

The Beginners Guide to
End-Times Eschatology

Robert L. *"Larry"* Pratt

PRESS

"LAST WORDS" WARNING!
The Beginners Guide to End-Times Eschatology
by Robert L. *"Larry"* Pratt

Printed in the United States of America

ISBN 9781628390834

Requests for information or to book a speaking engagement should be addressed to:
Berean Seminar Ministries
P.O. Box 1536, Lancaster, CA 93539-1536
www.bereanseminarministries.com

Published in the United States of American by Xulon Press, Maitland, Florida.

www.xulonpress.com

Special thanks to my entire family (especially my wife and best friend, Cindy) who have supported me in this ministry and are co-laborers with me in sharing the saving message of our Lord and Savior Jesus Christ!

To Him be all glory, honor, and praise!

Dedicated to my brother Cary, Mom, and Dad. I miss you and look forward to His shout, the voice of the archangel, and the trumpet of God.

Also dedicated to those who have suffered for our Lord and Savior, Jesus Christ, and to all the saints who will enter the 70th Week of Daniel. "Let no one in any way deceive you"(II Thessalonians 2:3). When you see the sign in the sun, moon, and stars look up—for your redemption is drawing near!

CONTENTS

Acknowledgements vii
Introduction: *The Journey*. . . . . *ix*
Part I: *Setting the Foundation*
1 What is eschatology? 17
2 Why study eschatology? 31
3 What is systematic theology?. 43
Part II: *The Plumb Line*
4 How do I study God's Word?. 61
Part III: *Further Influences on Eschatology*
5 What are biblical covenants? 77
6 What are dispensations?. 94
7 What are the Feasts of Leviticus 23? 109
Part IV: *Critical Answers and Discovery*
8 The "Who, What, When, Where, Why, and How?"
of the Rapture 129
Section 1 Who?. 132
Section 2 What? 162
Section 3 When? 188
Section 4 Where? 195
Section 5 Why?. 204
Section 6 How?. 213
Part V: *Key Elements and Self-Examination*
9 The Day of the Lord's Wrath 223
10 Summary-Are you ready? 229
Endnotes. 239
About the Author 245

ACKNOWLEDGEMENTS

F irst and foremost, I give thanks to my Lord and Savior Jesus Christ. He has given me so, so much. He has provided my every need throughout my entire life. He called me out of darkness and forgave my past, present, and future sins. He has always been there for me—even when I distanced myself from Him. He promises to be with me to the end of the age, and He will one day call me home. What amazing, overwhelming love, grace, and mercy! I look forward to His appearing and thank Him for placing a desire in my heart to write a book about His return. I pray that it will honor Him. Thank you Lord for giving us your precious Word!

Thank you Cindy, my incredible wife. Writing a book is no trivial matter. Research and rewrites take time away from family. You have helped along the way and supported my every effort, whether it be career advancement or making the decision to retire, write a book, and develop a ministry. Nobody has done more for me than you apart from my Lord. He has used you to motivate, encourage, love, assist in research, and support my every passion. This book would not be possible without your unselfish love and sacrifice. I love you!

Thank you Beth Billings for editing this work and your patient endurance with me. You have provided the clear expression of my passion.

Thank you to all my great pastors and teachers. Many of you hold a different position on the timing of the Rapture than I, but you are the ones who have taught me the importance of studying God's Word. You provided the tools and example, and you will forever be my heroes.

Thank you Garo Panossian for designing the graphics and your unending support.

Thank you to Mike, Marlo, Nancy, Sheila, Bruce, and Dale for weekly encouragement.

Thank you Daniel, T.C., Melanie, Jesse, Stephanie, and Amanda. My quiver and heart are full! Thank you for the twelve incredible grandchildren!

Thank you Pastor Allen Hadidian. You are a mentor to me. You have taught me a great deal, and your endorsement of this work means so much.

Thank you Alan Kurschner for always answering my questions and for being a solid student of God's Word. What a great example you are. You have blessed me with your endorsement.

Thank you to all the folks at Xulon Press for making this possible!

INTRODUCTION: THE JOURNEY

I t is New Years Day, January 1, 2012. A beautiful day in the Antelope Valley, located in the High Desert of Southern California. I am taking in the magnificent view from a hillside as I walk our nine-year-old Boxer dog, Abby. What a wonderful example she is of how one can persevere and remain passionate about things loved, regardless of age. She is focused and full of zeal as she takes in every sight, sound, and smell.

The sky is crystal clear, and the sun's warmth feels soothing. I am contemplating the many blessings in my life and how wonderful the last few days have been. Everyone in our family is healthy. (My wife Cindy and I have six grown children and twelve grandchildren, so that is a blessing in itself.)

Yesterday I spent the morning at a prophecy conference with Cindy and my oldest son, Daniel. That same evening (New Year's Eve), I was doing one of my favorite things, playing music with my friends in our band, Flashback. Daniel (a gifted musician) controlled the soundboard and sat in on a few tunes.

I received a text from our youngest son, Jesse, announcing that he had just been promoted to the Head Pro position at an exclusive golf course where he works, and just days earlier, our oldest daughter, Melanie, had sent a picture of her left hand, displaying a beautiful engagement ring on the third finger that her fiancé had just given her for Christmas. Our youngest daughter, Amanda, is active in her church, and God is providing for our middle son, Thomas ("T.C."), while he is out of work—even blessing him with a new Bible!

Cindy stayed home from work during the Christmas holiday and enjoyed a yearly tradition of decorating gingerbread houses with our grandchildren. She also spent quality time babysitting our newest grandbaby, belonging to our middle daughter, Stephanie. I am nearing the conclusion of a successful career and working on entering full-time ministry. Life is good.

But this is 2012—a year when the economy is at one of its lowest points in history. The country's debt is out of control; many in America have lost jobs, can't find work, and are losing homes; sickness and unemployment are on the rise; children are homeless; worldwide famine, wars, earthquakes, and floods are ever present; there is the constant threat and paranoia over terrorism; and the persecution of the Church is increasing. This is the year that some even say the world will come to an end due to an ancient calendar running out of days and years!

"How could life *possibly* be good?!"

It is good because the Lord *says* it is good. Psalm 118: 24 states, "This is the day which the Lord has made; Let us rejoice and be glad in it." His Word also tells us to "rejoice always, and to be thankful for everything"(Philippians 4:4-6).

How many times have you heard someone say "one day at a time"? Today is good for me, but I must admit that not every day is. There are days when I wonder and worry about many things. This is sin. Jesus said, "So do not worry about tomorrow; for tomorrow will care for itself. Each day has enough trouble of its own" (Matthew 6:34).

Our pastor says that we are either entering a trial, in it, or coming out of it. That is just the way life is. God's Word tells us that, "In the world you have tribulation" (John 16:33). What always causes me to rejoice amidst tribulation is the "blessed hope" to come and the knowledge and assurance that our Lord will never leave us nor forsake us no matter what our circumstance might be. The Apostle Paul said, "...If God is for us, who is against us?" (Romans 8:31b)—the point being, nobody is more powerful than our God, and therefore we will emerge victorious.

While I do not worry about tomorrow, I need not be ignorant regarding those things the Lord would have us understand, including the great deal of information that He has given us in His Word regarding His sure return.

There are many books on the subject of our Lord's return, His coming. There are periodicals, television ministries on the subject, movies, plays, and songs. The last thing we need is another book! Yet today, on January 1, 2012, after much prayer, counseling with friends, church leaders, and family—as well as just observing how the Lord has been orchestrating my life lately—I have committed to writing this book. This must seem contradictory because I've just stated that we have already been flooded with material about this topic, but this book is unlike the myriad of books that present an author's dogmatic view about the subject. This is a journey—an opportunity for every believer to examine the Scriptures and arrive at truth about the Lord's return.

This book also differs from others in that it serves as a warning for believers to heed the words that Jesus spoke of regarding the end-times. These warnings are considered "last words" warnings because they are some of Jesus' last words to His disciples during His earthly ministry, and ultimately to that generation which will experience the end-times. In what is referred to as the "Olivet Discourse" (Matthew 24:24-25), Jesus speaks to His disciples on the Mount of Olives regarding the events that must take place prior to His return. He explains in Matthew 24:24-25, "For false Christs and false prophets will arise and will show great signs and wonders, so as to *mislead*, if possible, even the elect. *Behold, I have told you in advance.*" [Emphasis mine.]

There is no excuse for the believer. Jesus has given us the truth *in advance* regarding His return! You may think you know the truth and may even be able to articulate some basic terms regarding end-times prophecy, but can you truly defend the truth as taught in the Bible? How tragic it would be for the Church to be caught unaware or uninformed. Will we be raptured away before the trouble of the tribulation that Jesus spoke of begins? Will you be ready? This book will challenge you to arrive at a clear, defensible conviction.

In this book, you will discover clear teaching on what is referred to as the 70th Week of Daniel (often erroneously referred to as the "tribulation" period). The 70th Week of Daniel is a phrase which comes from the book of Daniel in chapter nine, verses 24-27 and refers to the final seven-year period of human history and end-times prophecy.

My journey and passion for the study of God's Word and these prophetic things, which are yet to come, began many years ago. I took numerous courses that churches offered on subjects like hermeneutics [the art and science of biblical interpretation], eschatology [literally, "last words" or discourse; prophesy], evangelism, and more.

As a layperson, I listened to great teachers and men of faith as they carefully taught exegetically [verse by verse] through the Bible. They followed the pattern of Nehemiah 8:8 and encouraged us to study the Scriptures for ourselves. We were to be like the "Bereans" of Acts 17:11, who received the Word with great eagerness and examined the Scriptures daily to see if what the Apostle Paul had said was true.

The Bereans were the inhabitants of Berea (then part of Macedonia); today it would be in northern Greece. This was the place where Paul and Silas traveled after departing Thessalonica during Paul's second missionary journey. After being run out of Thessalonica, Paul, Timothy, and Silas went to Berea and preached the Gospel and many believed—Jews and Greeks alike. Some back in Thessalonica believed as well, and they eventually became a model church; they struggled, however, with the subject of the Lord's return. Sound familiar?

One of the differences between the church at Thessalonica and our great seminaries and churches in the West is the fact that the church at Thessalonica was just over three-weeks-old when Paul and his companions departed for Berea (Acts 17:2). They were under persecution and yet became a model church with a reputation reaching across all of Macedonia and Achaia (I Thessalonians 1:7-8). That is remarkable. They had young leaders with a young congregation of believers. No seminary education, no real experience, but great faith and reception to God's Word.

When I first became a believer, I was fascinated with the original language, translations, how we got our English Bible, the many resource materials available, and the fact that every Bible-believing Christian is capable of studying, understanding, and applying the Word of God to his or her life.

II Timothy 2:15 focuses on the study and rightly dividing of God's Word; meaning to accurately handle it. The psalmist tells us to treasure God's Word in our hearts so that we might not sin against Him (Psalm 119:11). The power of God's Word is incredible. It is the sum of God's Word that we must consider (Psalm 119:160). II Timothy 3:16 and II Peter 1:21 tell us that it really is God's Word and not a result of man.

I grabbed all the tools to study and when something did not sound right, I prayed about it and dug into the Scriptures. I could not reconcile a number of expositions on the subject and the timing of our Lord's return, and so, like a Berean, I began questioning.

The verses supporting popular, well-held positions seemed fragmented and confusing. There were those individuals who would say, "Well, it doesn't really matter because it will all pan out in the end." But this is God's Word, His love letter to us. These are His instructions, His exhortations, and vehicle for equipping the saints for every good work. Therefore, it must be clear and unambiguous at every level.

The more I prayed and studied, the more I was convinced that there were some errors with the interpretations. I read great contemporary views on the subject along with historical views and became convinced of a position, which will be highlighted in this book. I am not dogmatic on the view, yet must admit that once convinced of its truth, the entire Word of God became incredibly cohesive. It was as if a light was turned on and what had previously confused me became clear. My understanding went from black and white to full color. Through prayer and diligent study, God's Holy Spirit unveiled truth to me that I had never known before.

Before you get concerned, I must tell you that you will not find a specific hour or day predicting the Lord's return in this book. The Scriptures are clear. Jesus, speaking to His disciples on the subject of His return, said in Matthew 24:36, "But of that day and hour no one knows, not even the angels of heaven nor the Son, but the Father alone."

We are, however, commanded to watch, pray, be on the alert, sober, vigilant, and ready. We are exhorted to not be uninformed or ignorant regarding His return and about those who have gone before us, as those who have no hope (I Thessalonians 4:13). His return is our "blessed hope"!

The goal of this book is to tie the Scriptures about His return together in such a way that every believer can easily understand them and their clear message to the Church. While it's not meant to be scholarly, it tackles the complex study of eschatology ["last words" and prophecy] and systematic theology [major biblical themes systemized and developed by man as a means to understand the Bible and God's dealing with man throughout history] from a lay minister's perspective.

I will provide top-level information on the many views regarding the portion of eschatology that deals with our Lord Jesus Christ's return and ample support for the conclusions herein. I ask a question in each chapter and then attempt to answer it while providing the process for the conclusions presented.

Bottom Line Up Front, or BLUF as they say in military circles: this book presents a studied opinion on the subject of eschatology, but encourages the reader to search the Scriptures like a Berean and come to one's own conclusion. If at the end of the day we disagree, we still will have accomplished something together and that is the study of God's Word, which can never be a bad thing. I am always open to hearing the truth and not so proud as to not consider opposing viewpoints, so we would love to hear from anyone who would like to engage in further discussions about eschatology after reading this book.

I pray that you will be blessed and encouraged to dive even deeper into the wonderful truths of God's unchanging, infallible, and inerrant Word.

PART I
SETTING THE FOUNDATION

1
WHAT IS ESCHATOLOGY?

Since writing the introduction, another year has gone by. I retired on December 29, 2012, and have started working the full-time ministry I felt the Lord has led me to. It is called "Berean Seminar Ministries" and you can look us up at BereanSeminarMinistries.com. You may be interested in joining us at one of our seminars, so I would encourage you to keep an eye on the website for upcoming events.

Observing another beautiful morning in the Antelope Valley, it is now January 3, 2013, and I am back at writing this book with a goal of completing it before another year begins. I started the day in prayer while walking Abby, my Boxer, who is now 10-years-old. She still loves the walks and is every bit as passionate as she was a year ago, but is experiencing some effects of aging.

As we walked, my mind contemplated this first chapter. It could be as easy as giving a textbook definition of eschatology, or it could be as complicated as giving a full dissertation on the subject. What keeps me centered, however, is the basic, theological meaning of eschatology:

Last words.

Derived from the Greek combination of *éschato(s)*; meaning *last,* and *logos*; meaning *words,* we get "last words" or "last discourse". Some define it as end-times prophecy, death, judgment, or overall final things. Some say the end of the world. The real, literal translation *meaning,* however, is "last words".

As laypeople, we tend to think of "last words" differently than theologians do. We think of last will and testament or picture a person dying in someone's arms sharing a last thought. "Last words" makes us think about our own destiny or the legacy we might want to leave behind. It also causes us to take pause and consider what our own "last words" will be. If given the chance, wouldn't we want to say something of great importance to those we love and leave behind?

I must admit that when I first thought of "last words", I immediately thought of what that would mean to me. As I get older, "last words" mean a lot. I have seen many of my friends and relatives pass on. Just over the past two months, three friends have died. I have been blessed to live on this planet for over 62 years and often wonder where the time went.

"Last words", however, is not about where the time went, but rather about what is to come.

Theologians have combed through the Scriptures to understand the true, biblical meaning of eschatology and how "last words" reveal future things about the Lord's return as it pertains to prophetic events fulfilled and yet to be fulfilled.

Is prophecy important? Absolutely it is! Over one-fourth of the Bible is prophetic, and the book of Daniel tells us that in the last days, knowledge will increase. I believe we are seeing this today. I believe that Scripture—especially prophecy—is becoming clearer than ever before.

Eschatology covers a cohesive study of all prophetic Scripture from beginning to end. It addresses all of the Old and New Testament books. If studies are limited to one or two books alone, the proper interpretation of prophecy will be missed.

Because Jesus Christ is alive and gives us the gift of eternal life, eschatology, or "last words", does not seem appropriate. He is a living Savior and Lord. He is the first fruit of the resurrection. Jesus' words are not just "last words", but eternal words. They are timeless and ever relevant. I Peter 1:25 states: "But the word of the Lord endures forever and this is the word which was preached to you."

But before we delve further into the meaning, I believe it is important to pause briefly to address the very nature of the subject and the passionate debates surrounding it.

Eschatology is often a controversial subject among theologians, pastors, congregations, and seminaries. It need not be controversial or divisive, but often is. Some go as far as to accuse those who hold opposing views of committing heresy. The word "heresy" in the New Testament means *"choice, opinion, or sentiment"*. Paul refers to an accusation of heresy he received by the religious leaders of his day in Acts 24:14. Paul accused some in the Corinthian church of heresy in I Corinthians 11:19.

When one's opinion is so strong and self-willed that he or she no longer submits to the *truth of God's Word*, it can lead to factions and cause division and serious damage to the body of Christ; as noted in Galations 5:20, this is not good. The most damaging are those opinions/heresies that are contrary to what the Gospel teaches and are coupled with false teaching, "denying the Master who bought them" (II Peter 2:1). Peter gives a very strong warning to such false teachers. Differing opinions on the timing of the Rapture, however, do not fall into the category of false teaching.

Those who teach opposing views on the subject but still hold to the truth regarding Jesus Christ as Lord and Savior, therefore leading individuals to come to salvation through trusting in Jesus Christ alone, are not false teachers. Having said that, there is but one true interpretation of Scripture, and yet many great men of faith have unintentionally misinterpreted portions throughout history. For that reason, this book attempts to present all positions, however with the author's emphasis on one.

End-times as related to Scripture are the days that culminate all human history with the return of our Lord and Savior Jesus Christ—the climax of the story that the Bible reveals from the beginning to the end. It is all about Jesus. It is the summation of all systematic theology. It is when all humanity vectors toward that final collision course with our Creator God.

Jesus, speaking to His disciples, in what we refer to as the "Great Commission" said, "...All authority has been given to Me in heaven and on earth. Go therefore and *make disciples of all the nations*, baptizing them in the name of the Father and the Son and the Holy Spirit, teaching them to observe all that I commanded you; and lo, I am with you always, even to the *end of the age*." (Matthew 28:18-20)

[Emphasis mine.] The most important point is not that believers and theologians have opinions that differ; rather, it is what they *do* with these opinions that matter. We are called to make disciples and teach *all* that Jesus has commanded us.

Along with this commandment, Jesus gives us a promise, which is consistent throughout Scripture: He promises to be with us every step of the way, even to the end of the age. The Creator of the universe, the all-powerful, all-knowing God is going to be with us as we continue in His work and fulfill the purpose He has for our lives. I don't know about you, but that excites me! I always feel His presence when I am doing His will and carrying out this commandment. I am energized and so fulfilled when sharing His truth with others. We have the divinely appointed privilege of explaining to citizens of earth how to become citizens of heaven and the new earth to come. What greater joy could there be than to be used by the Lord to touch a life for eternity? We are invited by our Sovereign God to participate by planting the seeds of the Gospel! How exciting!

Quite a while ago when I was fairly young, I remember receiving a call from my grandmother-in-law. She was desperate as she shared how her daughter (my mother-in-law at the time) had passed out and needed emergency help. We were over 20 miles away. We quickly got in our car and rushed to the house. By the time we arrived, the paramedics were taking her to the ambulance and then to the hospital. She was unconscious and on life support. We prayed, but unfortunately she did not recover. I distinctly remember how surprised we were and the strong sense of not being sure of her destination. I was faced with the reality that life is but a vapor, a mere breath. I felt the hurt and shame. We do hope to see her again.

I knew about Christ, attended a "mega-church", but was not living the Christian life. That event and the subsequent loss of others impacted my life. Just prior to my 30th birthday, I became a believer. I wanted to share my newfound faith with any and everyone within my daily sphere of influence, and yet I knew that it was not me, but the Holy Spirit who would touch their hearts and draw them to salvation. Nobody comes to faith in Jesus Christ apart from the calling of the Father. Those who come to faith are the elect because they have been chosen and called by the Father. I was just planting seeds.

I had the whole election and pre-destination debate going on in my head and heart, yet I knew that salvation comes from faith, and that faith comes from hearing the Word. I also knew that He is the author and finisher of our faith, and that He will increase our faith as we call upon Him. I needed to share the Word and pray that the Lord would bring them to salvation. After all, it is His desire that no person perish.

I have not lived a perfect life. Far from it. I do however have a desire to follow the Lord, and if He can use me to further His Kingdom and bring Glory to Him, then I want to be a part of that while I still have breath. I cannot begin to tell you of the pain and sorrow over my many failures, even after coming to Christ, but I can tell you He still loves me and has purpose for my life. Let this be a hope and encouragement for you as well. You may have failed over and over again, but don't give up. God loves you and will complete His good work in your life. Just let Him.

By the way, trusting involves repentance [change of mind] regarding one's sinful past and turning away from it to follow Christ. If you have, there should be fruitful evidence of your true conversion. The fruit is the caboose, not the locomotive. You cannot produce fruit on your own; a sincere commitment to invite Jesus Christ to forgive, rule, and reign in your life is required. You cannot save yourself or get to heaven by good works (Ephesians 2:8-10).

We are all sinners, and we even sin from time-to-time after coming to Christ, but sin should not dominate our lives. I will share specifically how one receives the free gift of salvation in the last chapter. If you do not know for sure that you are going to heaven when you die, I would encourage you to go to the last chapter [Summary-Are You Ready?] of this book right now. Apart from salvation, the Scriptures cannot be clearly understood.

Paul, speaking to the church at Philippi in Philippians 1:21-24 said it this way, "For to me to live is Christ and to die is gain. But *if I am* to live on in the flesh, this *will mean* fruitful labor for me; and I do not know which to choose. But I am hard-pressed from both *directions*, having the desire to depart and be with Christ, for *that* is very much better; yet to remain on in the flesh is more necessary for your sake." Paul longed to be with His Lord, but realized the importance of fulfilling the Great Commission he was called to do while still living out his life.

He also referred to himself as the "chief of sinners." Paul struggled with the same issues we do. You can read about this in Romans chapter seven. Even though he would sin and struggle, he knew God had a purpose and plan for his life, and what God starts, He finishes (Philippians 1:6). We should all have this perspective. In other words, we should long to be with Christ in heaven, which is far better than the struggles of this life, but while we wait, we should be busy about the work and ministry He has called us to.

I was privileged to share with my older brother, father, and mother. All had accepted Christ. They are in the presence of our Lord today, and I know that one day I will see them again. Do you have a friend, relative, or next of kin with whom you need to share the Gospel? Let me encourage you to take that step of boldness and count on our Lord's promise that He will be with you in that very moment—and every moment you share—even until the end of the age. We have no guarantee that any of us will be here tomorrow, but for those who do enter the 70th week of Daniel, a clear understanding of that period of time is essential.

When it comes to end-times, some believe it could happen any moment. Some seem to want to hang out peering into the stars of heaven in their rapture-ready clothing waiting for the skies to open and the trumpet to sound. This belief is often referred to as "imminence", or any moment "rapture". Does this view align with Scripture? We will deal with the answer to this question as the book unfolds.

Eschatology not only deals with future things and the Lord's return as it pertains to prophetic events fulfilled and yet to be fulfilled, but *all* of Scripture as a cohesive whole from beginning to end.

When addressing eschatology, the word *"chiliasm"*[1] is sometimes used. It is referencing the millennium [one thousand years] kingdom; yet future. This period of a thousand years is most important. It is spoken of more than any other aspect regarding future events. The word millennium comes from two Latin words, *milli,* meaning one thousand and *annum*, meaning years.

It is used six times alone in Revelation chapter 20. It is a fulfillment of covenants, such as the Abrahamic Covenant in Genesis 12, where he is promised to bless many nations. It is the fulfillment of the Palestinian Covenant in Deuteronomy 30:1-10, where occupation and restoration are promised to Israel. It is the fulfillment of the Davidic Covenant, where Israel receives forgiveness and is saved, and where its true Messiah returns to rule and reign (II Samuel 7:8-16). It is a literal, one thousand year period and should never be allegorized. It is not a figure or abstract in Revelation 20. It is literal.

There are three predominate views on the millennium kingdom. The first is the "pre-millennialism" view. There are two views within pre-millennialism: dispensational pre-millennialism and historical pre-millennialism. Neither in their traditional description is wholly accurate, but the basic tenet is correct. This view simply states that Christ will return before the thousand-year reign or earthly kingdom is established. I would agree with that. I would also agree that the Church will be raptured prior to the Day of the Lord's wrath.

Where you place the Lord's wrath is essential in understanding the timing of the Rapture. The first, dispensational pre-millennialism states that Christ will return for His Church just prior to the beginning of the 70th week of Daniel, commonly, *but erroneously* referred to as the *tribulation* seven-year period. This position states that the entire seven-year period is referred to as the Lord's wrath against ungodly men who have not received Jesus Christ as Lord and Savior. This is somewhat forced due to man-made "dispensations".

The word dispensation does appear in Scripture and means "economy". Theologians created dispensations as a means to define how God has dealt with—and continues to deal with—mankind throughout specific periods of human history. I will do a chapter on this, so for now, we are simply stating that this view (dispensationalism) forces the theologian to separate Israel and the Church with regard to the events of the end-times, not permitting a concurrent dispensation.

At the conclusion of the seven-year period, there is a great battle. Jesus sets up His throne in the Holy City (the New Jerusalem) and rules the nations for one thousand years. Satan is bound during this thousand-year period and then loosed at the end of it for a final battle with the saints and Jesus Christ, which ends in judgment and the eternal state. Those who hold this view also believe the Rapture occurs pre-tribulation, or before the seven-year period they hold to be the Tribulation. Figure 1 below shows the progression/timeline of this most popular position, focusing primarily on the 70th Week of Daniel and what occurs prior to the millennial reign of Christ.

Note: The abbreviation "CA" refers to the Church Age, followed by a vertical line depicting where each position believes the Church Age ends.

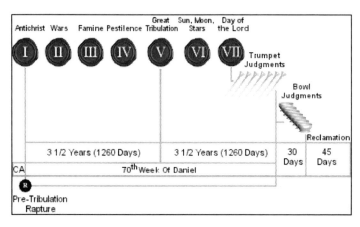

Figure 1: Dispensational Pre-Millennial Depiction

The historical pre-millennialism view, however, states that Christ will return just before the millennium, after the apostasy and the Great Tribulation. Those who hold this position believe that the falling away, defection, or the apostasy—is what ushers in the seven-year tribulation period, after which the Lord's wrath occurs and Jesus sets up His throne in the Holy City (the New Jerusalem) to rule the nations for one thousand years. Satan is bound during this thousand-year period and then loosed at the end of it for a final battle with the saints and Jesus Christ, which ends with judgment and the eternal state. This view mostly aligns with "mid-tribulation", meaning the Rapture would occur at the halfway point into the seven-year period, or 3 1/2 years, 1,260 days. It also aligns even closer with the "post-tribulation" view where the Church is not raptured until the end of the seven-year period and just prior to the millennial reign of Christ on earth.

Figure 2 below depicts the progression/timeline of what is often referred to as historical pre-millennialism, post-tribulation representing the traditional historical.

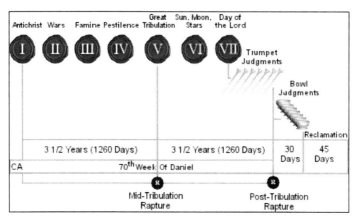

Figure 2: Often referred to as "Historical Pre-Millennialism" Depiction

It is my personal belief that there is some truth to both of the pre-millennialism positions previously noted. You will learn a bit more regarding dispensations later in the book, but the key element is where you place the Day of the Lord and the Day of the Lord's wrath. Both positions believe in a literal thousand-year earthly reign of Christ from the New Jerusalem. Both believe there is a seven-year period, often erroneously referred to as the Tribulation period. More accurately, it would be the 70th week of Daniel, but still seven years in duration.

I do, however, believe a more biblically accurate and true historical view places the Rapture not just prior to the 70th week of Daniel, not at the mid-point (just before the Great Tribulation), and not at the end of the seven-year period. My view is consistent with what has recently been referred to as the "pre-wrath"[2] position. That is to say, I hold to the belief that the Rapture or *harpazó* [caught up] takes place *just prior to the Lord's wrath*, which is after the Great Tribulation begins—not directly after, or what even some are calling a modified "mid-tribulation" view—but between the sixth and seventh seal of Revelation, with the seventh seal initiating the Day of the Lord and containing the trumpet and bowl judgments. See Figure 3.

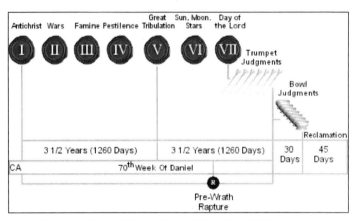

Figure 3: Pre-Millenialism, "Pre-Wrath" Depiction

Figure 3 may be a little confusing. The Church was born on the Day of Pentecost (Acts chapter two), when the pouring out of the Holy Spirit occurred and Peter preached to the gathered multitudes. During his powerful sermon, Peter quoted Joel 2:28-32. This was the start of the Church Age, or "Age of Grace", with a direct tie to the coming of the Lord and the sequence of events that will occur prior to His return as outlined in Joel 2:28-32.

A careful, normal reading of Acts chapter two will show consistency with the sixth seal of Revelation, as well as with the Olivet Discourse passage in Matthew 24. It is normally depicted as separate and absolutely distinct from the 70th week of Daniel or the Tribulation period. In Figure 3 above, however, the block where the Church Age is depicted is intended to illustrate the fact that the Church did have a distinct beginning and period/economy [dispensation], and that this age *does continue* into the future 70th week of Daniel until the timing of the Lord's appearing. Those of you who would like to have a very comprehensive chart illustrating the pre-wrath position can obtain one from ThePreWrathChart.com[3]. Allen Hadidian (author of *ThePreWrathChart*) has developed this very detailed chart describing the events of the 70th Week of Daniel.

Figure 4 illustrates a comparison of the major views with respect to the timing of the Rapture.

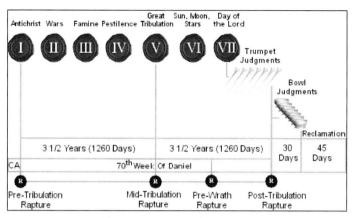

Figure 4: Comparison View

As we go into detail regarding the specific positions in chapter eight and nine, clear timelines will emerge. We should also note that the seventh seal contains the seven trumpet judgments, and the seventh trumpet contains the seven bowl judgments. These are all part of the Day of the Lord's wrath, and the bowl judgments continue into the 30 additional 1,290 days of Daniel 12:12.

It's okay if you need to brush up on the seals, trumpets, and bowl judgments—you can take a peek ahead into chapter 8, if you wish! A careful study of Matthew 24, Revelation 6, I Thessalonians 4 & 5, II Thessalonians 2, as well as Old Testament books like Isaiah, Joel, Amos, and Zephaniah will also unravel the timeline above.

What I am referring to as the pre-millennialism, pre-wrath view is not really new. It dates back to before A.D. 70. Some great contemporary Bible scholars recently popularized the pre-wrath position and, most notably, Marvin Rosenthal in his book, *The Pre-Wrath Rapture of the Church*[4], hence the name "pre-wrath".

A second view is the "post-millennium" view, which simply believes Christ does not return until after the thousand-year period. Those who espouse this view believe that we are currently in that thousand-year period, good will eventually overcome evil, and then the Lord will return. There is no biblical basis for such a view, and one merely need look around to see that the world is not getting morally better.

27

The third view does not believe in a literal thousand-year period and is referred to as "amillennialism". Those who hold this view believe that upon the resurrection of Christ, He rules in the hearts of men, and that His reign is actually in the spiritual kingdom of each believer's heart, as opposed to a literal thousand-year reign on earth. There is no biblical basis for this view in this author's opinion.

As we look at the timelines and events associated with Christ's return, it should become very apparent to the reader that the pre-millennium position is consistent with Scripture. As such, this book will assume pre-millennialism as the basis for the discussions which follow.

We already touched on the basic timing of the Rapture positions, but here are the five predominate positions as related to the subject of eschatology:

1. Pre-Tribulation: Christ returns for His Church prior to the 70th Week of Daniel.
2. Mid-Tribulation: Christ returns for His Church at the mid-point of the 70th Week of Daniel when the Great Tribulation commences, exactly 3½ years into the seven-year period of Daniel's 70th Week.
3. Post-Tribulation: Christ returns for His Church at the conclusion of the seven-year period of the 70th Week of Daniel.
4. Pre-Wrath: Christ returns for His Church after the mid-point of the 70th Week of Daniel, between the sixth and seventh seals of Revelation on the Day of the Lord. The Great Tribulation is cut short by His coming.
5. Partial Rapture: Only a portion of the believers will be raptured. This is a view that has no biblical basis at all and is merely mentioned here because you may hear of it.

A quick word on the 70th Week of Daniel is necessary in completing this first chapter overview. It comes from the book of Daniel, chapter 9, verses 24 and 27 where it states, "Seventy weeks have been decreed for your people and your holy city, to finish the transgression, to make an end of sin, to make atonement for iniquity, to bring in everlasting righteousness, to seal up vision and prophecy and to anoint the most holy place." (v.24) "And he (the Antichrist) will make a firm covenant with the many for one week, but in the middle of the week he will put a stop to sacrifice and grain offering; and on the wing of abominations will come one who makes desolate, even until a complete destruction, one that is decreed, is poured out on the one who makes desolate." (v.27) [Parenthesis mine.]

The first 69 weeks have already taken place in human history. There remains one final (the 70th) week. So you may say, "how can a week equal seven years?" These 70 weeks are expressed in weeks of years as related to the modified Egyptian calendar used during the time of Daniel's writing. We know for instance that the modified Egyptian calendar has 360 days. In the book of Revelation chapter 11 verses 2-3 state: "Leave out the court which is outside the temple and do not measure it, for it has been given to the nations; and they will tread under foot the holy city for forty-two months. And I will grant authority to my two witnesses, and they will prophesy for twelve hundred and sixty days, clothed in sackcloth." The 42 months or 1,260 days is equal to 3½ years, with a year being 360 days.

The Revelation reference speaks of the last 3½ years of the seven-year period spoken of by the prophet Daniel. We also see that a week equals seven years in Genesis 29:26-30. We will discuss the 70 weeks in more detail in a later chapter. There are differing views as to the commencement of that time (445 B.C. or dating from time of Creation) and whether the reference to Daniel 9:25 where "Messiah" is used is a reference to Jesus Christ or poorly translated as *"Messiah"*, when it might be a reference to Jerusalem and the destruction of the temple and the city in A.D. 70. All agree that the 70th Week of Daniel is a yet future time consisting of seven years, apart from the "Preterist" position which holds that the 70 weeks have already taken place in history. For our consideration, we would believe a "Futurist" view and that is to say, we believe that the final seven-year period [70th Week of Daniel] is yet to come.

In summary, there is a yet future time period of seven years known as the 70th Week of Daniel, which will be an unparalleled time in human history. Often erroneously referred to as the Tribulation period, this time will commence with the signing of a covenant between the Antichrist and the nation of Israel. In the middle of the 70th Week (42 months or 1,260 days), the Antichrist will break the covenant and the Great Tribulation will commence with the Antichrist's terror against all who call upon the name of the Lord as well as Israel.

This period of time is a focus of future prophetic events. While terrible with horrific persecution, destruction, and death, it will be a time that will culminate all human history with the return of our Lord Jesus Christ. We all look forward to the blessed hope and glorious appearing of our great God and Savior, Jesus Christ. There is eternal hope for all who call on the name of the Lord. We look forward to a new heaven and a new earth where we will dwell with the Lord for eternity!

It would be a tragedy for the Church to enter into the 70th Week of Daniel unprepared or caught unaware. This is one of the reasons and passions behind the recent books and teaching on the subject.

We are about to study the subject of last words (eschatology). Our goal is to share truth concerning that critical time period, prepare believers, and to motivate each of us to share our faith with the lost in all our spheres of influence and beyond.

2

WHY STUDY ESCHATOLOGY?

This is a valid question. We defined eschatology as the study of prophecy or "last words". We talked about the importance of "last words", but this is a broader question as it relates to prophecy or eschatology in general. There are many Christians who attend church every week and participate in classroom or home Bible studies on a variety of topics. Eschatology is probably the least taught or studied, however we are seeing a much greater interest in the subject lately. Having said that, most believers are not able to biblically defend the position they have been taught or claim to hold.

Some might go as far as to say that it is too difficult to understand and that it will all pan out in the end anyhow so, "why bother?" They defend that, "Jesus will come when He comes." I would agree with the fact that "He will come when He comes," and in reality it *will* all pan out in the end, but the Bible states that there are some very significant implications that believers are to understand. To not take prophecy serious is to deny a true exegetical study of God's Word. With over one-fourth of the Bible being prophetic, it could hardly be argued that one should not consider the study of prophecy very seriously.

I believe there are some very basic reasons why we should study eschatology. The following are just some thoughts on the topic and not meant to be all-inclusive:

1. Over one-fourth of the Bible is prophetic. As mentioned earlier, it could be argued that the entire Bible is prophetic

in that it is literally God-breathed. This is God's Word. It is His instruction for us. It is His means for unveiling truth and allowing us to know Him. Bible prophecy helps us see His wonderful plan from creation to eternity. We are exhorted by Paul in II Timothy 2:15, "Be diligent to present yourself approved to God as a workman who does not need to be ashamed, accurately handling the word of truth." Chapter three, verses 16 and 17 say, "All Scripture is inspired by God and profitable for teaching, for reproof, for correction, for training in righteousness; so that the man of God may be adequate, equipped for every good work." You cannot take heed of these verses and not study eschatology.

2. The study of eschatology helps equip the believer for every good work. II Timothy 3:16-17 tells us that the Bible is God's Word and that it is for our equipping. It does not isolate what portions of God's Word are for equipping, but says "all." If you are going to be adequately equipped as a believer, you need to consider and understand *all* of God's Word. That is a tall order, and I believe that we are constantly learning and growing—or at least we should be. You cannot be a student of the Bible and not consider eschatology. It is impossible. With over one-fourth of the Bible being prophetic, you cannot avoid the topic.

3. Understanding eschatology helps us defend our faith. I Peter 3:15 says, "but sanctify Christ as Lord in your hearts, always *being* ready to make a defense to everyone who asks you to give an account *for the hope that is in you*, yet with gentleness and reverence;" [Emphasis mine.] What is that hope that is in you? Earlier in I Peter chapter one, verses three through seven we have a clear indication. "Blessed be the God and Father of our Lord Jesus Christ, who according to His great mercy, has caused us to be born again to a living hope through the resurrection of Jesus Christ from the dead, to *obtain* an inheritance *which* is imperishable and undefiled and will not fade away, reserved in heaven for you, who are protected by the power of God through faith for a salvation ready to be revealed in the last time. In this you greatly rejoice, even

though now for a little while, if necessary, you have been distressed by various trials, so that the proof of your faith, being more precious than gold which is perishable, even though tested by fire, may be found to result in praise and glory and honor at the revelation of Jesus Christ."

This is the living hope! This is what we should be able to defend. Titus 2:11-15 speaks about it as well. "For the grace of God has appeared, bringing salvation to all men, instructing us to deny ungodliness and worldly desires and to live sensibly, righteously and godly in the present age, looking for the blessed hope and the appearing of the glory of our great God and Savior, Christ Jesus, who gave Himself for us to redeem us from every lawless deed, and to purify for Himself a people for His own possession, zealous for good deeds. These things speak and exhort and reprove with all authority. Let no one disregard you." It cannot be any clearer. Our defense of our faith is in direct correlation to our hope. Our hope is in His return on the day He comes to redeem us at the Rapture.

There are three aspects of our salvation. The first is the redemption or deliverance from *the penalty of sin*, when we accept Jesus Christ as our Lord and Savior. He [Jesus Christ] purchased us out of the marketplace of sin, and when He was dying on the cross at Calvary He said, "it is finished." In the original language it meant that the debt was paid in full. Romans 6:23 tells us that the wages of sin is death, but He paid the debt that we owed in full. Through the Father's election and our decision to receive Him as Lord and Savior, we were redeemed.

The second aspect of our salvation is the redemption or deliverance over *the power of sin* in our life (Romans 6:14). It is not to say that we will not sin this side of Glory, but we are *no longer slaves to sin*. It does not have dominion over us. In chapter eight of Romans, the Apostle Paul speaks about the deliverance from the bondage of sin and even concludes the chapter with our "looking forward to the hope previously spoken about–not only us, but also all of creation." Paul

33

struggled with the two natures and sin (Romans 7:14-25), but he focused on the blessed hope.

We have all met very pious Christians who have been subject to gossip and hard on those of us who have sinned after coming to Christ. There is a place for confrontation, but we have to be careful and remember that we too are sinners saved by grace. I John 1:8-10 tells us that we all sin. Romans 3:10 tells us that there is none righteous, which is a quote from Psalm 14:1-3. Isaiah 64:6 states that "all our righteous deeds are like a filthy garment." A word study of this passage may surprise you; its literal meaning depicts how vile even our greatest efforts are because of the stain of sin. The Church's physical buildings are full of people stained by sin. As believers, however, it should never dominate our life and if it does, we need to examine ourselves and see if we are truly saved.

Lastly, one day we will be delivered from *the very presence of sin*. This is what we long for—that day when we see Him come in the clouds to redeem His bride. We live in a fallen world ruled by an evil deceiver who is like a roaring lion, seeking whom he may devour. When believers depart this world by rapture or death, we will no longer be subject to the fall and deception. We will be clothed in the righteousness of Jesus Christ.

I was recently asked to help plan and officiate a funeral for a young man who passed away in his prime. He was only 34-years-old when he passed. It is times like this that our blessed hope and our longing to be with Christ and our loved ones who have gone before us really comes home. It is despairing enough for a young family to suffer the loss of such a young person, but if there was no hope of a future with Christ and a reuniting with this loved one, we would be so, so miserable, which leads to the next reason to study it.

4. Learning eschatology gives us an assured hope of a future without sorrow and grief. I Thessalonians 4:13 states, "But we do not want you to be uninformed, brethren, about those who are asleep, so that you will not grieve as do the rest who

have no hope. For if we believe that Jesus died and rose again, even so God will bring with Him those who have fallen asleep in Jesus." In context, Paul then goes on to describe the classic rapture passage. If we merely have an "earthbound" perspective all of our life and seek only that which this world has to offer, we will grow weary. The Christian life has application for more than the here and now, but also for an eternity full of heavenly hope and perspective.

This is not to say that we should only make applications in this life as they pertain to godly living while we wait for His appearing. On the contrary, we are to live godly and righteously. Empowered by His indwelling Spirit, we are to live a blameless life motivated by the blessed hope He has given us. Paul said it this way in I Corinthians 15:19, "If we have hoped in Christ in this life only, we are of all men most to be pitied." Knowing that one day we will live in a place with no sin, sorrow, or pain and where joy is beyond our full comprehension is an incredible motivator for the Christian. We have a great cloud of witnesses who have gone before us and are cheering us on. How many times have you attended a funeral or heard of one where the person who passed away may not have accepted Christ as his/her Lord and Savior? The pastor struggles to speak through it because there is an uncertainty. I am glad that I discovered that the young man I referenced in the previous paragraph had placed his trust in Jesus when he was younger. He is no longer subject to this fallen world and has become a recipient of that blessed hope.

Hebrews chapter 9:27 states, "And inasmuch as it is appointed for men to die once and after this *comes* judgment." Eschatology teaches us about this aspect. It teaches us about the hope, the resurrection, *and* the judgment. Eschatology teaches us about judgments and what happens to us after we die. It also tells what the generation living when the Rapture takes place will experience.

To not have this hope is to live a life of futility. We are exhorted by Christ to store up our treasures in heaven, not on earth, yet so many believers are still worried about storing up things on earth. They buy and buy and buy, dismissing that when they pass from this life to the next, the things accumulated will end up in garage sales, junk yards, charities, or—worse yet—thrown away. We spend a great deal of our life preparing for things. Think about it. We prepare for sporting events, we prepare for retirement one day, we prepare for having children, we prepare for college, we prepare for vacations and trips, some prepare wills and living trusts, and on and on. Many of those things we prepare for come with some level of excitement in anticipation. How much more so, to look forward to and prepare in this life for eternity with Christ? We have so much to look forward to, and by studying this topic we are assured of the promises and strengthened in our daily walk.

5. Learning eschatology fulfills the exhortation to not be ignorant or uninformed. We just quoted I Thessalonians 4:13. Paul says we should not be uninformed or ignorant. The word *agnoein* means to not be unaware, ignorant, or uninformed. It is used some twenty-two-times in Scripture. It is emphatic and followed by an accusative of the object, which is the subject of His return. It carries the idea of willful ignorance. The church at Thessalonica was a young church, just over three weeks old. We know this from the book of Acts, where we find in chapter 17 that Paul taught in the synagogue for three Sabbaths. He [Paul] had apparently taught on this subject and had to remind them of this teaching (II Thessalonians 2:5). There is really no excuse for us to be ignorant concerning the Lord's return. We have the full canon of Scripture that clearly informs believers about the Lord's return therefore there is really no excuse for us to be uninformed about this subject.

6. Learning eschatology helps us understand the times we live in. When Jesus spoke to His disciples in the Olivet Discourse (Matthew 24), He spoke to them about a near and far prophecy. As they listened to Him explain about the destruction of the Temple built by Herod the Great, they must have been amazed. Here stood this remarkable Temple, no doubt the crowning jewel of its day. This Temple was the

most magnificent structure in all of Israel. It was the second Temple, for the first Temple built by Solomon was destroyed in 586 B.C. when the Jewish nation was exiled to Babylon. This also was the time of Daniel's writings, which will be an important consideration when we look at the different positions and build some timelines.

The disciples could not fathom that this second Temple could be destroyed in the manner Jesus spoke of and even asked when all this would take place. He gave a near and far prophecy. The near would be the destruction of the Temple that they were observing; the Temple built by Herod. This would take place in A.D. 70. Some would be alive when this happened. It is of interest to note that the Apostle John, who wrote the gospel and epistles, was alive when Titus destroyed Jerusalem and Herod's Temple. It is also interesting to note that as our Lord used John to pen His words in Revelation, that John did not give specifics regarding the A.D. 70 destruction of the Temple, but instead spoke of a future time. He penned the words around A.D. 90-95 from the Island of Patmos, where he was banished because of the Word of God and the testimony of Jesus (Revelation 1:9). This was 25 years after the destruction of Jerusalem and the Temple by Titus. It therefore makes no sense that the prophecies of the book of Revelation had already been fulfilled or even fulfilled in A.D. 70. This should be one of the compelling arguments against the Preterist view.

The disciples listened intently, so when the destruction took place in A.D. 70, they understood the times and it should have been no surprise to them. As Jesus continued speaking in Matthew 24, He told of a yet future time and made reference to Daniel's prophecy in Daniel 9:27 regarding the Abomination of Desolation, which would be followed by the Great Tribulation. He was speaking of the 70th Week of Daniel. That seven-year period has yet to take place. In verses four through eight He spoke of a series of things that would happen and would represent what He referred to as "merely the beginning of birth pangs."

This is a unique metaphor. If you are a mother, this is language you can understand. The beginning of birth pangs (pains) is generally followed by hard labor. In these verses, the beginning of birth pangs represents a world ruler coming to power, nations coming up against nations, kingdoms coming up against kingdoms, famines wasting away the people, and earthquakes shaking the lands. These have happened for many years in history, but the illustration suggests a greater intensity as though it would be a unique time.

The hard labor starts in Matthew 24, verses 9-22. Here, Jesus describes the hard labor or, Great Tribulation, which we know starts at the mid-point, or 3½ years into the seven-year period known as the 70th Week of Daniel. We would expect deliverance to follow the hard labor if we continue with the metaphor, and that is exactly what Jesus refers to in verses 22 through 31. The deliverance in verse 31 is speaking about the Rapture from this author's perspective.

So, we must understand the times we live in. We are told that the love of many will grow cold. We are told of wars, famines, and earthquakes, which we see. There are more earthquakes, tornados, and hurricanes like never before. The number of wars have been increasing, and perhaps the most significant watch item in history is the date of May 14, 1948, when Israel became a sovereign State.

We are told of a future world leader who will deceive and make a peace covenant with Israel, according to Daniel 9:27. If we understand these things, then we too will not be surprised or caught unaware. We know to expect these things. If we are not taking note of the times we live in and simply believe that we will be exempt from the 70th Week, we may be surprised. There is a warning Jesus gives in Matthew 24: 23-26. There is no excuse. We need to watch what is going on in our world and—especially in Israel. We need to prepare and share the Gospel with as many of those in our sphere of influence whom we can.

7. Learning eschatology keeps us from being deceived or misled. I find this to be of particular importance, especially for those

of us living in America. We are a nation founded on biblical principles and ethics. Our nation has slowly turned from those values and our culture is changing daily. Many who claim to be believers are accepting culturally and politically assigned values, or should I say, lack of values.

Many great men and women gave their lives to protect our freedoms and constitution, and we need to pray for our nation and leaders to preserve our heritage and rich freedoms. Our blessed freedom of religion has become a platform to deny Christianity and embrace all religions and cults. The "feel good" and "self-esteem" psychology of the day has led to millions of Americans being addicted to mind-altering prescription drugs. There are churches that have walked away from the infallible, inerrant Word of God and embraced this mentality, which has led to espousing homosexuality as an acceptable lifestyle—even populating pulpits with pastors who are openly homosexual.

So many have been misled and deceived by the beliefs and actions of men and women in today's culture; sin that was once recognized as sin has now become overlooked, homosexuality being only one. It will get much worse when the master deceiver comes on the scene. This may offend some reading this book, but the Scriptures must be our plumb line. The Word of God is truth and the bottom line for every true Christian. The individual practicing homosexuality is no guiltier than the person exceeding the speed limit. Both need a saving relationship with Christ. I only share this because I truly love them and desire for them to be a part of His elect and want to see them in heaven one day.

Paul, in the book of Romans 1:18-32 describes our modern culture well and gives a harsh warning to those who practice such things. Note that these verses start with the "wrath of God against such things" and speak about the fact that even though they knew God, they did not honor Him as God (verse 21). Verse 29 talks about deceit as being a trait that does not honor God, and verse 32 states that those who do these things also give a hearty approval to those who practice them.

These are strong warnings against the ebb and tide of our culture. Having said that, everyone who is a believer today came out of some sinful past. I Corinthians 6:9-11 says, "Or do you not know that the unrighteous will not inherit the kingdom of God? Do not be deceived; neither fornicators, nor idolaters, nor adulterers, not effeminate, nor homosexuals, 10 nor thieves, nor the covetous, nor drunkards, nor revilers, nor swindlers, will inherit the kingdom of God 11 Such were some of you; but you were washed, but you were sanctified, but you were justified in the name of the Lord Jesus Christ and in the Spirit of our God." I am not singling out homosexuals here; the list just given includes all of us prior to coming to Christ. We will still sin from time-to-time, but it cannot and must not dominate our life.

James 2:19 states, "you believe that God is one. You do well; the demons also believe, and shudder." We need to examine ourselves. If you are living a lifestyle spoken of in Romans chapter one, you need to pray and ask the Lord to forgive you and turn from it. We are all sinners and we need to recognize when we are opposing God. We can have victory over sin and bad habits through His indwelling Holy Spirit. We will sin, but it should not dominate our life. The sins listed in Romans chapter one are just some. We have all sinned. I have sinned and every great Christian leader has sinned. The Bible says, "For whoever keeps the whole law and yet stumbles in one point, he has become guilty of all" (James 2:10).

All of us need to turn from sin and allow Jesus to be the Lord of our life. Reading and memorizing His Word helps (Psalm 119:11). We need the fellowship of other believers to help hold us accountable. We need to pray daily. I am not speaking of a "works" salvation; I am speaking of practical Christian living that battles against a culture which is becoming less and less moral. You cannot live a victorious Christian life apart from Christ and His indwelling Holy Spirit. We need to put on the armor of God spoken of by the Apostle Paul in chapter six of his epistle to the church at Ephesus.

We are exhorted not to conform to this world in Romans 12, yet so many are. We are to be transformed by the renewing of our minds, so that we may prove what the will of God is (Romans 12:2). Being in the Word will not only prepare us for the events surrounding us, but the Lord will use it to grow us spiritually and increase our faith. It will keep us from being deceived or misled. Look at just some of the warnings in context to the last days: Matthew 24:23-26, Mark 13:9, 21-23, Luke 17:22-24, Luke 21:34-36, I Thessalonians 4:13, 5:3-9, II Thessalonians 2:3, 10-12, I Timothy 4:1-3, II Timothy 3:1-5, 4:1-5, I Peter 1:13, 3:15, 4:7 II Peter 3:17, and on and on. The Antichrist will be empowered by Satan who is the father of lies (John 8:44).

The deception, delusions, and trickery that will be part of the schemes in the last days will be like no other time. We study this subject to be informed and to share the truth with others. My personal conviction is that the Christian generation alive when the Antichrist comes to power *will not* be raptured prior to the 70th Week or what most refer to as pre-tribulation. I would suggest you continue to read and study all the positions which I will speak of and come to your own conclusion, however would it not be one of the greatest lies and schemes to convince believers that they will be raptured prior to the 70th Week, only to hear of an "Abomination of Desolation" in a Temple that demands for world-wide allegiance? Look at II Thessalonians 2:1-4. Look at II Peter 3:3-7. It leaves it wide-open for mockers who have heard pre-tribulation taught in so, so many American churches and around the world. I believe we are entering into the time Paul warned about in II Timothy 3:1, "But realize this, that in the last days difficult times will come. (vs 2) For men will be lovers of self, lovers of money, boastful, arrogant, revilers, disobedient to parents, ungrateful, unholy, (vs 3) unloving, irreconcilable, malicious gossips, without self-control, brutal, haters of good, (vs 4) treacherous, reckless, conceited, lovers of pleasure rather than lovers of God, (vs 5) holding to a form of godliness, although they have denied its power; Avoid such men as these."

It sounds like a commentary on our culture today. Not understanding the Scriptures and what is taught about the timing of the Rapture can lead to tragedy for the believer. In II Timothy 4:2-5, we are told to "reprove, rebuke, exhort with great patience and instruction." Why? He goes on to explain in verse three, "For the time will come when they will not endure sound doctrine; but wanting to have their ears tickled, they will accumulate for themselves teachers in accordance to their own desires." Now, having said this, I do believe the premise is correct on pre-tribulation. It states that the Church will be raptured prior to the wrath of God and I agree. Where you place the Day of the Lord's wrath is the issue.

I could go on and name many more reasons why we should study eschatology but the first reason should be enough. Over one-fourth of the Bible is prophetic. If you are a serious Christian, you are a serious student of the Word of God, and therefore the study of eschatology will be a part of your daily discipline as you search the Scriptures. Perhaps one of the most compelling reasons is found in Revelation 1:3, "Blessed is he who reads and those who hear the words of the prophecy, and heed the things which are written in it; for the time is near."

3
WHAT IS SYSTEMATIC THEOLOGY?

Systematic Theology is just that. It is a system developed by man (theologians) by which to understand the Bible and God's dealing with man throughout history. The major divisions of systematic theology cover broad topics, encompassing all of Scripture. A word of caution would be in order before we go too far into this chapter. Whenever man attempts to compartmentalize the Bible by systems or categories, there is always the risk that we could lose the true meaning of any given text. There is also the tendency to look at things from a systematic approach in establishing doctrine, and thereby bring these systematic assumptions into specific Bible verses and further exacerbate the text with an eisegetical interpretation. That is, isolating a text around a doctrine, which may not be consistent with the immediate, book or Bible context, which we will discuss in chapter four.

There is also great value in systematic theology in that it helps the layperson understand major theological themes. Great men have compiled systematic theology and taught it at reputable seminaries, which has also accounted for the major doctrines of churches today. For pastors who graduated from such institutions, it would be difficult to arrive at an opposing view than that which was taught in seminary. For this reason, I believe that many churches today and many leaders and teachers hold to what they were taught and are so comfortable with such, that they rarely question or dig in deep to come to any other conclusion.

It must be a struggle for them. They might reason in their mind that, "even though I cannot reconcile this truth as I am studying it for myself, I must be wrong because it does not align with what I have always been taught and surely they must know better." I am so thankful for those men and women who have counted the cost, been Bereans discovering new truths who are willing to take a stand for such. We owe so much to men like Martin Luther and so many others who devoted their lives to discovering the truth of God's Word. It is no different today. Whenever men go against great institutions of learning and challenge the status quo, there is going to be controversy.

In this brief chapter, we will look at systematic theology at a very top level. To understand it in depth, however, would encompass volumes of work. Our purpose here is simply to expose the reader to the subject and demonstrate that even in a man-made system approach to theological study, one will find that each segment or major subject is uniquely tied to each other as a whole. Eschatology in my view really touches each of the major divisions of systematic theology in an even more unique way in that it must consider the entire Bible along with the prophets, genealogies, attributes of God, angelic beings, and so on. Having a top level understanding of eschatology prepares the Bible student to look at the entire context of Scripture, and thereby become a better navigator of the Bible.

What are the traditional major divisions of systematic theology and why would I include the subject in a study on eschatology?
The following are the traditional major divisions:

Bibliology – The study of God's Word
Theology Proper – The study of God the Father
Angelology – The study of angelic beings
Anthropology – The study of mankind
Soteriology – The study of salvation
Ecclesiology – The study of the Church
Eschatology – The study of "last words" or end-times
Christology – The study of God the Son, Jesus Christ
Pneumatology – The study of God the Holy Spirit
Doctrinal Summarization – Study of doctrine

The terms used for systematic theology make sense. The reason I find this to be an important part of the study of eschatology is not only because it is one of the major divisions of systematic theology, but also because it is the one area that has a tie to all of the rest. One of the fascinating things that took place in my life as I ventured into the study of eschatology was the discovery of how cohesive the entire Bible is. It was as if a light had come on. With the proper interpretation of Scripture, one can easily see how relevant the Old and New Testament are to one another. The entire canon of Scripture comes alive. You begin to see how God has always had a plan and how it has been unfolding from the beginning. Systematic theology is just another way to look at this. I will attempt to explain.

Let's start with bibliology. This is where we establish the inerrancy and infallible nature of God's Word. This is extremely important in the sense that we must believe that His Word is true. It must therefore, of necessity, be without error and absolutely trustworthy. Bibliology looks at the supernatural origin of the Bible. II Timothy 3:16 and II Peter 1:21 have been discussed earlier, describing God's Word as being God-breathed and not a result of any man's interpretation. The beautiful words recorded in the longest chapter in the Bible are found in Psalm 119, which describe the character and profoundness of God's Word.

It is interesting to discover that the Bible has something to say about everything. During the 1800s, an English philosopher, biologist/ socialist named Herbert Spencer said that "time, force, energy, space and matter"[1] could explain everything. He was an evolutionist and believed that everything evolved from these five basic things. He wrote a number of books and was nominated for a Nobel Prize in literature in 1902 for his works. Those of us who believe God's Word is true and has the correct answer for everything did not have to wait until the late 1800s to discover this. The very first line in the Bible; Genesis 1:1, "In the beginning *(time)* God *(force)* created *(energy)* the heavens *(space)* and earth *(matter)*." [Parenthesis mine.]

There are numerous examples where the Bible has given us clear information about things that were discovered by man many, many years after it was written, only to find out that it agreed with writings from ancient times. Another example is the discovery that our world is round and not flat. At the time the Bible was written, the inhabitants of this planet earth assumed that the world was flat. Early science grew and eventually they discovered that the world was round. Our photographs from space telescopes, satellites, and the space station confirm this. Yet, over 2500 years ago the Scriptures declared, "Do you not know? Have you not heard? Has it not been declared to you from the beginning? Have you not understood from the foundations of the earth? It is He who sits above the **circle** of the earth, and its inhabitants are like grasshoppers, who stretches out the heavens like a curtain and spreads them out like a tent to dwell in" (Isaiah 40:21-22). The word "circle" in verse 22 is the word "sphere" in the Hebrew.

The Bible is the most unique and fascinating book in all of human history. It has set standards for ethics, morality, and law in virtually every culture around the world. The Ten Commandments themselves are a standard for civil law. It has the power to change lives, which no other book can claim. No matter how many times evil men have attempted to destroy the Bible, it has survived, which is a fulfillment of its own claim. The Word of the Lord endures forever. It is eternal in that it will last forever. God revealed His Word through various methods. He used direct voice, direct writing, dreams, men, the Creation itself, historic events, and the Holy Spirit.

The Bible is prophetic. There are hundreds of prophesies in the Bible concerning the birth, life, ministry, death, resurrection, and return of Christ. Every prophecy of the Bible has or will come true. The Bible and the study, make-up, divisions, time periods, dispensations, covenants, feasts, genealogies, prophets, and descriptions are all key in understanding eschatology. Bibliology helps the reader to systematically approach the Word to discover how all the relationships come together in fulfillment of God's plan. It helps us to understand God's special relationship with Israel and the Church and how they are distinct, yet come together concurrently in the last days as a fulfillment of biblical prophecy.

The Bible canon, or 66 books, determined to be the Bible is included in the study of bibliology. The book of Revelation itself warns of the plagues that would fall upon one, should they add or take away the words in those 66 books (Revelation 22:18-19).

This writer assumes that you believe that the Bible is God's Word and that you also believe that it is true. There are many good books on the authenticity of the Bible, fulfilled prophecy of the Bible, and the supernatural evidence of the Bible. By understanding the Bible and bibliology, it will help you understand how the whole of Scripture comes together to provide a clear understanding of end-times.

The next area of systematic theology is theology proper. This is the study of God the Father. By understanding God the Father, you understand His desire to create a people for His own and His glory. You discover Creation, the character of God along with His attributes. We discover that He is all-knowing and all-present. Nothing escapes His attention. He is infinite, while we are finite. He is huge and we are small and yet He chose to love us. He spoke the universe into existence, a universe so large that we have not been able to know its depth in space and we find new wonders everyday.

Instead of the dilemma often associated with pre-destination and election, we see the sense in how they are uniquely different and yet with the same goal and purpose in mind. We understand that His ways are far above our ways and that we do not have the ability to understand everything while we are housed in this mortal body. By studying theology proper, we get to know God. We see Him as both a just and loving God and how He is able to perfectly balance His justice with His love. We understand what true love is and that it is not mere sentimentalism, but comes from a sincere, honest, loving heart that poured out His justice on His only Son because He loved us so much and desired to honor His name. The study of theology proper helps us understand the names of God like Jehovah, Elohim, Adon, Adonai. His names speak of His character and attributes.

In relating theology proper to eschatology, we see God's plan from the beginning. His purpose for our lives, His divine imperatives, His justice, and His love are all part of theology proper. We learn that He is part of the Trinity. The study of theology proper speaks to God the Father, God the Son, and God the Holy Spirit.

As we learn this portion of systematic theology, we learn about the angels, fallen and un-fallen. We learn about the relationship between the Father and the Son and how His justice will culminate in the day of the Lord's wrath and the final judgment at the Great White

Throne. We learn of His desire to usher in a New Heaven and New Earth and that His original intent to fellowship among us is still His plan and will become a reality once again in a New Earth, which will no longer be subject to sin. Theology proper relates to eschatology because it gives us insight into God's plan along with His purpose, divine instructions, and how one day His Son will return to earth and set up a righteous kingdom.

Angelology is the portion of systematic theology that deals with angelic beings. Throughout the Scriptures we see how God uses angelic beings as His messengers. From Genesis through Revelation you cannot find a time when God did not use His angels. We learn that they are not human like we are, and yet we discover that they can communicate and do the will of God. We learn of the fallen angels. We see the origins of Satan [morning star, KJV translates Lucifer] and how pride caused him to fall (Isaiah 14:12). We learn of his desire to deceive man from the very beginning in the garden and his eventual destruction cast into the eternal lake of fire. We see where fallen angels sinned with humans, which caused God to judge the world and cause a flood, yet by His grace, saved eight individuals. We saw it in relation to Sodom and Gomorrah and the wrath of God, yet deliverance of the faithful.

The subject of angelology teaches us about the angel, Gabriel (Daniel 9:21). We learn about the guardian Michael, who will be key in understanding our study of eschatology (Daniel 12:1 and Revelation 12:7-9). We can look at the patterns of Scripture and see that angels carry out God's desires and judgments. By studying angelology, we can see a distinct pattern, which will bring insight into the Revelation chapter six through nine passages regarding the seal and trumpet judgments. The angel Michael is of particular interest because of his relationship to Israel and how immediately after he *arises*, there is the "time of distress such as never occurred since there was a nation until that time", mentioned in Daniel 12. In my view, the archangel Michael is the "restrainer" of II Thessalonians 2:6-7, which pre-tribulation rapture proponents would assign to either the Church or Holy Spirit. We will explain why that cannot be the case later as we go through the positions in detail.

By understanding angelology we learn about elect angels, cherubim, seraphim, living creatures, and the distinction of names. We learn about Satan's judgment at the cross. How tragic to have once been Lucifer, son of the morning (Isaiah 14:12) who fell because of pride. It is important to understand his fallen character and desire to devour us like a roaring lion. All good soldiers know that unless they can understand the enemy, they will be of little effect in defending themselves or winning in battle. We study angelology and see the final judgment upon Satan, the Antichrist and the False Prophet.

In chapter six of Revelation we see the seal judgments being poured out with the four horsemen. During the fifth seal, the martyrs cry out and still God has not yet poured out His vengeance. The sixth seal opens and the heavens open up, a trumpet sounds, and people are gathered from every tribe and nation from the four corners of the earth. The seventh seal is opened and then God's angels blow the trumpets. These seven trumpets and then the seven bowl judgments are clearly God's wrath. This will be an important point we will revisit in later chapters of this book. A proper understanding of angels helps us understand eschatology and where they are used in carrying out God's plan.

The next portion of systematic theology is <u>anthropology</u>. This is the study of mankind. Here we learn about the origin of man. Through study we see that man is made up of body, soul, and spirit. This is important when we consider the death of the saints and where man goes when he dies. We learn about man's ability to reason and understand his Creator even from the things that are made. We were made in the image of God, but we are flesh and mortal. We are finite, while God is infinite. We are limited in our knowledge while He is all-knowing. We were created to fellowship with God and we will one day receive a new body. We learn that the fall of man [Adam] caused sin to come upon all men from that point on, and that man has inherited sin as well as willful sin.

The study of anthropology as it relates to eschatology gives us insight into the way man has either ignored his God-given conscience or found him guilty of sin. We learn to love because He first loved us. Studying this portion of theology helps us understand God's plan for man, His divine will, His transforming love, grace, and mercy.

Unrepentant man inherited a prideful character from the fall, and throughout the Bible we see man wrestling with this sinful nature. We see the foolishness of man when he attempts to build a tower and ends with dispersion and differing languages. We see men challenge and kill the prophets. We even see good men strike the rock instead of speaking to it obediently (Moses). We see man fall over and over again and God's grace poured out over and over again. This pride will continue to emerge in the last days and a spirit of lawlessness will prevail along with the apostasy.

With all of the wonderful things man has accomplished, his sin of pride will eventually be his downfall. The evil one in the last days will deceive those who do not humbly receive Jesus Christ as their Lord and Savior, and they will eventually be the ones who hide in the caves when the heavens break open and our Lord appears. Those who have trusted in their wealth will become poor and those who have trusted in their weaponry will become defeated foes. How terrifying it will be to fall into the hands of a righteous and just God. The study of anthropology as it relates to eschatology is the study of man relating to his/her Creator.

Soteriology is that portion of systematic theology dealing with salvation. This must be right if we are to enter heaven with our Creator God. It covers everything from the Kingship of Christ through His genealogy and fulfillment of prophecy, to His act of redemption for the lost sinner. Many religions would have you believe that you can somehow earn your way to heaven, and that while they acknowledge Jesus Christ as a real living person, prophet, and teacher, they do not see Him as the Savior and Lord whom He truly is.

Using systematic theology in this sense helps us to see God's plan from the beginning of a Savior who would one day come to seek and to save that which was lost. This was fulfilled according to the Scriptures at His first coming (I Corinthians 15:3-4). Jesus Christ, God's only begotten Son gave His life for each and every one of us in order that we might be saved.

Soteriology looks at the person of the Savior from the pre-incarnate Christ to His ruling and reigning forever. He is Prophet, Priest, King, Son of God, the Living Word, and He is the Way, the Truth and the Life; no man comes to the Father but through Him (John 14:6).

"And there is salvation in no one else; for there is no other name under heaven that has been given among men by which we must be saved" (Acts 4:12). Soteriology informs us that we must have more than just a mere intellectual assent to these facts in order to be truly saved (James 2:19).

Through soteriology, we learn about the suffering of Christ and what that suffering accomplished for all who would call upon His name and receive Him as their personal Lord and Savior. We learn about His atoning work for the sinner and how He fulfilled the law. Soteriology has us look at forgiveness and remission, guilt, penalty for sin, propitiation and substitution, as well as the sacrifice that satisfied God the Father's love as well as His justice. We investigate what it means to be chosen, grafted in, and adopted; we can explore the calling of the believer and how God foreknew that we would one day receive Jesus Christ as Lord and Savior, but at the appointed time. The latter helps us understand the difference between predestination and election. We also learn how God the Father, God the Son, and God the Holy Spirit all participate in our election and calling.

The security of the believer is clear from the study of soteriology. There are those who say that one can lose his/her salvation, but the study of soteriology teaches us that we are secure in Christ and when one seems so far from where they once might have professed to be, it is not a matter of whether or not that individual has lost his/her salvation as much as it is whether they actually were saved in the first place. Many profess to know and believe in Jesus Christ. The Scripture says; "You believe that God is one. You do well; the demons also believe, and shutter" (James 2:19).

James emphasizes works as an evidence of our faith and appears to be in conflict with the Apostle Paul with regard to faith and works, however there is no conflict at all. Ephesians 2:8-9 is often quoted to illustrate that grace through faith saves us. "For by grace you have been saved through faith; and that not of yourselves, *it is* the gift of God; not as a result of works, so that no one may boast." [Emphasis mine.] But if you follow Paul's writing to verse 10, it becomes clear that it aligns with James teaching on faith and works. Verse 10 of Ephesians two states, "for we are His workmanship, created in Christ Jesus for good works, which God prepared beforehand so that we would walk in them." I have heard it said this way: "faith is the ignition key which turns on the Grace of God in our lives", meaning that we come to Christ by faith and then He begins the good work in us and carries it on until the day of Christ Jesus. Good works is the caboose, where faith is the locomotive. Apart from faith, you can tarry all you want and work hard at trying to please God but it will never work. Hebrews 11:6 states that, "and without faith it is impossible to please Him, for he who comes to God must believe that He is and that He is a rewarder of those who seek Him."

When a person truly comes to Christ he is a new creature (II Corinthians 5:17). There should always be fruit when one comes to a saving faith. One of my favorite verses in the Bible is Romans 8:38-39, which states, "For I am convinced that neither death, nor life, nor angels, nor principalities, nor things present, nor things to come, nor powers, not height, nor depth, nor any other created thing, will be able to separate us from the love of God, which is in Christ Jesus our Lord." Jesus speaking about our security says this in John 10:27-30, "My sheep hear My voice, and I know them, and they follow Me; (vs 28) and I give eternal life to them, and they will never perish; and no one will snatch them out of My hand. (vs 29) My Father, who has given them to Me, is greater than all; and no one is able to snatch them out of the Father's hand. (vs 30) I and the Father are one."

It is also interesting that the word "snatch" here is the same root word as used for "caught up" or Latin transliteration, "rapture". Here in context, Jesus speaks of nobody being able to come along and snatch them out of the Almighty Father's hands and when speaking about the Rapture in I Thessalonians 4:17, Paul tells us that we will physically be caught up or snatched up to be with the Lord if we are that generation alive at the time of His appearing.

Soteriology teaches us about salvation and being saved. These are interesting words in Scripture. In the Greek, "saved" is *sozo*, which means to save, safely and soundly and to rescue from danger or destruction. *Soteria* is Greek for "salvation" and means deliverance, preservation, and safety. The study of soteriology should have an obvious connection to eschatology in that we are being preserved and we will be delivered, rescued, and ushered home safely. There will be difficult days ahead and many are even suffering today, but

God will preserve us. Our ultimate victory will be in Christ and we long for His appearing.

We must be saved and believe that Jesus Christ is our Lord and Savior or we will not have a place in the Kingdom. There will be a future time where the believer will stand before the judgment seat of Christ, and our works will be judged, but we ourselves will not be (II Corinthians 5:10). The judgment seat is a place of reward or loss of reward, but there is also a future time where a righteous God will judge the unsaved world (Revelation 20:11-12). This judgment is referred to as the "Great White Throne" judgment.

Books will be opened and every word, thought, and deed will be there. As good as a person as you might be, you still fall short of the glory of God and are a sinner. Your life record will condemn you before a righteous judge. On the other hand, if you have received Jesus Christ as your Lord and Savior, your every word, thought, and deed has been laid upon Him at Calvary, where He paid the debt in full. He died in our place. He took the punishment we deserved at Calvary. You can clearly see where soteriology is connected to future events.

Ecclesiology is the portion of systematic theology that deals with the Church and her history. This is an area of caution in that it systemizes the Church. It calls for far too much distinction between Israel and the Church, which leads to some erroneous conclusions regarding the last days or the subject of eschatology. While contrasts and differences certainly do exist between the Church and Israel, the lines are not implying that God cannot work with both simultaneously. Both the member of the Church and true Israel are the elect. Those Jews who have received Jesus Christ as their Lord and Savior and their true Messiah are part of the Church. There is a time after the Rapture when Israel will have a remnant, which comes to believe He is indeed the promised Messiah.

Ecclesiology addresses the Church as an organism and organization. It covers the ordinances of the Church, the origin of the Church, the leaders, the seed of Abraham, and the new covenants. It describes the Church as the bride of Christ and the future of the Church. It deals with the two mountains, Mt Sinai, where the law was given to show men their sins and inability to save themselves, and Mt Zion where we are under the new covenant in His blood through the sacrifice of Jesus Christ. Here again, we see our relationship with Israel as described by the author of Hebrews in chapter 12.

We learn about baptizing and the wonderful picture of the newly born again believer identifying with Christ and his/her sins being buried with Christ and rising to newness in life. We learn about the names given to believers, the Apostles, the gifts, the commandments, and the commissions.

Learning about the Church and God's purpose and plan for all believers is critical to the subject of eschatology. One of His purposes for the Church was to bring jealousy to Israel in order that they might turn to Him as their longed for Messiah. Of course the subject of the Rapture is of paramount importance when talking about the Church because we learn about the resurrection and the indwelling Holy Spirit.

The Church was established on the day of Pentecost when Peter preached to the multitudes in Acts chapter two. I would submit that the Church was in the mind of God well before the foundation of the world and that it was always His divine plan. When we look at books like Matthew, many would say that the teaching in chapter 24 (the Olivet Discourse) is strictly to the Jews and Israel, and theologians would say that the audience in mind in Matthew is the Jews. While we see the genealogy of Christ coming out as clearly the Son of David and the Son of Abraham, it is not a book strictly for the Jews. The Church cannot argue the fact that the gospel of Matthew has much relevance to the Church throughout its pages.

For instance, when we look at Matthew chapter 16 and Peter's confession of Christ as the Son of the living God in verse 16, immediately following Jesus says in verse 18, "I also say to you that you are Peter, and upon this rock I will build My **Church**; and the gates of Hades will not overpower it." [Emphasis mine.] Matthew 18 is referenced to the Church today with regard to Church discipline in verses 15-20. Matthew 24 speaks of the "elect", which when comparing Scripture with Scripture we see that these are references to believers. In Matthew 26, we see where Jesus instituted communion in verses 26-29. In Matthew chapter 28, no Church member would claim that the "Great Commission" is not for the Church, but rather an explicit commandment for all believers in verses 19-20. Further, we find the same Olivet Discourse language in the gospel of Mark chapter 13, as well as in Luke chapter 17 and 21.

Church history or the study of ecclesiology helps us understand what the early Church fathers believed regarding the subject of eschatology. We look at things like the *"Didache"* dated between A.D. 50-120 which contained some significant teaching on the return of Christ. We learn that the seven churches of Revelation chapters two and three were actual churches in history and yet also represent the spirit and heart of the Church in the last days.

Eschatology has an obvious connection to our study, for it *is* our study. We defined it briefly in chapter one, so we will not repeat that teaching here. When studying eschatology, we learn about the major segments of the 70th Week of Daniel, such as the week itself being seven years in duration. We learn of two halves being 3 ½ years each, or 1,260 days, which makes a case for the 360-day year. We learn of the "covenant with death", which initiates the seven-year period of Daniel's 70th Week. We learn of the "Abomination of Desolation" which takes place 3 ½ years into the seven-year period and initiates the Great Tribulation when the covenant is broken by the Antichrist.

We see the significance of the Day of the Lord's wrath in connection with the timing of this seven-year period, as well as judgments, catching up of the Church, an additional 30 days and 45 days for the 1,290 and 1,335 spoken of by the Prophet Daniel. We learn of the Antichrist, False Prophet, Satan, the mark of the beast, the sealing of the 144,000, the trumpet and bowl judgments, a millennial kingdom, and eventual new heaven and new earth. We see the significance of the seven seals of Revelation and how they directly relate to teaching throughout the Bible. We learn that this theology touches all the rest.

Christology is the portion of systematic theology that deals with the deity of Christ and His participation in creation. Christology teaches us who He is, His divine attributes, and His equality and oneness with the Father. It identifies the types in the Old Testament (ie: Melchizedek in Psalm 110:4 as referenced in Hebrews 5:5-6), the over 300 prophecies concerning Him. It teaches us about a divine plan and a virgin birth promised as far back as the fall in Genesis 3:15.

We learn that Jesus is fully man and fully God; He alone would live a sinless life and be the perfect sacrifice for all who would receive Him as Savior and Lord. Jesus is the propitiation for our sins, our very substitute and the indication of how much the Father and the Son love us. We learn of His teaching, the beatitudes, and the fulfillment of the law, the Olivet Discourse, the Upper Room Discourse, and His miracles. We learn of the first advent, or His coming, and how it relates to our understanding of His second coming.

The word *parousia* means "coming" as it relates to His second coming. *Parousia* is found throughout the New Testament and is similar to His first coming in that His first coming is associated with His birth, life, ministry, death, burial, and resurrection. His second advent/coming, or *parousia*, will involve the Rapture of the Church, the Day of the Lord's wrath, the earthly reign, and the eternal kingdom. We will talk about that significance in later chapters. We learn of His own specific teaching on the subject of His return and whom He is returning for. Finally, we learn of His names and what significance they hold with respect to who He is. It is the study of Jesus Christ our Lord and Savior. There is no greater connection to His return than He Himself.

Pneumatology is that portion of systematic theology that deals with the deity of the Holy Spirit, who together with God the Father and God the Son, make up the triune Godhead. We learn of His divine attributes and work in creation. We learn of His equality with the Father and Son. We see the work of the Holy Spirit in prophecy and divine election. We see His work from the beginning and Adam, all the way to the return of Christ and beyond. We learn that He is our teacher and comforter and that He indwells the believer. He is the revealer of truth as we will discuss in chapter four on how to study the Bible. Without Him, we cannot fully arrive at truth. We learn of the baptism of the Holy Spirit and what that really means. We see that the Holy Spirit seals us unto the day of redemption.

As we become believers, He fills us and the result is a life of fruitful good works. There is caution in this segment of systematic theology in that some would assign the work of the "restrainer" of II Thessalonians chapter two as the Holy Spirit. This author does not agree with that stance. When we look at the work of the Holy Spirit, we find through our study in this segment of systematic theology that He does not restrain in the sense being defined in II Thessalonians chapter two. Believers can still willfully sin just the same as an unbeliever. They will be convicted of that sin because the Holy Spirit dwells within them. This should lead to repentance, but this side of glory, one is still more than capable of sinning. Pneumatology helps us to see the work of the Holy Spirit in relation to eschatology through the indwelling and divine prophecies.

Doctrinal Summarization would be that area of systematic theology that summarizes all the key doctrines. We said earlier that it is the sum of God's Word that makes up truth (Psalm 119:160). Doctrine is important and the timing of the Rapture is a doctrine. Many churches will include their position on the timing of the Rapture within their doctrinal statement. Many do not. The reason some do not is that they recognize that there are different opinions about the timing held by reputable Bible scholars, and so they choose not be dogmatic about a position. They may teach a position, but do not include it in their doctrinal statement.

While the timing of the Rapture is not a critical doctrine in the sense of salvation, it is still very important. Some, therefore, do include it in their doctrinal statements and have become dogmatic about it. This has led to church splits, accusations of heresy, and division within the body of Christ. Some of the doctrines historically held by the Church have come at great cost and much travail. I suspect that the doctrine of the Rapture will fall into that category until Christ's return.

The key focus with any of these systematic theology approaches or subjects is to understand that it was developed by man as a way to better understand truth as a whole and provide a somewhat comprehensive tool about how to understand God's Word. It is essentially important to always weigh any of these theologies against the true plumb line, which is the Word of God. Part II will discuss how to study God's Word, which is critical if we are going to be true Bereans.

PART II
THE PLUMB LINE

4

HOW DO I STUDY GOD'S WORD?

This is the second most important chapter in the book. The only one superseding it would be the last chapter [Summary-Are You Ready?], where the Gospel message is presented. This is also the chapter where I expect every seminary professor and graduate pastor to start banging their class rings on the table and declaring that a layperson cannot possibly arrive at truth apart from having had a formal, seminary education. If that were the case, this book would be an exercise in futility; if that were the case, no believer could be a Berean; if that were the case, the exhortation of II Timothy 2:15 would not make any sense.

Not only can you [as a layperson] arrive at truth, you will not be able to live a victorious Christian life apart from the ability to properly interpret Scripture. You will not be able to discern whether or not you are being deceived or misled by well-meaning teachers. You will become vulnerable and you will be weak in your ability to give a defense for the hope that is in you. It is never through human wisdom that we arrive at ultimate truth. I encourage you to read and consider what the Apostle Paul said in I Corinthians 1:18-31.

Now having said all of this, it is also important to equip yourself, and that may be through a reputable seminary or Christian college; but on the other hand, there are some fundamental approaches to studying God's Word that if practiced correctly, one can arrive at truth with confidence. We can learn these from trained theologians, seminary professors, pastors, teachers, and dedicated self-study. There are more good tools available for every believer today then ever before. If you are blessed to live in a free country where you can avail yourself of these tools, you should.

I spent an entire career in Research Development, Test and Evaluation (RDT&E) with the Air Force. You had to learn what the general and specific test objectives were, then plan and provision prior to executing the test. It required extreme discipline and proper planning. One of the objectives was learning how things would work when integrated. Components seemed to work fine on a bench or in a lab, but once they were integrated with other systems, it could impact the whole. The Bible is like that. We may think we have arrived at a certain truth or doctrine and on its own it seems to stand up to the test, but when we integrate that passage into the whole of Scripture, it may not. When that happens, we need to understand the integration or the broader context. I like a motto that the Empire Test Pilot School has. It states, *"Learn to Test, Test to Learn"*[1]. When we pray and learn how to apply some basic hermeneutics, we are learning how to test or search the Scripture for truth, and as we test the Scripture, we will learn and grow in the grace and knowledge of our Lord Jesus Christ.

The writer of Hebrews in chapter five talks about dullness and complacency (Hebrews 5:11-14). The book is addressed to Hebrew believers and non-believers. These Hebrew believers did not even know the oracles of God [basic Old Testament truths and laws]. They were like babies and could not digest the meatier things of God's Word. The analogy is given of babies and milk. A newborn infant is dependent on milk and little else. Parents like to take humor as they observe their babies wrestling with adult food, knowing full well that they can gnaw all they want but cannot eat it or digest it.

These folks addressed in the book of Hebrews, however, were expected to be well beyond the infant stage. They were to be like young adults who should be eating solid food, not remaining on milk only to sustain life. The types and pictures of the Old Testament are now revealed in the New, and we have the great truth before us in its complete revelation, but Christians are capable of becoming complacent and dependent on others to constantly feed them. I believe that we will continue to discover the deeper things of God's Word as long as we are on this side of eternity, but if we are not growing in the grace and knowledge of our Lord and Savior and pursuing truth, we are not going to mature in our faith. It is imperative for every follower of Christ to study His Word.

Our Lord provides gifted pastors and teachers (Ephesians 4:11), and every believer grows under their instruction. It does not, however, negate our responsibility to study and understand the Scriptures to both arrive at truth and discern whether or not those who are teaching us are sharing a proper interpretation of the Word. It troubles me deeply to see many contemporary churches teach with all the wonderful electronic media, where the Scripture is displayed on large screens with few in the congregation having a Bible in their hands. Many leave church, go have breakfast with each other, and then never pick up the Bible during the week. It troubles me to hear of folks who have professed belief for many years and yet are still uncomfortable sharing the Gospel, which is very basic truth. This is the milk, and we need to move on to the meat if we are to mature.

My wife and I attended a prophecy conference in late 2011 with a couple hundred other folks and I was so encouraged by the attendees. A few younger individuals attended but the majority were older, mature believers. Many of these wonderful believers were retired and well over 60 years of age. One was over 90. What impressed me were the worn Bibles, which were heavily marked with notes in the margins, binders separated—even taped in some cases. They were true Bereans.

During the breaks and throughout the conference, free time was spent in the hallways, around dinner and virtually everywhere, sharing truth with zeal and passion. It was *"iron sharpening iron"* (Proverbs 27:17). We should all be like that. Your interest in this subject is evidence of your desire to arrive at truth. Studying God's Word is like exercise; most of us fight it, but once we start we want more. It takes discipline, commitment, and dedication. You will need to set a specific time aside in your busy schedule to pursue it and recognize when you are being distracted by less important things. It happens to all of us, but it is easy to get back on track, you just need to constantly remind yourself. Once you establish a habit, it will become one.

I have a saying that all my kids and grandkids have heard many times. It goes like this: *"The sign of an un-kept person and un-kept things, is the sign of an un-kept life."* We can get distracted so easily, and before you know it, we become poor stewards of the possessions the Lord has blessed us with and the gifts He so graciously bestows upon us. If the habit persists, it will eventually wreak havoc in our life and even manifest itself in our appearance. We are so blessed to live in a free country where we can purchase Bibles, study books, and fellowship with one another. It is time to dust off the Bible, dig in, and be good stewards of these wonderful gifts and truths He has for us.

As we consider some of the mechanics and structure of studying Scripture, it will be important to emphasize that no matter how well educated you become in the fundamental principles of how to study the Scriptures or even if you are an expert in Hebrew, Greek, and Aramaic, you must first be a believer in order to arrive at the true meaning. Seminaries are probably full of individuals who have not accepted Jesus Christ as Lord and Savior, students who may do well in courses like hermeneutics.

The moment a person receives Jesus Christ as Lord and Savior of their life, the Holy Spirit indwells them and they are sealed unto the day of redemption (Ephesians 1:13,14). Romans 8:9 tell us that anyone who does not have the Spirit, he is not of Christ. All Christians are indwelt with the Holy Spirit (I Corinthians 12:13). The Holy Spirit convicts us of our sin upon hearing the Word, and when we respond in faith—realizing we cannot save ourselves and need Jesus Christ to save us—and then receive him through prayer, confessing with our mouth and believing in our heart, the Holy Spirit takes up residence within us. He [Holy Spirit] continues to work in our life teaching us, gifting us, leading us, purifying us, interceding for us, and producing fruit. Here, in context, we are focusing on the teaching aspect of the Holy Spirit. One of the greatest privileges we have as believers is to know that the Holy Spirit will teach us (John 14:26). He is a comforter, helper, and source of strength; He is our teacher, always present, always accessible.

During the introduction and in a previous paragraph, I mentioned II Timothy 2:15, which states: "Be diligent to present yourself approved to God as a workman who does not need to be ashamed, accurately handling the word of truth." The word "diligent" here is sometimes translated study. It is the Greek verb, *spoudazō,* meaning to exert oneself, and so diligence is a great translation. It does not convey a casual approach to the study of Scripture. It signifies a diligent pursuit of truth, involving time and discipline. It is not describing a believer who purchases a commentary and settles for what someone else has said. Commentaries are great and they do have their purpose. Many great teachers and theologians have spent much of their life work in giving us great commentaries, but you are exhorted to "be diligent" and to "accurately handle the word of truth."

As previously mentioned, the Holy Spirit will teach us. The word "teach" in John 14:26 is the Greek verb, *didaskō*, meaning to give instruction. As you pursue the study of Scripture, always start with prayer and ask the Holy Spirit to teach (instruct) you. This is the fundamental starting point. Be disciplined and when you arrive at truth, the Holy Spirit will not only bring to remembrance, but He will also create the passion and zeal within you to present the newfound truth to others.

Now, let's look at some basic things which must be considered when studying Scripture. Bibliology is that portion of systematic theology, which is the glue for all other doctrine and divisions of systematic theology. It is the study of the Bible, how we got it, the makeup, divisions, prophecy, dispensations, et cetera. The word Bible simply means books. There are 66 books in the Christian Bible. There are 39 in the Old Testament and 27 in the New Testament. One way I learned that was to take the 39 and make it three times nine and that would give you the number in the New [27]. We will talk more specifically about the make-up of the Bible later, but why do we have it? God loves us and desires to communicate with us. He has chosen to do this through the Scriptures. Because we are hard headed and stubborn, God revealed the Word to us through His Son, where the Word became flesh and dwelt among us (John 1:1, 14).

He continues to reveal His plan and purpose for our lives through His Word, so it starts with revelation or the unveiling of God's Word. Then He chose to breathe His Word into men, who then penned His truth (II Peter 1:21). The Bible tells us that all Scripture is "inspired" by God (II Timothy 3:16). Inspired means "God breathed". It is not like any other writing that has ever existed or ever will. The 66 books of the Bible are complete and often referred to as the canon of Scripture. In other words, there had to be a bar or standard set by which to measure that the Scripture met the criteria to be one of the 66 books that make up our Bible.

Not only did all prophecy have to be one hundred percent accurate, but also the Scriptures had to harmonize and be part of a cohesive whole. They had to be measured against the ones who penned it; were they true prophets of God? Were they authenticated by true miracles? Was their work without contradiction? Does it have transforming life effect? Did those who it was originally presented to accept it as God's Word?

So in review, revelation was first, God choosing to reveal His truth; then He chose to speak through men, recording the truth without error, which is inspiration; and then finally, the original Hebrew and Greek manuscripts had to be copied with exacting detail, which is transmission. Once copied and preserved, these original Scriptures and copies were translated into languages. This is the translation segment where it is important to refer back to the original language in order to arrive at a more accurate translation. Little irritates me more than to hear a pastor define a word used in the Bible with an English Dictionary.

Having the Scriptures in our own language, the next link is interpretation and illumination. This is where we seek to understand the Scripture through proper interpretation and where the Holy Spirit illuminates the Word to us (I Corinthians 2:9-13). I really like verse 13, "which things we also speak, not in words taught by human wisdom, but in those taught by the Spirit, combining spiritual thoughts with spiritual words." You cannot arrive at the full truth by human wisdom. Man in his pride has always gotten it wrong apart from God (Proverbs 14:12). The word of the cross and salvation does not make sense to man in his own wisdom (I Corinthians 1:18-21).

Once you discover the truth, it is important to apply the truth, which is a critical link. We must be doers of the Word (James 1:22-24). As a result of this, we should have changed lives and exhibit fruit. When we become complacent, we set ourselves up for failure. I have been there and so have many of you. The good news is that He will continue the work in us until He comes and beyond. He loves us and is merciful and gracious, but we should not take advantage of that fact. Staying in His Word is one way of staying on course (Psalm 119:11).

Having understood that God desires to communicate with us and chose His Word to do so, we now need to apply the basic principles of hermeneutics. Here are some basics:

1. **All Scripture has a literal meaning.** There is the plain literal and figurative literal, but all is literal and you must avoid falling into the trap of allegorizing Scripture. Do not try to read something into it that is not there. If it makes sense as written, do not seek another sense. Do not try to trap me here by saying that there are allegories and figures in Scripture. That would be a misunderstanding of what I am saying. There is no doubt figurative language, allegorical inferences, and symbolic presentations in God's Word, but understanding the figure, allegory, and/or symbols will lead to the literal meaning that God is conveying.

   Jesus spoke in parables and the religious leaders of the day did not understand them. He used them to conceal and reveal truth. The figures used are typical in language, such as a metaphors, euphemisms, hyperbole, similes, et cetera, but always with the intent of presenting a greater literal truth. The allegories or analogies are presented to help the reader understand the greater literal truth. This is why we must **not** emphasize the figure or the allegory, but rather look for the meaning attempting to be conveyed.

2. You must **consider word meanings and relationships**. It is important to go back to the original language. You can use a number of tools to do that. You should have a good exhaustive concordance (not just the one in the back of your Bible) and couple it with good expository dictionaries for both the Old and New Testaments. I would suggest taking a course in Greek and Hebrew if your church offers such. There are wonderful works on biblical figures of speech and cross-referencing guides available.

3. You must **consider the historical and cultural implications** of the time it was written. Some use a slightly modified "*six*

serving men"[2] concept, asking "who, what, when, where, why, and how?" regarding any passage. Who is being addressed by the author, what is the subject, when did the discussion take place, where are they and the significance of the time and place, why is the instruction being given, and how, with what illustration, is the author trying to reach them.

There are many good tools that give the historical setting of the Bible along with maps and explanations of what was taking place in every period of history. There are tools, which speak to the customs of the day and even the sayings, which will help you to understand the setting. Additionally, there are good tools for understanding the figures used in Scripture.

4. Context is very, very important. **There are three contexts to any Scripture: 1. Immediate, 2. Book, 3. Bible.** If you simply take a passage and attempt to build your doctrine around it without considering context, you may miss the true meaning. Scripture must be cohesive. It must agree with itself and never contradict. It should not only find its way consistently through the New Testament, but should also be true in the Old Testament. There are good tools available along with search engines to look up common language passages along with themes. Always compare Scripture with Scripture. The Internet has some great sites for this; just make sure it is a reputable one. Ask your pastor for a recommendation.

5. **Contradictions are never acceptable.** There are times that a contradiction might be apparent, but a careful search and study should eliminate all contradictions. Look at commentaries and works by trained theologians, but always compare it to the plumb line of Scripture and ensure that it aligns correctly.

6. **Recognize the near and far implications and applications of Scripture.** There are types in the Old Testament and there are passages where there are both near (relevant to the time written) and far (prophetic or future) implications as you will see when we look at the various times and periods and how they relate to the end-times.

7. **Avoid using terms to describe your conclusions that are not biblical.** Much of the confusion surrounding the 70th Week of

Daniel results from using terms to describe events and times, which are not biblical. There are some translations like the word *"rapture"*, which is really a Latin transliteration, but I would prefer to use the term *harpazó*, which is the Greek word for catch or "caught up", as used in I Thessalonians 4:17. I would also avoid words like *"tribulation period"* in reference to the 70th Week of Daniel. It does not appear in Scripture. "Rapture" (while present in a Latin Bible) and "Tribulation Period" are terms not found in the English Bible, but the concept is well known as they relate to the 70th Week of Daniel, and so we may refer to them throughout this book so as to not confuse the reader. Just know that they are words used by theologians to describe an event and period of time, much like theologians describe time periods in history using dispensations.

Yes, the Bible does talk about the tribulation of *those days* (in context referring to the Great Tribulation) and it certainly talks about the "Great Tribulation", but that starts 3½ years into the 70th Week of Daniel and nowhere is the entire seven-year period referred to as the "tribulation period" in Scripture. Will there be trouble during the entire seven-year period? No question, but nowhere is it referred to as the "tribulation period" in the Bible. I would use the term *parousia* in the Greek to describe Jesus' "coming". It means arrival and presence with. I would also use "Day of the Lord" in reference to God's wrath as opposed to "tribulation". Stick to biblical terms and then use all the tools above to cross-reference and determine if they fit or not. Again, we are going to break my own rule here as we refer to some events and times based on the traditional use of the terms, but where we do, we will indicate whether or not it is man's reference or the Bible for the use of such terminology.

8. Once you have applied these basic principles, it is not a bad idea to **research others' work and compare** what they have said to your own conclusions. Check their background and basis for their conclusions. Did they apply a good herme-neutic? I find this to be valuable in many ways. First, it causes me to dig deeper at times. Second, it confirms my conclusions

at times, and third, it helps me form a basis for defending my conclusions.

It is also very important to memorize Scripture, meditate on it, and share it. We should seek after the Word like it is a hidden treasure, waiting to be discovered (Proverbs 2:4).

Here are just some of the basic terms and references we will use as we study the subject of eschatology:

- The 70th Week of Daniel (Daniel 9:24-27)
- Caught up (*harpazó*) (I Thessalonians 4:17)
- The Great Tribulation (Matthew 24: 21, Revelation 7:14)
- Coming (*parousia*) (Matthew 24:3, 27, 37, 39, I Thessalonians 4:15, II Thessalonians 2:1,8,9, James 5:7, 8, II Peter 1:16, 3:4, 3:12, I John 2:28)
- False Prophet (Revelation 19:20)
- "Keep you from the hour" (Revelation 3:10)
- Seven seals (Revelation 5:1)
- Antichrist or the Beast (over 80 descriptive references, I John 2:18, Revelation 16:13)
- Abomination of Desolation (Matthew 24:15, Mark 13:14, Daniel 9:27)
- Day of the Lord (Isaiah 7:18-25, 13:6, Ezekiel 30:3, Joel 2:1, 31, Zephaniah 1:7, 14-18, Revelation 6:16-17, chapter 8, 16:14, II Peter 3:10)
- Beginning of birth pangs (Mark 13:8, Matthew 24:8)
- A thousand years (six times in Revelation chapter 20)
- Gathering (II Thessalonians 2:1, Matthew 24:31)

These are but a few of the terms and phrases which must be considered. The correlation as we compare Scripture with Scripture later will be astounding. Other phrases like *"the sun, moon, and stars"* and how they relate to the Lord's return will also be key in understanding the timing of the Rapture.

Let's take a brief look at the books of the Bible. Theologians typically break down the Old Testament into five major divisions:

1. **The Law** (the first five books, or the Pentateuch as it is often referred to). The word Pentateuch comes from two words, *penta* meaning five, and *teuchos* meaning scrolls, hence five books. It is the law or often referred to as the Torah. Moses penned these first five books. You will hear the phrase *Mosaic Law*. There are some 613 of them.
2. **History and Government** (Joshua through Esther). God ruled under a theocracy using judges, and then because of man's hard heart, He allowed human government and rule, beginning with King Saul. King David would succeed him.
3. **Poetry** (Job through Song of Solomon). While considered under the category of poetic, these books speak of human victory and failure along with wisdom and divine counsel. For instance, the book of Proverbs is often referred to as the book of *wisdom*.
4. **Major Prophets** (Isaiah through Daniel). Major, mainly due to the size of the books.
5. **Minor Prophets** (Hosea through Malachi). Minor, mainly due to the size of the books.

The New Testament divisions are:

1. **History** (Matthew through Acts). The synoptic Gospels and the history of the Church.
2. **Teaching** (Romans through Philemon). These are the 13 letters to both churches and individuals, written by the Apostle Paul.
3. **General Letters** (Hebrews through Jude). To Hebrew believers and unbelievers, letters of instruction by individuals to all believers.
4. **Prophecy** (Revelation). The final book of the 66 Books of the Bible in both words and time. It concludes with a warning to those who would add to its content. Any religion who uses the Bible in conjunction with other books that they regard with equal inspiration are in danger here. While this is arguably the New Testament book of prophecy, it could and should be said that over one-fourth of the Bible is prophetic, which

also includes key prophetic passages in other books contained within the New Testament.

Now that we have a pretty good idea of what basic tools we need to work with, let's look at what considerations are necessary when studying Scripture, how the Bible itself is constructed, and some basic truths about prophecy itself.

We get the word prophecy from the Greek noun *prophēteia*. It simply means to speak forth the mind and counsel of God. Both in the Old and New Testament it refers to the prophet as one who not only speaks forth the mind and counsel of God, but also speaks of future events. The true test of a prophet in the Old Testament was that he had to be one hundred percent accurate, one hundred percent of the time (Deuteronomy 18:18-22).

Are there prophets today? With the full canon of Scripture, I would say no. Is there the gift of prophecy today? There are two sides to that word meaning: (1) The gift as it relates to forth-telling of future events (predicting based on a direct revelation from God) (2) The gift as it relates to speaking forth what is already written. I would say that the latter gift (I Corinthians 12:10) as it relates to gifted pastors and teachers or having the ability to speak forth the written Word of God as great orators is true of today.

There have been many who have made predictions, which have not come true. Many well meaning Christians have attempted over history to predict dates or even specific days. Once again, the Bible is always the plumb line for truth, and it is clear from Matthew 24:36 that nobody will know the hour or the day of our Lord's return. Having said that, there is a tremendous amount of prophecy in the Bible. Over one-fourth of the Bible contains prophecy. It could be argued that the entire Bible is prophetic in that it is God-breathed, not a result of man. Individuals, however, were chosen by God to pen the words in the Bible and were moved by the Holy Spirit (II Peter 1:21). For over 40 authors from such diverse backgrounds, spanning over 1,500 years and from different places around the world, to produce 66 books which are in absolute harmony with one another speaks of the fact that it is the result of God.

There are even wonderful parallels in the Jewish canon. If you were to break down their important writings, it would look something like this:

Torah (the Law or the Pentateuch) would be Genesis through Deuteronomy.

The Neveeim would be the books of the prophets; the former prophets being Joshua through Kings, the latter prophets being Isaiah through Ezekiel, and then the twelve (the minor prophets) were reckoned as one book.

The Kethuvim would contain the "Other Writings" which would be Psalms, Proverbs, Job, Song of Songs, Ruth, Lamentations, Ecclesiastes, Esther, Daniel, Ezra, Nehemiah (1) and Chronicles.

Note that Daniel falls within the other writings. The only reason for mentioning this construct is to illustrate to the Gentile that there are parallels we can use to share with our Jewish friends. I recall a time when I read Isaiah chapter 53 to a Jewish friend of mine and asked him who he thought the writing was referring to without giving a reference. He immediately said Jesus Christ. I then shared with him that it was from Isaiah, considered one of the latter prophets in the Neveeim. He read it for himself, and while he was not ready to make a decision for Christ, he said that he needed to study more. I pray to this day that he has made that decision.

Our relationship with those who are the sons and daughters of Abraham is paramount. Our relationship with the sovereign State of Israel is critical, and we must continue to bless Israel if we are going to be blessed as a nation. It is through Abraham that all the nations have been blessed. It is through Abraham that Christ came and through whom we are adopted.

As you study God's Word you will find that Israel is a tremendous key to understanding prophecy, so we do well in making ourselves aware of the mindset, culture, and history of the Jewish people. My wife and I were blessed to take a trip to Israel back in 2000 and we hope to have the opportunity to travel there again. Ultimately, we will return there one day, and we look forward to the time that Jesus Christ will reign and the throne of David in the New Jerusalem is re-established.

Another area of research should be the early counsels and conferences. By looking at where some of systematic theology evolved from and what proponents championed various doctrines, we can investigate their research and conclusions to see if they are valid when compared to Scripture. Great scholars and men of faith have poured their lives into research and have endured confrontational debates and forums in order to share what they believe is truth.

When looking at the pre-tribulation doctrine for instance, you will discover that it was within the late 1800s that this view reached the United States, some fifty or so years after its origin. With the release of the second edition of the *Scofield Study Bible*[3] in 1917, containing study notes on the subject, it became a part of American fundamental Christian doctrine. From here it was taught in all the major seminaries across America and remains the most popular doctrine to this day. Does that make it correct? We will look into this in later chapters, where we go into greater detail on each position.

I can tell you that you will not find it in the Apostles Creed, the Nicene Creed, the Athanasian Creed, Westminster Confession of Faith, Baptist Conference of 1689, or the Philadelphia Confession of Faith, among other important forums and conferences of the early Church. While men like John Darby of the Plymouth Brethren supported this view, he had contemporaries like Benjamin Wills Newton who did not and who wrote on the topic of last days as well.

In 1879, Newton wrote the third edition of *The Prophecy of the Lord Jesus, as contained in Matthew XXIV and XXV*[4]. His writing indicated that he believed that the Church would enter the 70th Week of Daniel. Other early historical writings, such as the *Didache*, which dates back to the time of the apostles, indicated that they believed we [the Church] would enter the 70th Week of Daniel.

PART III

FURTHER INFLUENCES
ON ESCHATOLOGY

5

WHAT ARE BIBLICAL COVENANTS?

M y intent here is not to present a detailed or scholarly answer to this question. There are entire volumes of works on this subject, which can give you greater insight and detail than I can. My purpose in even mentioning this is to expose the reader to the fact that there are many man-made systems and interpretations that have resulted in doctrine being established only after fitting into these systems. This is true of systematic theology, mentioned earlier, and it is true of the dispensationalist approach, which we will discuss in the next chapter. Having said that, all of these systems have value and purpose when viewed in an appropriate context. Please do not misunderstand me; I am in no way attempting to discredit these tremendous works by great men of faith. What I am saying is that we must always submit to the final authority of God's Word and not allow systems to determine ultimate truth. I believe those same men of faith who developed these great works would ultimately agree with that.

Biblical covenants may be a bit different in that these are truth contained in Scripture, which are more explicit. Most seminaries will teach that there are seven biblical covenants. Before we mention what they are and give a brief explanation of each, we should understand what a covenant is. Simply put, a covenant is an agreement. So, a biblical covenant is an agreement between God and a person or peoples. Some are to mankind as a whole and some are to individuals with relationship to Israel as a people. One could easily argue with that definition and say that there are many promises within Scripture, both within the Old Testament and New Testament, but again, we are speaking of a system that takes a general overall view and provides specific covenants consistent with both systematic theology and a dispensational approach, not just promises.

The reason for including the subjects of systematic theology and dispensations in our study of eschatology is to provide some insight and understanding as to how certain doctrine emerged within the Church and, in particular, the wide-spread Western beliefs concerning the return of Christ. If you build your reasoning around these systems as evidence for your exposition of doctrine, you appear to have a defense, which fits nicely into these systematic approaches. The systems then become your basis for defense along with some isolated text found within the Bible. On the other hand, if you reason strictly from Scripture and take a normal approach to understanding the language within Scripture as your sole basis for arriving at truth, you may find some inconsistencies with the aforementioned approach. The danger with any man-made approach to defining Scripture as a subset for understanding could lead to the next level, which has resulted in allowing culture to define truth. I believe that is why some faiths within "Christianity" have compromised and permitted a departure from the moral teaching of God's Word. This too fits into prophecy and the literal churches mentioned in Revelation chapters two and three. It is also serves as warning to us.

Covenants are important. We make covenants every day. Some are conditional and some are unconditional. The difference between God and us of course is that He is always faithful to keep His covenants. We are not so good at it. That is apparent with the evidence of divorce in our nation. We are sinful people and many of us have had divorce in our life. It was because of our hardness of heart that divorce even came about. It was never God's desire for us. He is a gracious and forgiving God, so do not lose heart if you have had divorce in your past. Regardless of what you may feel or have been told, God still loves you and has a purpose for your life.

God loves Israel and yet they were unfaithful to the covenant (Hosea 6:7). Jeremiah was despondent. He never saw a convert as far as we know. In chapter three of Jeremiah we see the Lord's anger at Israel and Judah, and their unfaithfulness is compared to that of a harlot in verse six. As a result, the Lord issued her a writ of divorce in verse eight. The word for divorce here is *kerithuth* in the Hebrew, which means "cutting off". Some would even say that they have been cut off completely/permanently and that the Lord will not deal with them again, but that would be extreme replacement theology, which is not biblical in my view. One need only to look at Jeremiah 3:11-14 in that same context to see that the Lord invites them to return, and He will not look upon them with anger forever.

We should turn to Romans chapter 11 for evidence that God is not done with Israel. In verse 11 Paul states, "I say then, they did not stumble so as to fall, did they? May it never be! But by their transgression salvation *has* come to the Gentiles, to make them jealous." Going down to Romans 11:22 we read, "Behold then the kindness and severity of God; to those who fell, severity, but to you, God's kindness, if you continue in His kindness; otherwise you also will be *cut off*." [Emphasis mine.] They [Israel] were cut off due to their unfaithfulness and pursuit of idols. Gentiles can be guilty of that too.

Look now at verse 25 of Romans chapter 11, "For I do not want you, brethren to be uninformed of this mystery—so that you will not be wise in your own estimation—that a partial hardening has happened to Israel until the fullness of the Gentiles has come in; and so all Israel will be saved; just as it is written, "The Deliverer will come from Zion, He will remove ungodliness from Jacob", "This is My covenant with them when I take away their sins."

One day, Israel, who currently does not accept Jesus Christ as their Messiah, will. If a Jew believes now, he/she becomes a member of the Church and are true Israelites. Some, at the time when Jesus had His earthly ministry, were looking for a "Messiah Ben David", and some a "Messiah Ben Joseph". They were looking for a son representative of a conquering king [Ben David] to restore, rule, and reign with them and therefore could not see the suffering Messiah [Ben Joseph] who would come to take away their sins once and for all. The word Ben is used as a Jewish surname, meaning *son of*.

When Jesus rode into Jerusalem on a colt in Matthew 21, He was rejected. He confronted the religious leaders of the day, yet as He was getting ready to depart the city in Matthew 23:37-39, we read this: "Jerusalem, Jerusalem, who kills the prophets and stones those who are sent to her! How often I wanted to gather your children together, the way a hen gathers her chicks under her wings, and you were unwilling. Behold, your house is being left to you desolate! For I say to you, from now on you will not see Me until you say, 'Blessed is He who comes in the name of the Lord!'" Jesus fulfills I Kings 9:7 and Jeremiah 22:5 by cutting them off for a time, but not forever, otherwise the part where He says, "you will not see Me until you say, 'Blessed is He who comes in the name of the Lord!'" would not make sense.

Immediately following this verse in Matthew 23, He goes out from the temple and to the Mount of Olives to share with His disciples regarding a near and far prophecy. The near would be in Matthew 24:1, which would be fulfilled in A.D. 70, and the far is the Olivet Discourse portion referring to the 70th Week of Daniel with specific reference in verse 15. He is no longer speaking to Israel but to those who would become the Church. The apostles were Jews but also the leaders of the Church when established on the day of Pentecost in Acts chapter two. All this to say that the Lord will remain faithful to His covenants and can continue to draw Israel while concurrently blessing the Church, even into the 70th Week of Daniel.

There are conditional covenants and unconditional covenants in the Bible, as we will discuss later. I remember years ago working on building a decorative sidewalk beside my house in the backyard. I had one of those neat molds that you pour your mix of concrete into and then continue to join sections together to form your patio or sidewalk. I had to lay a pretty good base down first so it would not crack when stepped upon. I told my middle daughter that if she and her cousin helped, I would take them to a theme park. I made a conditional covenant with them. Their part was to help and my part was to take them to the theme park. They were faithful to their part and worked really hard. They met the conditions of the covenant and so I kept my end of the agreement and took them to the theme park of their choice. I will always love my kids and grandkids no matter what. That is an unconditional covenant. I do not have to formalize it, but I always tell them I love them and I really mean it as well as demonstrating it in different ways. The biblical covenants are also conditional and unconditional, as we will see among these seven.

You will hear terms like covenant theology or terms like replacement theology. These are not one in the same. I would encourage you to research these and gain some understanding as to their meaning. Basically, covenant theology is used as one baseline of biblical interpretation, which is why we think it is important to remember that the Scriptures should be interpreted in their normal sense and not on a pre-defined set of covenants.

There are times when covenant theology will contrast with dispensationalism, but not always. As a matter of fact, it can go hand-in-hand with dispensationalism when strictly following the teaching of John Calvin[1] as it pertains to a system of theology. This is more of an outgrowth and continuation of the reformation—or reformed Church—and/or Calvinistic perspective. I would tend to agree with the greater body of John Calvin's theology, but I still contend that we should hold up the Scriptures as the final authority on all matters of doctrine and dogma.

Covenant theology looks at three broad covenants being that of works, grace, and redemption. All the seven we will speak about briefly fit into those categories. Replacement Theology says that God is done with Israel because of their unfaithfulness, which is not biblical as demonstrated in an earlier paragraph. Are you starting to get the issue we have with this means of interpretation? Confused yet? Hang in there; we will give a brief overview.

When approaching the text in the Olivet Discourse found in Matthew 24 (where Jesus spoke to His disciples from the Mount of Olives after being rejected and departing Jerusalem), these systems would state a separate and distinct difference between the Church and Israel, and in some writings, even demand that the Olivet Discourse is spoken to Israel alone and has nothing to do with the Church. We believe that Israel is distinct from the Church, but that does not mean that God cannot work out His plan with them concurrently. Others would claim that those who believe that the Church will enter the 70th Week of Daniel do not understand the distinction, dispensations, or covenants. The fact that the covenants, in particular the Palestinian and Davidic, and the future, spoken of by the Prophet Daniel, were to

Israel, eliminates in their minds the Church as a consideration during the 70th Week. This is faulty logic. They would say that since the Church was not in the first 69 Weeks of Daniel's prophecy, therefore they will not be in the 70th and that Daniel is clearly to Israel. There is no biblical basis for this rationale.

If one looks at Mark 13, you will see the same reference to the Olivet Discourse teaching of Jesus. Similar words appear in Luke 17 and Luke 21. The language in all accounts match up with the book of Revelation and Old Testament books such as Isaiah, Joel, Amos, Zephaniah, et cetera. The idea that the Church is not in view in any of these passages, where Jesus taught His disciples concerning His *coming*, is unfortunate, and as we will see later, may not be true. So, what are these seven covenants?

1. The Adamic Covenant – As one could guess from the title, this would be a covenant between God and Adam. This is also a covenant for all mankind. It is generally referred to in Genesis 3:15-19. Adam and Eve were responsible for obeying God in the Garden of Eden. They could eat of any of the fruit, but they could not eat of the tree of the knowledge of good and evil. You know the story. They disobeyed and that disobedience became inherited sin for all born after. We have inherited sin and we have sin because of choices we make. The Adamic Covenant provided justice and grace. God would cause the ground to be full of thorns and thistles, man would work hard all his days, and a woman would have pain in childbirth. The very ground was cursed. The ultimate was that they would experience physical death. I find it amazing that in Romans 8:19 we read, "For the anxious longing of the Creation waits eagerly for the revealing of the sons of God."

   It makes sense. Creation itself was cursed at the fall of man and it too longs for Jesus' return and restoration. In this covenant, God also provided a promise and grace. We see this in Genesis 3:15, "And I will put enmity between you and the woman, and between your seed and her seed; He shall bruise you on the head and you shall bruise him on the heel." This was the promise of the virgin birth and victory at the cross of our Lord and Savior Jesus Christ. God made a provision for the sin of man and the inherited sin of all mankind throughout the ages to come. We have seen that part of the promise fulfilled when Jesus Christ died on the cross for our sins and was resurrected on the third day. The future will yield deliverance from the cursed ground, the hard labor, and those things that plague us each day of our mortal existence. Once Jesus comes He will establish a kingdom and then a new heaven and new earth without the conditions which resulted from the fall in the Garden.

2. The Noahic Covenant – This is the covenant between God and Noah, but not just Noah. It is a covenant with all mankind. This covenant is referenced in Genesis 6:18 as a specific covenant between God and Noah, and in general for all mankind in Genesis 9:8-17. Man had become so corrupt and evil (Genesis 6:5), but God found favor in Noah. God's heart grieved and we can grieve the Holy Spirit today when we sin. Ephesians 4:30 states, "Do not grieve the Holy Spirit of God, by whom you were sealed for the day of redemption." God was going to wipe out all of mankind, but because He found favor with Noah, He provided grace and mercy.

    We see God's judgment when He in fact flooded the world (Genesis 7:17). All flesh not in the Ark perished (Genesis 7:21). God provided grace to Noah in that He gave him [Noah] a way of deliverance with forewarning. Noah was faithful and built an Ark just like God directed. It had never rained before and it had not flooded before. He was unique and did what he was directed by God to do, whether it made sense to him or not based on the culture or surroundings of his day. The return of Christ will be like that. For those who have called upon His name and received Him as Lord and Savior, He will deliver through the Rapture, but at that same hour, just like in the days of Noah, He will pour out His judgment on the wicked during the Day of the Lord's wrath.

    God found favor with Noah and spared him and his family and two of every kind of animal, and on the very day that Noah entered the Ark, the floods came and it was too late for anyone else to be delivered. They would perish. It will be like that in the last days. We are not in darkness that His wrath should overtake us by surprise or like a thief, but it will be a surprise for the wicked, just like it was in the moment Noah entered the Ark. We will be delivered at the Rapture if we are alive when He comes and we have placed our trust in Jesus Christ alone as our Lord and Savior.

The other part of the covenant with Noah was the one for all mankind. It is found in Genesis chapter nine. It is the covenant sign of the rainbow, where God promises to never flood the whole world again (Genesis 9:8-17). There are those in recent years who have perished by flood. You may even know of a family who has lost members to some of the devastating floods of this past decade resulting from earthquakes or hurricanes. This does not mean that God did not keep His promise, for these were not worldwide floods. Nevertheless, these were devastating to those of you who may have lost someone and we pray that you would be consoled in your grief and loss. We never know when these things will occur for sure, but most of the time, there is some level of warning.

I have a sister in New Jersey who lives near the coast in the southern portion of the state. Weather forecasts during the recent storms indicated a severe path and good chance of flooding in her area. The authorities and news outlets advised residents in those areas to evacuate. There was a point where they said that they would not provide emergency services in those areas, and that if people did not evacuate they would be on their own. She and a neighbor waited until the last minute. She called and did not know what to do. I called the authorities there and they said she was on her own and that she should leave right away. This was not the news she wanted to hear. Together with her neighbor, they drove north of the area with what little they had in their hands and a couple of pets. It turned out that her home was not damaged and she was not harmed. The Scriptures are more explicit in terms of the last days than most Christians are aware of. We can take heed to the warnings Jesus gives in the Olivet Discourse or what Paul gives in his epistles, or we can wait until the last minute. Either way, we are told to be vigilant, to watch and pray, to be alert, to be sober, to be informed, and not be misled. Believers will ultimately be delivered, but they may have to give their life if they do not pay attention, and even if they do, we are approaching a time when we may have to lay down our life for our faith. For the wicked, there will be no emergency services and they will perish under the wrath of God. It will be like the days of Noah. By the way, my sister is a believer.

3. The Abrahamic Covenant – Here is a covenant between God and Abram, who would be called Abraham. This is a covenant for Israel. We find this covenant in Genesis 12:1-3. Prior to this man started down the path of corruption and wickedness again. There was the tower of Babel, where God chose to scatter them and confuse their language. Would it not have been wonderful if we all spoke the same language? Well, folks messed that up for us. Abram's father was Terah. "Terah took Abram his son, and Lot the son of Haran, his grandson, and Sarai his daughter-in-law (*who would become Sarah*), his son Abram's wife; and they went out together from Ur of the Chaldeans in order to enter the land of Canaan; and they went as far as Haran, and settled there." (Genesis11:31-32). The Lord told Abram to leave that country to a land He would show him. Then the covenant in Genesis 12:2-3, "And I will make you a great nation. And I will bless you, and make your name great; and so you shall be a blessing; and I will bless those who bless you, and the one who curses you I will curse. And in you all the families of the earth will be blessed."

God would change his name to Abraham. The promise continues in chapter 15 where his descendants would be numbered as the stars. In chapter 16 Abram has a child with Sarai's Egyptian maid, Hagar. He would be Ishmael. In chapter 17 we see the specific covenant (Genesis17:3-5). Abraham was ninety-nine years old when this covenant happened. Still, Abraham would need a son from his line. We see where he would be circumcised and that every male among them who is eight-days-old would be circumcised. Abraham was 100-years-old when told he would have a son with Sarah who was 90. What an amazing God! In chapter 15 Isaac was born just as the promise declared, and the line would continue through Jacob and so on. Israel would become a people from this line. Abraham believed God and is the father of faith. If we believe, we too are the spiritual descendants of Abraham and have been grafted in. Galatians 3:7-9, "Therefore, be sure that it is those who are of faith who are sons of Abraham.

The Scripture, foreseeing that God would justify the Gentiles by faith, preached the Gospel beforehand to Abraham, saying, "All the nations will be blessed in you." So then those who are of faith are blessed with Abraham, the believer." In the same chapter, verse 29 states, "And if you belong to Christ, then you are Abraham's descendants, heirs according to promise." This is how the grace is extended through the covenant with Abraham to all the families of the earth. The direct descendants would become unfaithful and be placed in captivity at times, but He will call them back one day. They are once again in the land, and on May 14, 1948, they became a recognized sovereign State. In 1967, they re-gained East Jerusalem.

We are living in a unique period of human history like no other. We talked about the writ of divorce earlier in this chapter of the book, but God is by no means done with the nation or direct descendants of Israel. Once the Church is raptured we see a remnant of Israel sealed with protection from the coming wrath of God in Revelation 7:4-8. These would be the 12,000 from each of the 12 tribes for 144,000. When the Church is raptured, God is not left without a *"people,"* however the Bible does not say anything in context about these 144,000 witnessing during this period. We are told that the 144,000 are sealed, blameless, and identified with Christ, but nothing is specifically stated about witnessing. These 144,000 are divinely protected and have His name and the name of His Father written on their foreheads (Revelation 14), which is the exact opposite of the Antichrist and the mark of the beast, which the wicked will take on their forehead or on their hand and therefore will be subject to God's wrath (Revelation 14:9-11). They are the first fruits that come to Christ after the Rapture. This is just as prophesied in Ezekiel 20:35, 37. Those who do call upon the name of the Lord are light and salt, but as to their exact function, I cannot say. We do know that there are going to be two witnesses who come upon the scene for 1,260 days, as stated in Revelation chapter 11. There are a number of thoughts as to who they are, but I cannot say. We see what they do in chapter 11 and that they will be slain by the beast after completing their purpose in giving testimony. Their dead bodies will be placed in the streets as a spectacle in the great city, but will come alive after 3 ½ days and go up into heaven as their enemies watch, followed by wrath being poured out on the earth. Many will be terrified, and in verse 13, as a result of that terror, those who survived give "glory to the God of heaven".

4. The Palestinian Covenant – This is a covenant with Israel. It is found in Deuteronomy 29:1-29 and Deuteronomy 30. This covenant is unconditional. It really comes after the Mosaic Covenant, which we will discuss next. God is not done with the Israelites and He will eventually bring them back as a nation. It will be different than the nation/state of Israel today that still largely does not accept Jesus Christ as Messiah. Those who have received Him are members of the Church just like the early apostles, who were also Jewish in descent. The national covenant here is the earthly kingdom where they will be ruled under the throne of David once again. Some assign this to the millennial kingdom. God did bring them back to the land in 1948. He will one day circumcise their hearts with love for Him. He will divinely protect them like never before in that He will judge Israel's enemies.

I truly believe that God has always preserved His chosen people and divinely protected them from complete destruction. So many have risen up against Israel and yet the God of Abraham, Isaac, and Jacob will not let those who threaten her demise be fully successful. We have a history of miracle upon miracle where they have survived the worst persecutions and attacks both nationally and individually. This covenant is coupled to the covenant with Abraham and God where He will bless those nations who bless Israel and curse those nations who curse her.

Lastly, God will cause them to prosper. There is a near and far application to this covenant. The United States has historically stood with Israel since 1948, and President Truman was instrumental in their recognition for being a sovereign State. I believe that because of our nation's founding based largely upon Judeo-Christian values and our standing with Israel, that we have been a blessed nation. We need to continue to pray that the United States will always bless Israel or we may be cursed ourselves. We should continue to reach out to the sons and daughters of Abraham with the saving message of Jesus Christ.

5. <u>The Mosaic Covenant</u> – As you would guess, this is a covenant between God and Moses for Israel. This would be a conditional covenant for the most part. Some would reason that covenants, while appearing to be conditional with the use of terms such as "*if*", are still the result of the establishment and origin of God and therefore find fulfillment in the will of God. This is true when looking at the fact that it is God who establishes His covenants, and it is this same Sovereign God who will bring about His purposes, not necessarily viewing the covenants as separate and distinct, as much as purposeful with intent. In other words, there is always a divine purpose for the covenants, which find their ultimate fulfillment in accordance with the plan of God.

In Exodus chapter 19, we see that in the third month after the sons of Israel had gone out of Egypt, God called Moses up to Mt Sinai. There He established a covenant with Moses in Exodus 19:5-6, where God said, "Now then, if you will indeed obey My voice and keep My covenant, then you shall be My own possession among all the peoples, for all the earth is Mine; and you shall be to Me a kingdom of priests and a holy nation. These are the words that you shall speak to the sons of Israel."

The word "holy" here means set apart. They [Israel] would have a distinct purpose in God's plan. If we turn to Deuteronomy chapter 11 verses 26-28, we read, "See, I am setting before you today a blessing and a curse: the blessing, if you listen to the commandments of the Lord your God, which I am commanding you today; and the curse, if you do not listen to the commandments of the Lord your God, but turn aside from the way which I am commanding you today, by following other gods which you have not known." Here we see what appears to be a condition. If you listen to the commandments, blessing; if you do not, cursing. Israel, as a nation, set apart for the purposes and plans of God has experienced both. We read earlier that God had cut them off because of their disobedience and actually issued a figurative writ of divorce, but we also read that God offered them the blessing, should they obey and return to Him and one day they will.

The Mosaic Law is often thought of as the "Ten Commandments". When we look at all the laws in Leviticus, we find that there are some 613 commandments or laws. When we look at Romans chapter three, we see God's plan for the law. Verse 19-20 states, "Now we know that whatever the Law says, it speaks to those who are under the Law, so that every mouth may be closed and all the world may become accountable to God; because by the works of the Law no flesh will be justified in His sight; for through the Law *comes* the knowledge of sin."

Jesus spoke of the Law as a means of exposing sin with the intent of the hearer acknowledging his/her need for a Savior. James tells us in James 2:10, "For whoever keeps the whole law and yet stumbles in one point, he has become guilty of all." The Law cannot save us. Works cannot save us. The Law was given as our *"tutor"*, showing us our sin and leading us to justification by faith (Galatians 3:24). Does Israel still attempt to keep the Law? I would say yes and no. Yes, there is a desire to continue the Levitical priesthood and the calling for obedience to the Law of Moses, but we know that nobody can keep the entire law. All are condemned under the Law, but are justified by faith in Jesus Christ alone for their salvation, Jew and Gentile. Will Israel be saved? Yes, there is a yet future time coming when Israel will be saved (Romans 11:25-27). That is after the Great Tribulation spoken of by Jesus in the Olivet Discourse and in Revelation chapter 6. We find this new covenant in Jeremiah 31:31-37.

6. The Davidic Covenant – This covenant, as the wording suggests, is a covenant between God and David and is for Israel. The message of this covenant is found in II Samuel 7:8-17. God is going to work out His divine plan in many ways according to this covenant. He will make David a great name and appoint a place for His people Israel. He will send forth One who will come from his [David] descendants and establish His [Jesus] Kingdom. There will come a time when Israel's enemies will no longer disturb them or attack them. When the Lord comes, He will establish His throne and it will be an everlasting kingdom, v.13.

Many times, we gloss over the genealogy presented within the Bible, but it is given for our understanding and provides a wonderful key to unlocking prophetic truth. The first line in Matthew starts out, "The record of the genealogy of Jesus the Messiah the son of David, the son of Abraham", v.1. We see where the near and far prophetic truth comes in. Jesus comes from the descendants of David. Jesus is the promised Messiah who will also one day establish His throne as one with the title deed to the earth and the holy city. He alone will be exalted on that day, and He will conquer those who have come against Him and His people. He will punish the wicked and rescue and reward the faithful.

We cannot think of a time in history when Israel has not had an enemy who has wanted to conquer and destroy her. The day after Israel was recognized as an independent sovereign State, May 14, 1948, they were immediately attacked on May 15. They gained East Jerusalem during the Holy War of 1967, and they have been surrounded by enemies ever since. They long for a time of peace, which is why they may be deceived by the Antichrist when he promises peace they have never known. They will establish this agreement with the Beast [Antichrist] and in the middle of the Week [70th Week of Daniel] he will break that agreement and once again attack her. It is a covenant with death (Isaiah 28:15,18); it will be so disguised that they will be deceived. This Davidic Covenant will not be fulfilled completely until Jesus comes again, but make no mistake, He *will* come again and He will establish the throne of David in the holy city and He will conquer all Israel's enemies just as He promised. We see this in Zechariah 12 and 13.

We live in unparalleled times. You can hardly turn on the news without some mention of what is happening in the Middle East—especially with regard to how Israel fits into the various scenarios with other countries. Today Iran and Egypt are speaking. Iran, an enemy of Israel who desires to annihilate her and Egypt who at one time had a peace agreement, but is now under new rule and typically not a rule favoring Israel.

The United States is involved in what is referred to as the P-5 plus One[2] negotiation with Iran to prevent the further development of nuclear weapon capability. The P-5 stands for five countries of the United Nations Security Council: United States, Britain, France, China, and Russia. The plus one is Germany[3]. Strange relationships to say the least, yet these are the combined countries that are currently negotiating with Iran at the time of this writing. There is fighting taking place as civil war within the Arab countries surrounding Israel in what is being referred to as the "Arab Spring". There is economic unrest and uncertainty, which all lead to the potential for what Jesus refers to as the "beginning of birth pangs" in Matthew 24:8 and Mark 13:8.

7. The "New Covenant"—I placed this in quotes because there are a number of different interpretations as to what this truly is referring to. We see a reference to it in Jeremiah 31:31-34 where we read, "Behold, days are coming," declares the Lord, "when I will make a new covenant with the house of Israel and with the house of Judah, not like the covenant which I made

with their fathers in the day I took them by the hand to bring them out of the land of Egypt, My covenant which they broke, although I was a husband to them, " declares the Lord, "But this is the covenant which I will make with the house of Israel after those days," declares the Lord, I will put My law within them and on their heart I will write it; and I will be their God, and they shall be My people. "They will not teach again, each man his neighbor and each man his brother, saying, 'Know the Lord,' for they will all know Me, from the least of them to the greatest of them," declares the Lord, "for I will forgive their iniquity, and their sin I will remember no more."

There is a time coming when Israel will acknowledge Jesus Christ, *Yeshua* as their promised Messiah. As the name *Yeshua* implies, He [Jesus Christ] will be their rescuer and deliverer. He will be accepted as Messiah and will forgive their sins, both Jews and Gentiles who have accepted Him. He will write His law within their hearts and they will no longer be subject to the penalty of sin, which results from disobeying the Law given to Moses. This new covenant will reach far beyond the descendants of Israel, for we too would become recipients of this new covenant. It is often quoted as we take communion, where Jesus spoke to His disciples at the "last supper" and said, "In the same way He took the cup also after supper saying, "This cup is the new covenant in My blood; do this, as often as you drink it, in remembrance of Me" (I Corinthians 11:25).

Paul would be a minister of the new covenant and it would reach beyond the Jew to the Gentile also (II Corinthians 3:6). Gentiles would become partakers of this promise (Ephesians 3:6). What a wonderful blending of this magnificent promise, originally given to Jeremiah. In Galatians 3:29, believers are heirs of the promise and become descendants of Abraham. We were grafted in. We are adopted. How incredible to be adopted by the most High God! (Galatians 4:5).

I was adopted as an infant. My parents did not seek to hide it from me. As a matter of fact from as far back as I can remember, I have always known. I was made to feel incredibly special. My mom would say, "Just remember, we chose you, which makes you special." Parents who adopt are the salt of the earth. I was blessed with the best. In my case, my parents chose me and always made me feel special. I always wondered about my birth family, and God blessed me by allowing me to discover them when I was thirty-eight. I have a great relationship with them as well. That could be a book in itself.

This covenant is one of the examples of how God can and does work with both Jew and Gentile simultaneously. We can see how this also fulfills the promise to Abraham to be a blessing to many nations. Some take this covenant too far, in my opinion. You may hear of "covenant theology" which we spoke about earlier in this chapter. It basically covers the covenants we have talked about and sees a very clear distinction between Israel and the Church. On the other hand, there is what some would refer to as "replacement theology". They would take this covenant to the extent that God is done with Israel and that the Church has replaced her and there only remains a future "spiritual Israel". I would not agree with that position at all.

There are many good studies on the biblical covenants and so I would encourage you to study this topic and become somewhat familiar with it and how it fits into eschatology.

6
WHAT ARE DISPENSATIONS?

H ere again, it is not my intent to give a full dissertation on dispensations or the idea of dispensational theology. There is a great deal of work on this topic as well. The purpose in this book is to expose the reader to the topic and to see how doctrine can sometimes be established based on fitting it into these man-made systems as opposed to letting Scripture interpret Scripture. Having said that, dispensationalists would claim that they are the only ones who do take Scripture literally and rightly divide it. I would say that is probably true in just about every area with the exception of eschatology. I will explain the reason for that comment later in this chapter.

This is a man-made system for the most part. I say for the most part because you will find the word in the King James Bible, but when you go back to the original text we find a bit different translation, so in Ephesians 1:10 we see "administration" for instance in the NASB. The word is translated "management" in Luke 16:3, "stewardship" in I Corinthians 9:17, and so on. The point I am making is that dispensation in terms of a theology is not necessarily a biblical term. What theologians have attempted to do is look at dispensations of time or the "economy" of time and how God has dealt with man through these various defined periods. So, for the purposes of our understanding here, we will define this as major periods of human history from a biblical perspective and how God has demonstrated a pattern through each. This author does not have a problem if allowed to define it as such. There are patterns in Scripture and it helps us to understand the character and attributes of God and how He relates to us. The patterns are repeatable as we observe the major divisions of dispensations described in theology.

There are seven major dispensations according to most theologians. Dr. Lewis Sperry Chafer provides a good explanation in his *"Chafer Systematic Theology"* series. *Dr. Lewis Sperry Chafer in his "Chafer Systematic Theology" in volume eight "Biographical Sketch and Indexes" page 11, 3.b notes the seven.* We will quote the seven he lists, but will provide our own summation of what those are with some different wording than found in the greater volumes by Dr. Chafer[1].

One of the key points we are attempting to make again, is that if we form a doctrine by forcing it to fit into one of these man-made systems, such as dispensations, we may miss the point of Scripture and lose overall biblical context. This is where we would suggest that a normal interpretation of the language given in the Bible stand on its own as the final authority when taken in proper context.

We will look at these seven major divisions of dispensations and give a brief explanation of each. The pattern should emerge clearly, which was the intent of the theologians who gave us these major divisions to begin with.

The patterns throughout each dispensation can be broken down into four major events: 1) God's Ordinance, 2) Man's Opposition, 3) God's Outpoured Judgment, and 4) God's Overwhelming Grace.

According to *Dr. Chafer*[2] these seven major periods are:
1. "Dispensation of Innocence"
2. "Dispensation of Conscience"
3. "Dispensation of Human Government"
4. "Dispensation of Promise"
5. "Dispensation of Law"
6. "Dispensation of Grace"
7. "Dispensation of Kingdom Rule"

Let's take a look at these individually and see how theologians have established the four patterns we listed (my interpretation of their words).

1. Dispensation of Innocence – Everything has to start somewhere, so we start in the beginning. This dispensation began with Adam and Eve in the Garden. First, we see God's ordinance in Genesis 2:15-17. God created Adam first, and in these verses we see where God gave Adam the stewardship over the Garden to cultivate it. He also told him that he could eat from any tree freely, but he could not eat from the tree of the knowledge of good and evil. Pretty simple, perfect paradise, all the food you need, just one command: don't eat from the tree of the knowledge of good and evil.

   Adam was created by God from the dust of the ground and placed in the Garden of Eden. It must have been absolutely magnificent. God decided to give Adam a helper and so created Eve from Adam's rib. We see the passage in Genesis 2:24 quoted often at weddings. Here God created the perfect couple, in perfect paradise. No sin at this time. They were innocent and hence the dispensation of innocence. All they had to do was not eat of this one tree. So, that command was *God's Ordinance*. If they did eat of the tree of knowledge of good and evil, they would die.

   Then comes the tempter, the serpent in chapter three. He is crafty and deceitful and tried to convince Eve that they would not die if they ate of the tree of the knowledge of good and evil. She bought into the lie and she not only ate of the tree, she gave its fruit to Adam and he ate also. We see this in Genesis 3:6. This would be *Man's Opposition*. From Genesis 3:14-24 all kinds of things happen. Basically, we see *God's Outpoured Judgment*. God would deal with Eve first and He told her He would "greatly multiply your pain in childbirth, in pain you will bring forth children; yet your desire will be for your husband, and he will rule over you", Genesis 3:16. God then went on to punish Adam and said, "Because you have listened to the voice of your wife, and have eaten from the tree about which I commanded you saying, 'You shall not eat from it'; Cursed is the ground because of you; In toil you will eat of it All the days of your life. Both thorns and thistles it shall grow for you; and you will eat the plants of the field;

By the sweat of your face you will eat bread, till you return to the ground because from it you were taken; for you are dust, and to dust you shall return" (Genesis 3:17-19).

It resulted in removal from the Garden and eventual physical death. This is where God once walked among them. Adam lived 930 years and then died (Genesis 5:5). God created Adam in His likeness and blessed him. The fall of Adam and Eve would pass on to all men and women (Romans 5:12). This inherited sin would cause spiritual separation from God.

God judged the serpent as well and had him cursed more than all the beasts and placed on his belly all the days of his life (Genesis 3:14-15). In verse 15, we see *God's Overwhelming Grace* in that He made a provision to overcome Satan, which is where we see the first prophetic truth/promise regarding the first coming of Jesus referencing the virgin birth. The woman does not have a seed, only the man. Further, God would be gracious and merciful in making garments of skin for them to wear. Prior to the eating of the tree of the knowledge of good and evil, their nakedness was not an issue. This act of disobedience and fall of man would be the end of the dispensation of innocence.

When people say that the world is going to get better, I do not think they take these verses into account. The earth we live in today is cursed and the very evidence of labor pain during birth, man sweating to earn a living, farmers dealing with weeds and thistles, physical death, and separation from God are not indications that things are getting better. On the other hand, one day it will when the King of kings comes in all His Glory with the title deed to earth and reclaims it and establishes His Kingdom. We should long for that time. We should continue to live for Him and we should lay up our treasures in Heaven and not be so earth-bound. God made a provision at the end of this dispensation with the promise of His Son. Those who have accepted His finished work on the cross no longer are separated from God and will one day spend eternity with Him. Those who have not accepted are still under the judgment of sin from the day that Adam and Eve fell.

2. <u>Dispensation of Conscience</u>–After the fall, man was given another ordinance. In Genesis 3:22-24 we see where man was now aware of good and evil. He has a conscience. This is interesting to me because we all have a conscience, and we all know basic right from wrong. Romans 1:18-19 tells us that truth is evident within us. Man [Adam] was removed from the Garden. *God's Ordinance* was for man to do well and not sin. We read that in Genesis 4:7. Here is the story of Cain and Abel. Cain became jealous of Abel and as a consequence, Cain sinned and killed Abel (Genesis 4:8). We read that Enoch, who was the son of Jared, was translated or *"took"* by God (Genesis 5:24). As chapter six unfolds, we see more and more corruption and wickedness. Genesis 6:5-6, "Then the Lord saw that the wickedness of man was great on the earth, and that every intent of the thoughts of his heart was only evil continually. The Lord was sorry that He had made man on the earth, and He was grieved in His heart." How incredibly sad this must have been yet it is still true today. Men are still evil. The Bible says that none of us are righteous. Thanks be to God for Jesus Christ. Here in chapter six we see this wickedness or *Man's Opposition.*

The next thing is that God in His righteous anger decided to destroy the world with a flood. This would be *God's Outpoured Judgment.* In Genesis 6:17-24 we see where God floods the entire world and all its inhabitants yet in the midst of this world of corruption and wickedness that broke God's heart, He finds a faithful man named Noah. God in His *Overwhelming Grace* would command Noah to build an Ark to specific dimensions and what to specifically inhabit it with. This would include Noah's family and the animals and birds in numbers He specifically told Noah to take. The flood would conclude the dispensation of conscience.

Don't get the wrong impression that these first two dispensations were quite short because you read all this in the first few chapters of Genesis. One need only look at the age of the descendants of Adam to see how God was long suffering with man. Noah was six-hundred-years old when he entered the Ark.

There are people who do not believe there was a literal worldwide flood, but fossil records validate that there was. As a young boy, my dad used to take us kids to a rock area a number of miles from the ocean where we would dig for fossils. It was a fascinating adventure for a young boy to see all those imprints of sea creatures upon the rock so high above and far from the ocean. In the 1950s, us kids readily accepted the fact that there was a worldwide flood. It made perfect sense. I also have full confidence that God's Word is infallible (trustworthy) and without error.

With the end of this dispensation of conscience and having just a remnant to go into the next dispensation, we will see the pattern continue.

3. <u>Dispensation of Human Government</u>—God spared Noah, his wife, his sons, and his sons' wives. They were now going to populate the world and multiply. With blessing, mercy, and grace comes responsibility. Noah and his family were to obey God and govern this earth for His glory. We see where God told him this in Genesis 9:1-7. We also see where this time relates to the covenant with Noah, which we spoke about in the previous chapter on covenants. He [God] would never flood the earth again. So this covenant was for all of mankind. The key here is that God is to be glorified and exalted, not man. God always expects obedience and it is no different here. The floods subsided and Noah and his family were to be fruitful and multiply and do as God commanded. They were to govern. This was *God's Ordinance*.

As the family multiplied and continued to multiply, things seemed to be going pretty well until you come to Genesis chapter 11. Up to this point, everyone on the earth spoke the same language. How wonderful that must have been. Once these descendants came into the land of Shinar, they became proud and started to build a tower to reach into heaven. Here is where we see the pattern of *Man's Opposition* come in. They were at a point where they thought they could do anything—even reach into heaven with a man-made tower. This actually goes back to chapter 10 where we learn about a mighty one on the earth who was the son of Cush. His name was Nimrod. Part of his kingdom was Babel in Shinar. We could park here for a while and talk about Babylon and a lot more, but our point here is that God wanted them to govern rightly and follow His commands.

Because man became proud and built a tower in opposition to God, the pattern continues within the dispensation of *God's Outpoured Judgment*. We see in Genesis 11:7-9 that God confused their language and dispersed them. The effects are still being felt today. This was a specific time in history when we see human government, but this is not to say that we do not have human government today or that it was confined to this period alone, which is obvious as we still have human government. By the way, we are still commanded to govern responsibly. There is no authority on this planet that God has not ordained (Romans 13:1). Not all governments are good and many are bad, but nonetheless they are there only because God ordains it. Bad government is never the fault of God anymore now then it was in the time of Nimrod and Babel. God will also deal with bad government and leaders who are opposed to His precepts and principles. This takes us to the last portion of the pattern in the call of Abram as *God's Overwhelming Grace*. He would become Abraham and once again God would bless the nations of the earth. The next dispensation would be that of "Promise".

4. Dispensation of Promise – This dispensation begins with the call of Abram to go forth from Ur of Chaldeans to a land God would give him: Canaan. We see this in Genesis 12. The promises of God were to make his a great name [Abraham] and a great nation [Israel] that would be blessings to all the families of the earth. Abraham and his descendants were to believe these promises and act upon them. That was the *Ordinance of God*.

As with the previous dispensations, this starts out well. Abraham believed God and it was counted unto him as righteousness. He is the father of faith. He had a nephew named Lot. Abraham was rich in livestock and Lot not so much.

There arose strife between the two herdsmen in chapter 13. There was enough good land over the vast territory to bless each of them, so Abraham settled in Canaan and Lot headed to Sodom. War would break out with Bera, king of Sodom and Birsha, king of Gomorrah among other territories and kings as allies against other kings and territories according to Genesis chapter 14. There were four kings against five we are told in verse nine. The kings of Sodom and Gomorrah fled and fell into tar pits. Those who survived headed for the hills.

The conquering kings took all their food and Lot. A fugitive went to Abram and told him what had happened. Abram responded by putting together his forces and pursuing them. Abram won the battles and secured Lot as well as his possessions. The king of Sodom blessed Abram, but he would not take anything from the king. In chapter 15 we see where Abram is promised a son. Here is where we connect with the Abrahamic covenant and where Abram is promised to have descendants that would be like the stars of heaven. He believed God.

In chapter 16 we see Sarai, his wife, and Hagar, her maidservant. Abram would have a child with Hagar named Ishmael. The covenant continues in chapter 17, where he is promised that he would be the father of a multitude of nations and his name changed to Abraham, verses four-five. Chapter 18 continues the promise fulfillment with the birth of Isaac and the line of descendants where all the nations of the world and the eventual people of Israel would be blessed. Sarai would become Sarah. In chapter 19 we see the beginning of *Man's Opposition* with the doom of Sodom and Gomorrah. It continues with the birth of Esau and Jacob and the stealing of Esau's blessing/birthright (Genesis chapters 25-27).

We see Joseph hated by his jealous brothers and how he was sold into slavery to Egypt in Genesis 37, and yet God used him to take care of his family in grace and mercy. As a result of the disobedience and man's opposition, we see *God's Outpoured Judgment* where He places them in bondage in Egypt (Exodus 1:8-11). Here is the bondage of Israel within

Egypt under taskmasters who would afflict them daily. The pattern continues with *God's Overwhelming Grace* as He uses Moses to deliver them out of Egypt. This would conclude this specific age of promise and yet all of us know that when we look at the covenant with Abraham that the promise will continue and has with the blessings of those who would be grafted in. This will take us into the next dispensation.

5. <u>Dispensation of Law</u> – Moses led the people of Israel out of Egypt and across the Red Sea, and the Lord "saved Israel that day from the hand of the Egyptians" (Exodus 14:30). This dispensation starts with Moses being called to Mt Sinai and receiving the commandments from God. This would be the Ten Commandments spoken of in chapter 20 of Exodus. This would be *God's Ordinance*. There would be a number of ordinances, some 613 Mosaic Laws. Even while Moses was on Mt Sinai, the people began to rebel and build an idol. Aaron caved under the pressure and they built the golden calf. Amazing, that these people who had just witnessed God's miraculous hand in delivering them out of Egypt among huge opposition, would move to idolatry.

We are such a sinful people. Moses was not happy and neither was God. Israel would wander in the desert for 40 years. Even Moses at one point would strike the rock instead of speaking to it obediently and as a result, he could only view the Promised Land and not enter it. The period of the judges would begin within this dispensation and Israel, not wanting to be under a theocracy, pushed to be under a king, and so the period of kings began with Saul.

They would break God's Law's continuously, and so we see *Man's Opposition*. David came to the throne and we see over and over again how God poured out His favor on this disobedient people. We see a connection within this dispensation with the Davidic covenant and how that one day Christ will come again and establish His Kingdom. He would come from the line of David. Within this period as a result of their repeated disobedience, we see the pattern of

God's Outpoured Judgment in the Babylonian captivity and dispersion throughout the nations.

The first Temple was destroyed and then there came a period of restoration when the second Temple was built. The Law was given to show them their sin and need for a Savior, but they missed it. During this period, there would be prophets, but the people would not listen to them—and even killed them in many cases. The religious leaders would add to the Law and burden the people even more.

There would be corruption and yet as the pattern continues, we see *God's Overwhelming Grace* in the period between the Old Testament and New Testament and the birth of Christ, the Messiah, who would come to die for man's sin and repeated disobedience and opposition to God. Jesus would come among them and teach within their synagogues and gain followers who would become His disciples, apostles, and friends. He would lay down His life for their and our disobedience. He would fulfill the law and fulfill God's justice. Jesus would experience death on the cross, but would rise again after three days. He would promise to send a Comforter and Teacher. The third person of the Triune God, the Holy Spirit would come and fill those who have received Jesus Christ as Lord and Savior, which would lead to the next dispensation.

6. Dispensation of Grace—This dispensation is also referred to as the dispensation of the Church age. This dispensation started on the day of Pentecost in Acts chapter two. The day of Pentecost, or "fiftieth day", was a day where they came together to celebrate the Feast of Weeks or Shavuot. It was first fruits. It was so called because it was to take place *"seven complete weeks, or fifty days, after the Passover"*[3]. The Sanhedrin would associate this with the giving of the Law to Moses on Mt Sinai, which caught on, but it really was to be the giving of the first loaves made from the wheat harvest to the Lord.

On this particular day in Acts two, we see where there was a loud noise from heaven like rushing wind and the Holy Spirit came upon the apostles. All who gathered there could understand what the apostles were saying in their own language. Peter gave his great spirit-filled sermon starting in verse 14, and he quoted the Prophet Joel. He preached of Christ Jesus and His crucifixion. He spoke about the resurrection of Christ. Three thousand were added to the Church that day and thus the Church age, or dispensation of grace, began.

This is the age, or dispensation, that we are currently in today. We would expect the pattern to be the same in this dispensation as in the earlier dispensations. That is to say, that we would expect it to contain the same elements as in the previous dispensations: *God's Ordinance, Man's Opposition, God's Outpoured Judgment and, God's Overwhelming Grace.* The fact is that we will see all these elements within this current age, right to the end of the age that Jesus spoke about in the Olivet Discourse.

This is where there is some disagreement as to how this age should be interpreted in light of eschatology. As far as *God's Ordinance*, we are to see ourselves as lost sinners in need of a Savior and accept God's grace, believing that Christ paid the penalty for our sin—past, present and future. We are to accept Him as Lord of our life. We are to obey His commandments in the power of the Holy Spirit, who resides within us upon accepting Him as our Lord and Savior.

We are to love one another, fulfill the "Great Commission", and reflect His light here in a dark world. For those who have placed their trust in Jesus Christ, they are now members of the Church body and are the bride of Christ. During this dispensation, however, many *have not, still do not* and *will not* accept His grace, refusing to believe in Christ as Lord and Savior. *Man's Opposition* will come to a climax during the 70th Week of Daniel, and those who follow the Antichrist will receive his mark.

Those who have trusted Christ will be delivered, and those who have not will be subject to the Day of the Lord's wrath. We will see *God's Outpoured Judgment* during the Day of the Lord's wrath, which begins on the same day that we see *God's Overwhelming Grace* in the rapture of the Church, His bride.

As far as patterns go, this does appear to be consistent. We have such a long-suffering, patient God. He loves us and calls us, and we are His elect. This will lead to the last dispensation, which is Christ's Kingdom, or the millennium.

7. <u>Dispensation of Christ's Kingdom (millennium)</u>–As mentioned earlier in the book, the millennium is one thousand years. We said that we hold to the pre-millennial position, which is to say that Christ will return for His Church prior to the initiation of the thousand-year reign. We also said that we believe this to be a literal one thousand years, as seen in Revelation chapter 20. It is mentioned there, no less than six times. So for this to be a dispensation as the others are categorized, we would expect the same pattern or elements. This period begins after the 70th Week of Daniel. It is after the battle of Armageddon [1,290 days of Daniel 12]. It is after the last forty-five days [1,335 days of Daniel 12]. Satan is bound during this period. There will be those who have come to believe during the 70th Week of Daniel who will enter this period.

We start again with *God's Ordinance*. Christ has established His earthly kingdom and rule. The throne of David is re-established and man is expected to know Christ as Savior and Lord and obey Him. Some might wonder, "for those who came out of the 70th Week of Daniel without taking the mark and who received Him as Savior, are they not saved believers?" The answer is yes. They will, however, have offspring and, believe it or not, some of these offspring will rebel against Him. Satan will be released at the end of the one thousand years and will deceive the nations. Those subject to this deception are likely to be some of the offspring. Here we see *Man's Opposition* and failure. There will be rebellion and war. This will lead to *God's Outpoured Judgment*, where God sends fire out of heaven to destroy them (II Peter 3:7, 10-12). This will culminate with the Great White Throne judgment and the casting of the lost along with Satan into the Lake of Fire forever (Revelation 20:10). The beast and the false prophet are also there forever.

As with the other dispensations, we see *God's Overwhelming Grace* in the new heaven and new earth, where we will spend eternity with God. No more sorrow, no more pain, no more dying, no more thorns and thistles. Heaven is not just a place where we float around playing harps all day and night around the throne. We will forever praise Him and enjoy His glory and presence as we worship Him, but we will also have new bodies and will be part of the new earth. We will see God in all His majesty and glory, which we only get a glimpse of today as the heavens declare His glory. It will be magnificent beyond anything we could ever imagine.

These were brief explanations on the topic of dispensations, not meant to be a theological lesson. I would encourage you to study this topic in more depth and learn about these dispensations. Some believe that you cannot be a dispensationalist and believe in a pre-wrath rapture. I would disagree with that. Again, I would contend that the whole idea of dispensations is the result of a man-made system, yet it *does* have value in understanding how God has dealt with man from creation through all the ages. There does appear to be a pattern, which is consistent. I do not believe, however, that it would invalidate my eschatological view on the timing of the Rapture.

The reason I say this is because I do see the pattern, and I can see that even when using this pattern, pre-wrath makes sense. Those who hold to the dispensations would say that in every period of time, man was tested, failed the test, and was judged, yet God provided grace. If we say that we are raptured prior to any of the real testing, then I would say that it violates this pattern. On the other hand, if we are permitted to go through the testing and remain faithful, we can expect to be delivered, while those who are disobedient are subject to His wrath.

For those who hold the pre-tribulation position, their contention is that the Church was not present during the first 69 Weeks of Daniel's prophecy or the dispensations prior to the Church age. Because of this, they believe that Christians will not enter into the 70th Week of Daniel. This is faulty logic.

There is no biblical basis for that conclusion; it is merely an assumption.

Part of their faulty logic includes the fact that the Church was not mentioned in the Old Testament and Daniel's prophecy concerns only Israel; there was a gap between the 69th Week of Daniel and when the Church came into existence, hence the Church Age. They insist that the Church will and must be raptured before God can continue His economy of time again with Israel, who will go into the 70th Week. Again, there is no biblical evidence to support this. The fact that the Church is not mentioned in the Old Testament does not mean that the Church will not be present during the 70th Week. There are too many Scriptures, in my view, to suggest that the Church will be present along with Israel.

One of the things we should observe when we look at each of the seven dispensations is that the people mentioned in each previous dispensation enter into the next. If we look at it from a pure dispensation, where one ends and another begins, we would expect the people to follow the same "start and stop" pattern, but that would be faulty logic on our part. I believe that those who are part of this current *Church Age* or *Dispensation of Grace* will enter the 70th Week. I will talk about this more in chapter eight of this book when we take a close look at the Olivet Discourse and ask the "six serving men"[4] questions.

It is worth mentioning again that great scholars over many years of time have poured their sincere hearts into giving us great writings on theology, whether it is systematic theology, covenant theology, or dispensation theology. All of these major themes and works have been and are still invaluable for the serious student of theology, and we should be indebted to these wonderful, faithful followers of Christ.

I can personally tell you that during my journey as a Christian, I have learned a great deal about the Bible due to the help of many of these works. I have been able to truly examine the Scriptures and determine what I believe and why I believe it. These men have been inspirational to me, and it is so apparent that they loved the Lord and His Word. I will never discount these works, but no matter how great they are, we must always weigh doctrine against the plumb line of absolute truth, which can only be found in the Bible. Whenever a great work appears to contradict or force us into a position that is inconsistent with the whole of Scripture, we must study and ask all the right questions, while applying a good hermeneutic to ultimately arrive at truth, upon which we can form a conviction and be prepared to defend.

7

WHAT ARE THE FEASTS OF LEVITICUS 23?

This is another one of those widely debated topics. There are already a number of great works available about the feasts in Leviticus that examine whether or not there is a correlation between the feasts and Jesus' first and second comings, but the purpose of this book is to look at the symbolic nature of the feasts and allow the reader to come to his or her own conclusion about how each feast relates to the Scriptures as a whole. This is not intended to be a cop-out, I will just simply tell you when I am not sure about something.

The fact of the matter is that these feasts in Leviticus chapter 23, or "appointed times", are the Lord's. Appointed times are important when looking at eschatology, just like the other topics we have discussed. These are *His* feasts or *His* appointed times, which are *His* "holy convocations" (Leviticus 23:1-2). In other words, these are important because *they belong to the Lord*. These feasts include:

1. Passover – Leviticus 23:5
2. Unleavened Bread – Leviticus 23:6
3. First Fruits – Leviticus 23:9-10
4. Weeks – Leviticus 23:15
5. Trumpets – Leviticus 23:24
6. Atonement – Leviticus 23:27
7. Tabernacles – Leviticus 23:34

We spent a little time going over the various covenants and dispensations and saw how distinct these were for Israel with regard to promises and specifics for individuals and the descendants of Israel. We saw how all the nations of the world would be blessed through the descendants of Abraham, and indeed that has happened for both Jew and Gentile who have embraced Jesus Christ as Lord and Savior. These feasts fall into the dispensation of the Law and the Mosaic Covenant in the sense that they were instructions given to Moses by God. I do believe there is a clear distinction between Israel and the Church. I believe there are distinct instructions given in the Law to Moses for Israel which may not be for the Gentiles; we also are told, however, that Gentile sojourners could participate if certain conditions were met (Exodus 12:47-49). In other words, they were not totally excluded from celebrating, but it is clear from Scripture that these ordinances were/are for Israel. I also believe that Jesus came to fulfill the Law and the prophets. He *did not* come to abolish the Law.

Regarding the book of Leviticus, Alfred Edersheim in his *Bible History Old Testament*, states, "The Book of Leviticus is intended for Israel as the people of God; it is the statute-book of Israel's spiritual life; and, on both these grounds, it is neither simply legal, in the sense of ordinary law, nor yet merely ceremonial, but *throughout symbolical and typical.* Accordingly, its deeper truths apply to all times and to all men"[1].

I do believe that these feasts, just like many of the types in the Old Testament, have a symbolic significance for all believers in that they point us to God's greater plan and purpose. Consider verses found in Colossians 2:17, Hebrews 8:5, and Hebrews 10:1-10. Each use a term "shadow" of things to come when referring to the feasts and sacrifices associated with them. It carries the idea of a reflection. We have all seen our shadow or that of an object cast when the sun is in the right position. It is not the object or person itself, but rather a reflection. In the case of the feasts, it could be argued that they cast a reflection or shadow of things to come as a broader intent by God as noted in the Colossian and Hebrews passages.

When we look at these feasts in the context of Leviticus 23:1-2, we gain insight into the significance of these special times. "The Lord spoke again *to Moses*, saying, *Speak to the sons of Israel* and say to them, '*The Lord's appointed times* which *you* shall *proclaim as holy convocations-My appointed times* are these:" [Emphasis mine.] These verses provide four crucial points regarding the feasts: 1) The command from the Lord was to Moses, 2) They were to be given to the sons of Israel, 3) These are the Lord's appointed times, and 4) They [Israel] shall proclaim them as holy convocations. Here we see the distinction as being specifically for the sons of Israel, and yet they [Israel] were to be the channel through which God would bless all nations. Herein lies the debate. Again, my intent here is to address the symbolic nature of the feasts as they point to His [Jesus Christ] *coming(s)*.

Many Christians today are finding a new appreciation for these appointed times of the Lord. Many are even embracing and celebrating these feasts. Is this wrong? I would say that it is not. This is a matter of conscience in my opinion, but certainly it is not wrong to celebrate them in a proper context. These appointed times/feasts belong to the Lord and were commanded to Moses and Israel to keep. We will use the word "keep" because these were part of the law for Israel and so they must keep them as in keeping the law. We see them observed while Jesus was in His earthly ministry and we see His apostles keeping them as well, but we should remember that they [the apostles] were from the line of Abraham, Isaac, and Jacob. While Gentiles are not commanded to keep these feasts specifically given to Moses, we should nonetheless know about them and what significance they have with regard to "appointed times". I would also be careful when using verses like Colossians 2:14-17 as a means to say that these feasts are no longer relevant. I believe that we have freedom in this area as believers and members of the Church. As we take a brief look at these feasts and the *apparent* relationship to Christ's first and second comings, we should also know that these were/are feasts that the descendants of Israel were commanded to keep in *all* generations (Leviticus 23:21, 31, 41).

The feasts are another area where we see some division within the Church, and this should not be. I said earlier that this is a matter of conscience, and I see this specifically in Romans chapter 14. We need to be careful not to place a stumbling block before our brothers and sisters in Christ, and we also need to maintain sensitivity in love.

We all know that we cannot work our way to heaven—or at least we *should* know this fundamental truth. On the other hand, we want to strive to be obedient to Christ and submit to His Lordship over our lives. Every one of us is growing at various levels, and it is only as we study God's Word, see God working in us, and pray for understanding that we will form convictions, which ultimately will mold and shape our lives. I would suggest, however, that if a Gentile were to keep these feasts to the letter of the Law, he or she would see some issues, since some are very specific and relevant to Israel only.

Some believe that the first four feasts, Passover (Leviticus 23:5), Unleavened Bread (Leviticus 23:6), First Fruits (Leviticus 23:9-10), and Weeks (Leviticus 23:15) points to the first coming of Christ, while that the last three, Trumpets (Leviticus 23:24), Atonement (Leviticus 23:27), and Tabernacles (Leviticus 23:34) point to His second coming. Using the analogy of a shadow of things to come, we can see why some would think this; within the text itself, however, we do not find this explicitly stated. There are some clear parallels, but again we are not dogmatic on these.

All of these feasts really are *appointed times*. They are specific with regard to when and how they are to be carried out. Each is based on the Jewish calendar, which is different than our modern Gregorian calendar. It is more of a lunar calendar, but not *purely* lunar, for the pure lunar calendar contains 354.37 days. Due to the lunar cycles, they [the feasts] do not fall on the exact day each year.

The first three fall within the month of Nisan, which would be springtime. The fourth (Weeks or First Fruits) falls in the month of Sivan, which would be late spring or early summer, depending on the cycle. The remaining three fall in the month of Tishri, or the fall season. Appointed times are cyclical just like this. Each has a very specific command associated with time and characteristics. Let's take a look at each feast and see if there is an apparent "shadow" or inference to His coming(s).

1. Passover—Leviticus 23:5 states, "In the first month, on the fourteenth day of the month at twilight is the Lord's Passover." The Hebrew word for Passover is *Pesach*, which carries the idea of leaping over or delivering from punishment. *Wilson's*

Old Testament Word Studies defines it this way; "to leap over, to pass over; more specifically, to ward off a blow, to bend or spring forward, as bending or kneeling on one knee...in act and posture to ward off either a stroke, or to oppose the threatened entrance of an enemy"[2]. It is to be observed on Nisan 14. The specifics about the origin of this feast are found in Exodus chapter 12. It was initiated during the Israelites' captivity in Egypt. In verse two, the Lord establishes the beginning of months for them. All the Israelites were to take a lamb for themselves on the tenth of the month (Nisan 10) for each household. Small households could take one with their neighbor and divide it. It had to be an unblemished, one-year old male (verse five), from a sheep or goat. They would keep it until the fourteenth day of that same month. The whole assembly of Israel was to kill it at twilight and then take the blood and place it on the doorposts and the lintel of the houses. Prior to the captivity, this was the month of Abid. During the Babylonian captivity it became the month of Nisan. You may see it referenced as either, but it always occurred on the fourteenth day of the first month. They were to eat it in haste with their loins girded, sandals on their feet, and staff in hand (verse 11).

This was the Lord's Passover. The blood was to be a sign of those who followed and revered Him and when the Lord saw the blood, He would pass over their households and no plague would come upon and destroy them prior to their departure from Egypt. This was done in haste and with readiness to move. This was not a comfortable sit-down meal. They were commanded to keep this Passover of the Lord as a reminder of the Lord's deliverance from Egypt (Deuteronomy 16:1).

The shadow of things to come is symbolic of the blood of the Lamb of God who is without spot or blemish. Jesus Christ came to seek and to save that which was lost. He came to die for lost sinners. He came to deliver us from our sins. He would be the Passover Lamb who would ward off the coming wrath of God and deliver us. Jesus Christ, God's only Son became sin for us "that we might become the righteousness of God in

Him" (II Corinthians 5:21). Hebrews 10:10 tells us that "we have been sanctified through the offering of the body of Jesus Christ once for all." There appears to be a relationship between the Passover and the deliverance associated with it for Israel, and the fact that those of us who have accepted the finished work on the cross and His perfect sacrifice at His first coming will be delivered from the wrath to come at His second coming.

Jesus spent the eighth and ninth Nisan at Martha's house (John 12:1-2). The day changed at sunset, and verse two tells us He had supper with them, hence eighth and ninth Nisan. The next day, would have been the 10th Nisan when Jesus entered Jerusalem. He entered during the time that the Passover lamb would be gathered and held in preparation for the 14th Nisan. He would be the Passover Lamb. He would be crucified on the 14th Nisan. Jesus had cleansed the Temple, had spent the Passover preparation meal with His disciples prior to the Passover. He became the perfect sacrifice for sin. We can see how this symbolic feast cast as a shadow of things to come would find it's fulfillment when Jesus first came and was crucified as the Passover Lamb, as the words of John the Baptist echo "Behold the Lamb of God who takes away the sin of the world" (John 1:29)!

2. Unleavened Bread–Leviticus 23:6 states, "Then on the fifteenth day of the same month there is the Feast of Unleavened Bread to the Lord; for seven days you shall eat unleavened bread." This feast would start on Nisan 15 on the day after Passover. We can see the specifics in Exodus chapter 12. This feast was to serve as a reminder of the Israelite's deliverance out of Egypt, and it was to be kept for all generations. It too had some very strict ordinances. It was to be a "Feast to the Lord"; it was to be a permanent ordinance (verse 14). They were required to eat unleavened bread (bread without yeast) for seven days and they had to remove all leaven from their houses. Anyone who ate leaven would be cut off from Israel (verse 15). The first and seventh days were a holy assembly of the people.

I am not a very good cook, so when I make a feeble attempt at preparing a meal, I typically need some remedial training from my wife, who is a great cook. As I am writing this today, I am going to attempt to put together some stuffed bell peppers for dinner tonight. Last night, I asked my wife some key questions about the recipe and the basic steps on how to prepare the meat. At one point she talked about rice or breadcrumbs and explained that they serve as a "thickening/bonding agent". Cooking agents have a cause and effect.

For bread, we use yeast typically to complete the fermentation process and cause the bread to "rise". Yeast is actually a microorganism from the fungal species. It converts the fermentable sugars in the dough into gas oxide, which causes the bread to rise. During baking, the yeast dies and you are left with the expanded loaf of bread. When the Lord gave the ordinance to Moses and the Israelites to eat unleavened bread for seven days as a reminder of how He delivered them out of Egypt, it demonstrated the haste in which they had to leave in connection with the Passover.

These two feasts are closely related. There was no time to sit and eat the Passover as we mentioned earlier, and there was no time to include yeast or an agent to cause the bread to rise. They were to eat it without that agent. They also had to remove all the yeast from their homes. Today you may think of *matstah*, which is the Hebrew word where we get matzo. It is the word for unleavened bread as used in Exodus 12:8,18 and Deuteronomy 16:3 and 8.

How does this relate to His first coming? Yeast is used as a metaphor in the New Testament for sin or corruptible things. In I Corinthians chapter five, Paul rebukes a member within the church at Corinth who was engaged in immoral behavior. This individual was committing sexual sin with his father's wife. When we come to verse six, we see the metaphor of the leaven used. Paul writes, "Your boasting is not good. Do you not know that a little leaven leavens the whole lump of dough?" He then goes on to say, "Clean out the old leaven so that you may be a new lump, just as you are in fact unleavened. For Christ our Passover also has been sacrificed." Here we can see the connection made by Paul that

Jesus Christ was the Passover as the shadow of things that were to come. In verse eight Paul goes on to say, "Therefore let us celebrate the feast, not with old leaven, nor with the leaven of malice and wickedness, but with the unleavened bread of sincerity and truth."

Paul associates the leaven with sin throughout this passage, and he makes the analogy that a little leaven will spread and corrupt. He also makes the connection between the Passover and these statements regarding leaven and unleavened in the same context. Leaven, we said earlier was an agent used to cause the bread to rise or expand. It is a foreign agent and comes from fungi. It dies when cooked, but while alive, it is a microorganism, which spreads. Sin in the body of Christ, His Church will have the same effect according to Paul. Jesus died for our sins, and in that sense we can see the connection. Some have connected this to mean that after Jesus died, His body did not decay or become corrupt. I am not able to agree or disagree on this point. One thing that is clear from the writings of Paul in I Corinthians chapter five is that he *does* make a connection with Christ as the Passover and, in the same context, speaks about the leaven and unleavened consequences, calling for a feast without the leaven of sin. Leaven [sin in context] must be dealt with in the Church.

Let me take a slight diversion here. One of the most difficult things for a church to do is to discipline those within the body who are engaged in perpetual sin. We see in Matthew 18:15-20 that the Lord calls for us to do this, and He gives us explicit steps on how to carry it out. When the Church is obedient to this, often the sinning brother or sister will turn from his or her sin and there is no need to go any further. On the other hand, there are times when one does not and, as a result, the Church is no longer to associate with this individual as a brother. Paul gives the strongest of exhortation in that they may even lose their life, but still be saved. In the case with the disobedient brother in I Corinthians chapter five, we see the church's call to restore him and reaffirm their love for him in II Corinthians 2:7-11. This is a step that is left out at times. People are people, and when there is emotional injury due to sin, it tends to stay with individuals, making it slow and difficult to forgive and restore, even if that person has clearly demonstrated repentance. This is a sad commentary for the Church. I would encourage all who read this to take heed to Paul's exhortation in II Corinthians chapter two and reaffirm love and restoration to a repentant brother or sister. The Lord has removed all our sin as far as the east is from the west, so why would you hunt for it in gossip and bring it up again? He will remember it no more.

Another interesting thing about Church discipline is that those churches that practice it will always refer to Matthew 18 as the premise for such. I believe it is the correct premise. We see that it is important to deal with the "leaven". When this happens, however, it must be in accordance with the Word of God; this is where the Church has to exercise wisdom and not discipline an individual just because the members of the body do not agree with him or her on non-essential issues. In the case in Corinth, we can see the clear "leaven". If we go to II Corinthians chapter two, we see the restoration. Matthew is not a book written to the Jews only. It is for the Church as well. This will be an important point when we look at the "Olivet Discourse" later on.

Because Passover and Unleavened Bread Feasts are so closely connected and often seen as one, we could see where one might conclude that there is a symbolic relationship between this Feast and His first coming. There is no doubt that there was no "leaven" in the person of Jesus Christ. He was without sin. His body did not decay in the grave during those three days. In Mark 15:46-47, we see where Joseph of Arimathea took the body of Jesus and wrapped Him in fine linen cloth and laid Him in the tomb. Mark 16:1 tells us that, "When the Sabbath was over, Mary Magdalene, and Mary the mother of James, and Salome, bought spices, so that they might come and anoint Him." Of course, when they arrived the stone was rolled away and the body was gone. The spices were part of the preparation of a body, but there was no need here for the body had not decayed—He had risen. Praise God!

Having said all of this, it is still clear that this feast of the Lord was also one that was specifically given to Israel as a constant reminder of how the Lord delivered them out of Egypt. They [Israelites] are to keep this for all generations and they do. This is why I cannot be dogmatic on my own conclusion with regard to this particular feast.

3. First Fruits – Leviticus 23:9-10 states, "Then the Lord spoke to Moses, saying, Speak to the sons of Israel and say to them, 'When you enter the land which I am going to give you and reap its harvest, then you shall bring in the sheaf of the first fruits of your harvest to the priest." This feast is traditionally celebrated on Nisan 16. There are a number of interesting conditions here. First, it is when "you enter the land", speaking to Israel. In Exodus, it is referring to the first-born, or offspring, of every womb and every beast. Here in Leviticus, it is referring to the beginning of harvest. They were to bring the priest and a sheaf of the first grain the day after the Sabbath. This was to show that the harvest belonged to the Lord and He would have the first fruits; because of this, they would reap the benefit of a full harvest.

There were other requirements as well. They were to bring a one-year old lamb without blemish, two-tenths of Ephah with fine flow, oil, and one-quarter Hin of wine. They were not to eat bread—roasted or new grain—until the day of offering. These are strange terms for us, "Ephah" and "Hin". They were measurements. An Ephah was a little over an English bushel or around eight gallons and, a Hin is somewhere around 12 pints according to *The American Heritage® Dictionary of the English Language, Fourth Edition*[3].

This is another feast, which is specific to Israel. Here it is in reference to entering the Land, which the Lord promised to them. Back in 2000 my wife and I had the wonderful privilege and blessing to go on a trip with our church to Israel. One of the most outstanding things apart from all the rich biblical history and walking in the footsteps of Jesus was the abundant fruit and harvest. There are many places in Israel where the soil produces incredible crops. When these chosen people of God entered the land He had given them, they were to give the first fruits to Him as an offering. He would bless their crops and they would reap a harvest and still are today. The words first fruits are not isolated to the Old Testament. We see the term or phrase used by Paul in I Corinthians 15:20 and 23. Paul gives an overwhelming defense for the resurrection and our eventual resurrection also, tying it into the "first fruit", being the resurrection of Christ. He would say that we are the most miserable people on the planet if we have hope in this life only (my paraphrase). There are many Scriptures in the New Testament that demonstrate that because He rose as the first fruits of the resurrection, we can cling to the promise of a future resurrection. We see this in verses like Acts 26:23, Romans 8:11, Colossians 1:18, I Peter 1:3, and even in Revelation 1:5.

If we follow the pattern and symbolism of the previous feasts and attempt to correlate them to the first coming of Christ, the resurrection would represent the "first fruits". Some would say this is a bit of a stretch, but because Paul uses such a phrase in reference to the resurrection of Christ, it may not be that far off. Once again, this is a feast that was specific to Israel and reference to their entrance into the Land. It is also one that they are to keep as a lasting ordinance to all generations and in all their dwelling places. The orthodox still keep this feast. Another very interesting use of this phrase is found in Revelation 14:4, where we see the 144,000 referred to as the "first fruits" to God and to the Lamb; certainly we can see that this refers to Israel. This would only be possible because of the "first fruit" resurrection of Christ.

4. <u>Weeks or Pentecost</u> – Leviticus 23:15-16 states, "You shall also count for yourselves from the day after the Sabbath, from the day when you brought in the sheaf of the wave offering; there shall be seven complete Sabbaths. You shall count fifty days to the day after the seventh Sabbath; then you shall present a new grain offering to the Lord." The Feast of Weeks is another lasting ordinance for the people

of Israel. This time period places it on the sixth day of the month of Sivan on the Jewish calendar. This was fifty days after the first fruits. We see seven, one-year old male lambs without defect, one young bull, and two rams. There was also the requirement for one male goat sin offering and two lambs, one-year old each for a fellowship offering. What is interesting about this feast is that it includes two loaves of bread baked *with* leaven (Leviticus 23:17). It would become the day of Pentecost, meaning fiftieth. We see Pentecost, or this Feast of Weeks, referenced in the New Testament in the book of Acts 2:1 and Acts 20:16. We also see it referred to in I Corinthians 16:8. In both Acts 20:16 and I Corinthians 16:8, Paul is referring to the same occasion. As a Jew, he would continue to celebrate Pentecost and was anxious to leave Ephesus to go to Jerusalem and celebrate it.

Great things happened in Acts chapter two when the day of Pentecost had come. It was fifty days after the feast of "first fruits" and, in this case, fifty days after our Lord's resurrection. The barrier between Jew and Gentile had been broken down by Christ death, burial, and resurrection. Devout Jews from every nation were in Jerusalem to celebrate Pentecost, but on this occasion, the promised Holy Spirit came upon the disciples and Peter gave that incredible sermon, which led to three thousand accepting Christ. This marked the day that the Church was born.

The walls were broken down and there could be fellowship among all believers, Jew and Gentile. Here again is the apparent connection between the feasts of the Old Testament given to Israel and the New Testament with Christ's first coming. I believe it is more than a coincidence that fifty days after His resurrection, the Church would be born. It is also interesting that the original ordinance given to Israel to keep for all generations involved two loaves of leaven bread this time. You remember that leaven was associated with sin in the New Testament in I Corinthians chapter five. Those who would be added to the Church were sinners. There would be sin from time-to-time in all believers' lives, and yet it would not—or should not—be dominate. One day we will be free from the presence of sin, when given new bodies (I Corinthians 15:42-49).

Here again is a feast of Israel and yet some would see a connection between the Old Testament, Leviticus Feast of Weeks/Pentecost, the birth of the Church, and the giving of the Holy Spirit in the New Testament. The descendants of Israel continue to keep the Feast of Weeks today. You can understand why some see this connection.

Those who would see a connection between the feasts in Leviticus 23 and Christ's first and second coming would believe that the first four had a connection symbolically to His first coming. The remaining three would pertain to His second coming.

5. Trumpets – Leviticus 23:24 states, "Speak to the sons of Israel, saying 'In the seventh month on the first of the month you shall have a rest, a reminder by blowing trumpets, a holy convocation." This would be in the month of Tishri on the Jewish calendar, Tishri 1. There would be no work. There would be an offering made by fire. This was an assembling (convocation). Today this is observed as Rosh Hashanah. The trumpet was always used as a means of assembling, and in many cases, assembling for battle.

There are many references to trumpets in the New Testament. Some of the more obvious references are found in I Corinthians 15:52 and I Thessalonians 4:16. These trumpets in context speak about a future gathering of the elect at the *harpazó* or Rapture. The trumpets are also found in the book of Revelation in chapter eight and beyond where we see the wrath of God being poured out on the wicked. There are seven seals preceding the pouring out of God's wrath, the seventh seal contains seven trumpets, and the seventh trumpet contains the seven bowl judgments. Some would make the connection between the Feast of Trumpets in Leviticus 23 and the future trumpet call and assembling/gathering of the Church at the *harpazó*.

Trumpets are also associated with the Day of the Lord as seen in places like Zephaniah 1:16, Joel 2:1, 15, Amos 2:2,

3:6, and so on. Again, it is interesting that the trumpet is for calling an assembly, and we can see where a connection can be made symbolically between this feast, the future *harpazó* and Day of the Lord. There is also an obvious issue with this in that if we knew what the feast day was (Tishri 1), then we could correlate this with the Rapture, meaning we would know when the Rapture would occur, yet we know from Matthew 24:36 that no man knows the hour or *day*. Some would argue that since this starts at the Jewish New Year and the crescent moon, that it is difficult to say which specific day it falls on because it is a two-day celebration. It could also be argued that we do not know in which New Year, Tishri 1, this would take place during the 70th Week of Daniel, therefore making it impossible to know the day or hour.

The Feast of Trumpets is still celebrated today. There is another possible relationship to the Trumpet Feast of Leviticus 23 which might fit within the period of future time where the nations are judged, the earth is renovated, and the period of 45 days; 15 belonging to the three remaining feasts, trumpets, atonement, and tabernacles. These remaining feast days certainly do add up to 15 days. If you consider 30 days for the judgment of the nations and the renovation of the earth, you could come up with 45 days, however there is no explicit verse for these 30 days separate from the 15. There is a period of 30 days that take place prior to the 45 days, but those are related to the bowl judgments.

6. Atonement – Leviticus 23:27 states, " On exactly the tenth day of this seventh month is the day of atonement; it shall be a holy convocation for you, and you shall humble your souls and present an offering by fire to the Lord." This too would be a lasting ordinance for Israel. The Feast of Atonement would fall on the Tishri 10. This feast is known as Yom Kippur today. Here, one denies oneself, fasts, and does no work. The idea or meaning associated with Kippur is "covering". There were sacrifices, a day of reflection, repentance, and an inventory of the sins committed over the previous year. It is the most holy of days for Israelites. We read in Hebrews 10:3-10 that

year after year of sacrifices for sin could not accomplish what Jesus Christ accomplished on the cross, sanctifying those who receive Him as the perfect sacrifice once for all.

Today, Israel still does not accept Jesus Christ as their Messiah. One day they will resume the daily and yearly sacrifice, and today they still celebrate Yom Kippur as their high holy day. One day Israel will receive Him as its promised Messiah, who did much more than merely cover sin. He *became* sin for us that we might be the righteousness in Him. There are many folks who give all kinds of answers to the question, "who do you think crucified Jesus Christ?" Some say the Romans, some say the Jews, and others say all of us. The fact of the matter is that God the Father crucified His only begotten Son in order to complete His justice and make a propitiation for our sins once and for all, thereby honoring His name. Take a careful reading of Romans 3:23-26.

One day Israel will be saved (Romans 11:25-27). One day she will realize the covenant God has made for her people when He takes away their sins. We know that it is a yet future time. Is there a correlation between this feast and the future time when all Israel will be saved? Is this part of the last 15 days of the 45, fulfilling the feast for Israel? Is this a reference to the Rapture as a shadow of things to come? I will leave that up to you to determine.

7. <u>Tabernacles or Booths</u> – Leviticus 23:34 states, "Speak to the sons of Israel, saying, 'On the fifteenth of this seventh month is the Feast of Booths for seven days to the Lord." Once they had gathered their crops on the 15th day of the month of Tishri, they were to celebrate the feast of the Lord for seven days, resting on the first and eighth day (Leviticus 23:39). They were to live in booths for the seven days. This was to remind them of how they lived in booths when the Lord brought them out of Egypt. It would represent His divine providence and care over them during those years of wandering in the desert. This was a joyous occasion and celebration. There were the sacrifices, but this was a joyous festival.

There is a future time when God will dwell among men. He will set up His tabernacle among men (Revelation 21:3-4). Is there a connection between this feast of booths and that future time when God will set up His tabernacle among men? As far as symbols go and the provision of God, one could say yes. As far as the literal correlation, I cannot say.

In conclusion with regard to the correlation between the Feasts of Leviticus 23 and the first and second coming of our Lord, I can tell you that the parallels are remarkable. I can tell you that there are some that appear clear and apparent, such as the Passover, First Fruits, and even Pentecost regarding His first coming. As far as each one, I cannot be dogmatic and can only suggest that we continue to search the Scriptures and ask the Lord to guide our understanding on such references.

The fact remains that these feasts were given as instructions to Moses for the sons of Israel, and to take them beyond that might be presuming too much. Far greater men and Bible scholars have said "yes" and some have said "no". What we *can* say is that there is a pattern and purpose in God's plan and provision for man, and we do know that the things that were given beforehand are mentioned as shadows of things to come, and so we will remain open to the possibility that these things are so. Is Jesus our Passover? Absolutely. Is Jesus the unleavened bread? In the sense that there was no "leaven" in Him or that His body did not decay, yes. Is Jesus the First Fruits? He is undoubtedly the first fruit of the resurrection. Were the birth of the Church and the giving of the Holy Spirit, Pentecost? Yes, on the day of Pentecost. As far as feast relationship, this is hard to say, but one cannot deny that it is interesting that this happened fifty days after first fruits, the resurrection, and that there was forgiveness offered to all men for sins (leavened), both Jew and Gentile, comprising the Church. Does the Trumpet Feast relate to the Rapture? Again, hard to say, but there is no doubt that this is a call to assembly and gathering. Some believe there is a correlation between the trumpet feast of Leviticus 23 and the final 15 days of the 45, making up the 1,335 total. Whether it was the straight belled silver trumpet or the shofar, we can be sure that one day a trumpet will sound and the dead in Christ will rise first and those elect who are alive during that generation will be gathered from one end of the heavens to the other. Could it be a fulfillment of the trumpet feast in Leviticus to the nation of Israel during those final fifteen days of the forty-five? It would seem appropriate prior to ushering in the Kingdom, but I cannot be dogmatic on either case. Is the Feast of Atonement related to the future state of a saved Israel? This certainly is a beautiful picture of such and we do know that they |Israel| will be saved based on our reading in Romans 11. Is the Feast of Tabernacles or Booths related to Christ setting up His earthly kingdom among men in the future? Hard to say, but certainly we see His tabernacle among men yet future in Revelation 21.

There are a number of beautiful pictures, patterns and types in God's Word. We have to be careful not to take them too far or move them out of their intended context. It is clear that all these Feasts were for the sons of Israel and that they still keep them to this day. They may also have been given, as were many pictures, to show the sons of Israel a clearer picture, displaying the character and plan of God. You decide.

PART IV

CRITICAL ANSWERS
AND DISCOVERY

8

THE "WHO, WHAT, WHEN, WHERE, WHY AND HOW?" OF THE RAPTURE

Some have referred to this concept of study as "the six serving men". The idea comes from a short story, *The Elephant's Child* by 19th Century author, Rudyard Kipling. In the short story he includes a poem, and the first part goes like this: "I keep six honest serving-men (they taught me all I knew); their names are what, and why and when and how and where and who"[1].

In chapter two we discussed how to study God's Word. As we employ good principles of hermeneutics previously outlined regarding word meanings and relationships, historical and cultural considerations, immediate, book, and Bible context, we can gain even greater insight into the passage by asking these basic questions during the process.

When you think about it, these basic questions serve as a means to arrive at truth in just about every aspect of life. You could ask myriad of who, what, when, where, why, and how questions during your investigation for arriving at truth, or you may have an obvious, plain literal statement, which removes all doubt as to the answer being sought. I along with others have found it to be an effective means for arriving at truth. Let me give you an example: I was assigned to a jury trial a while back. The examinations and cross-examinations went on and on for days. Once the lawyers were done giving their closing arguments, it was time for us to go to the jury room, discuss the merits of the case, and arrive at a unanimous verdict if possible.

We started out with three individuals wanting a guilty verdict and the remaining nine wanting a not-guilty verdict. We discussed the details as best we could. More than once we had the stenographer come into the room and read back several details about the case. We had come to the conclusion that we were not going to arrive at a unanimous verdict, and so we elected to re-enter the jury box and disclose our finding to the judge. This would have resulted in a hung jury. We soon discovered that the court is very firm about a jury arriving at a verdict and will therefore press the jurors to work harder to arrive at one if at all possible. The judge encouraged us to take another look at the case. We went back into the jury room and went over the details again. We did make some progress, with all jurors—minus one—arriving at a not-guilty verdict. We did all we could without coercing the sole juror to see what our differences were, and yet the individual remained set on a guilty verdict. We felt we had done the best we could, so we re-entered the courtroom again. Seeing that we had made some progress, the judge requested that we take one more look at the case, so back to the jury room we went!

We were all becoming a little frustrated at this point, feeling that we had done the very best we could. That is when I thought of the "six serving men"[2] concept. I reasoned that it works well when studying Scripture, so why not here? I asked the panel if they had ever heard of the "six serving men" and they said no. I explained the concept briefly and suggested that we take six pieces of the poster paper they had given us and label them, "Who", "What", "When", "Where", "Why", and "How", and then post them on the wall. I was not the foreman of the jury, but they asked me to direct the conversation since I understood the process.

We started with "Who", and immediately details were uncovered that we had not clearly seen in the original process. We wrote down our answers on each paper as we went through the six-step process. By the time we completed "How", we had collectively uncovered a path to arrive at a unanimous verdict. Looking at each question individually and then as a cohesive whole, the truth emerged. The one individual still had some emotions due to the nature of the case, but had changed the verdict to not guilty based on the collective facts.

Even though I had used this process in virtually every leadership position I found myself in or when faced with challenges and important decisions, I was somewhat surprised to see it work in this setting. It was just another example of how effective the process is for arriving at truth. So many details within God's Word are not thoroughly examined and can lead to erroneous conclusions if we are not careful. Applying good hermeneutics, praying for the Holy Spirit's promised guidance, and employing these simple, yet profound questions, should yield results in which you can be confident.

Before I ask and answer these six questions in this chapter about the subject of the Rapture, let me state right up front that these are by no means intended to be all the iterations of the questions which could possibly be asked. You may have others that you might ask, and I encourage you to do so. I found that upon asking these six questions, however, I was able to form my own conviction(s) and hold firm to them. You will have to judge for yourself and, by all means, if you have not arrived at a verdict, keep asking the questions. While you read the answers in this book that I've found to be true, I encourage you to examine all the Scriptures for yourself as I've included only a sampling to provide a consistent, immediate book and Bible context.

As the chapter title suggests, these questions are intended to uncover the answers about the Rapture, or *harpazó* in the Greek, in regards to the study of eschatology. We have already given some background on the different man-made systems and dispensations. We will now look at the context of Scripture while asking these questions apart from the man-made systematic assumptions or dispensations. I will purposely avoid referring to men who have given their opinions on the subject and simply consult God's Word to collect the evidence for arriving at truth. In order to arrive at context, we will consider a number of Old Testament and New Testament books, and a consistent truth will emerge. We will also consider the commonality among the various positions held regarding the timing of the Rapture and also what makes them different.

SECTION 1 WHO?

We start with the question, "Who?" The first context I want to examine is found in Matthew 24, the Olivet Discourse. **Who is the author of Matthew?** Believe it or not, there is not an easy, clear-cut answer to this. The Gospel according to Matthew is actually found as a title on some early manuscripts. We know that Matthew was a tax collector as noted in Matthew 9:9 when Jesus first calls Matthew to follow Him as one of the twelve disciples. We also know from Mark 2:14 that he was also referred to as Levi the son of Alphaeus. Luke also refers to Matthew as Levi in Luke 5:27 when referring to the same calling. This may or may not mean a lot, but it is interesting. One of the arguments often used that Matthew did not write this Gospel is that he refers to himself in the third person. There is no explicit reference in the Gospel where he identifies himself as the author, but that was fairly common in early writings. The fact that he refers to himself as Matthew when he is called by Jesus is interesting in that it seems to indicate that this is the name that Jesus called him after Matthew chose to follow Him.

When we look at the Epistles, Paul and Peter (who undeniably wrote these books) both use their "post-following" names; Paul was formally Saul, and Peter was formally Simon. In their writings, they refer to themselves as Paul the apostle and Peter the apostle. In the book of Jude, Jude refers to himself as "Jude a bond-servant of Jesus Christ and brother of James" (Jude 1:1). James, in the book of James, refers to himself as "James, a bond-servant of God and of the Lord Jesus Christ" (James 1:1).

Within the book of Matthew, we also see details regarding taxes and accounting, which are not outlined in detail within the other Gospel accounts. This can be attributed to the fact that the author was a tax collector with a financial background. Early church leaders, historians, and writers also assign this Gospel to Matthew as the author. We can see this in the writings of first century writer, Papias, and second century writer Iraneaus. Most theologians and scholars believe that Matthew was written around A.D. 50 and Mark followed around A.D. 68.

The Olivet Discourse is discussed in the Gospel of Mark as well, and Mark was a disciple of Peter (I Peter 5:13). He is also referred to as John Mark in Acts 12:12. There is some debate about the authorship of this Gospel as there is no specific self-reference within the text from Mark that positively identifies him as the author. Historians as well as writers, Papias and Iraneaus, also attribute the authorship of Mark to Mark.

Luke also speaks about the Olivet Discourse in his Gospel, and John speaks about the return of Christ in his Gospel. They, too, did not identify themselves within the text as the authors. We know that Luke is a physician (Colossians 4:14), and we also believe that he is the author of the book of Acts. The reference to Theophilus in Acts 1:1 is an interesting parallel to his mention in Luke 1:3. The Gospel of Luke also provides more detail with the medical language than the other Gospels do. Again, early writers like Iraneaus attribute the authorship to Luke. Luke was written sometime between Matthew and Mark around A.D. 60 and John after sometime between A.D. 85-90.

John is one of the twelve as was Matthew, and in John 1:14, speaking of Jesus as the Word becoming flesh, John uses the words "we saw His glory". The word "we" speaks of personal acquaintance or beholding. John beheld His glory. The external, historical writers also attribute the authorship of the Gospel of John to John the apostle.

We could spend a lot of time attempting to provide a defense for the authorship of these Gospels, but that is not the emphasis of this book or the purpose. Ultimately, it is God's Word, which makes up the full canon of Scripture. It is precisely what He desired to be penned (II Peter 1:20-21). There is a great deal of material on authorship defense. I am of the conviction that Matthew wrote Matthew, Mark wrote Mark, Luke wrote Luke, and John wrote John. Since all accounts speak about the return of Christ and three speak specifically about the Olivet Discourse, we will move on to the next who question.

Who are the readers or audience Jesus is addressing in the Olivet Discourse? Matthew provides more references to the Old Testament than do the other Gospel writers. He provides a distinct genealogy of Jesus pointing to His Kingship and Messianic role, coming from the line of David and Abraham. Mark provides a more immediate urgency within his shorter Gospel account and does not go into the genealogy. Luke gives a good genealogy in chapter three beginning in verse 23 of his Gospel, and takes us all the way back to the beginning with Adam. John, much like Mark, does not go into the genealogy. We mention this because Matthew appears to be providing an emphasis to a particular audience with the descendants of Abraham. This, coupled with the abundance of Old Testament references, leads us to believe that the audience is predominately Jewish.

Matthew presents Jesus as Messiah and His Kingship, thus making the tie to King David and Abraham. Mark presents Jesus as the servant, so his emphasis is different. Luke presents Jesus as the Son of Man and takes us all the way back to Adam, while John starts off right away in chapter one speaking of Jesus as deity. Since each writer appears to have distinct purpose in how he presents Christ, they all have relevance to every believer, Jew and Gentile. For the purpose of our study, they all include language regarding Jesus' return, and three include the instructions given by Jesus to His disciples at the Mount of Olives, referred to as the Olivet Discourse.

To assign the Olivet Discourse to Israel only based on the fact that Matthew appears to be writing to a Jewish audience, would be misleading. Since the subject of His return appears in all accounts and the Olivet Discourse appears in three of the four accounts, we can see relevance for *all* audiences. I would also point out that there are a number of passages within Matthew that are relevant to the Church. This would include Peter's profession in Matthew 16, where Jesus specifically mentions the Church, Matthew 18 where we see the process for Church discipline, Matthew 24 as we will see referencing the elect, Matthew 26 where we see the ordinance of the Lord's Supper (Communion) instituted, and certainly Matthew 28 where we see the Great Commission of the Church. I would not disagree that there is an emphasis for the descendants of David and Abraham, but that does not negate the importance of the message for all believers. Since it is speaking of a future time when He will return, we can also believe that this is dealing with both Israel as a chosen people and the Church, which was made up of converted Jews to begin with and then Gentiles afterward. In Matthew 24, Jesus is specifically addressing His disciples. The same is true in Mark 13 and Luke 21.

Jesus had just departed Jerusalem in Matthew 23, where He was rejected by the Jews. He was deeply saddened by their rejection as noted in Matthew 23:37-39. He is clearly speaking to Israel and concludes the chapter by saying to them, "For I say to you, from now on you will not see Me until you say, "Blessed is He who comes in the name of the Lord!" These are His final words to them while He was in their midst. They wanted a conquering king who would put down the Roman oppression and set up the Kingdom right then and there. They could not comprehend or believe in a suffering Messiah and even though they uttered those words during His triumphal entry in chapter 21, they did not believe. Jesus quotes Psalm 118:26, but they do not accept Him as their true Messiah. We should take note that He uses the word "until" in Matthew 23:39. God is faithful to His promises and covenants. He will remain faithful to preserving a chosen people [Israel], and one day they will acknowledge Him as their true Messiah as it says in Romans 11:26-27, "and so all Israel will be saved; just as it is written, the Deliverer will come from Zion, He will remove ungodliness from Jacob. This is My covenant with them, when I take away their sins."

One of the errors that can emerge from dispensationalism is that which leads to what has been previously referred to as "replacement theology". Those who espouse to this theology believe that since Israel rejected Jesus, that He has forever forsaken them as a uniquely and divinely chosen people and replaced them with the Church. This is simply not true, because if it were, it would negate God's covenants. Passages such as Jeremiah 31:31-37 and Zechariah 12:8-10, 13:8-9 tell us that there is a future time when they [Israel] will believe. We see in Revelation 14:4 that the 144,000 are the "first fruits" of this national repentance. They are sealed and protected in Revelation chapter seven. We will talk more about them in this section later. Not many who believe in dispensations believe in replacement theology, but they do believe in distinct times and would say that since the Church was not in the first 69 Weeks of Daniel's prophecy, they will not be in the 70th. They believe that this present age is the "Church Age" or "Age of Grace", which will cease with the Rapture and then revert back to God dealing specifically with Israel during the 70th Week of Daniel. As I stated earlier, I believe that you can see the pattern throughout the history of man and how God has dealt with us, but you can also take dispensationalism too far. We have to exercise caution and not allow a system to define our doctrinal beliefs.

When we come to Matthew 24 and the Olivet Discourse, we are now seeing the disciples as the direct recipients of Jesus' message. This is true in Mark and Luke as well. Jesus is also the one speaking about His return to His disciples in John chapter 14, which took place just a day or two after the Olivet Discourse when Jesus was having the preparation supper with His disciples (John 13:1).

It is clear in my view, that the message of Matthew 24, Mark 13, and Luke 21 are to believers, and since Israel rejected Christ and still do to this day, we can believe that the message is relevant to the Church, which started with these first Jewish disciples. As we continue to ask the "who" question with reference to the verbiage within chapter 24, this will become more apparent. He is clearly speaking to His disciples and answering their questions regarding "when will this happen, and what will be the sign of Your coming, and the end of the age?" (Matthew 24:3). Jesus is also addressing a future group of "readers" in Matthew 24:15 — those who will witness the Abomination of Desolation, as spoken of by the prophet Daniel.

Who are the "elect" in Matthew 24:22, 24, 31 and Mark 13:20, 22, 27? *Vine's Expository Dictionary of New Testament Words*[1] unabridged edition states, "*eklektos* lit. signifies picked out, chosen (*ek*, from, *legō*, to gather, pick out). (c) believers (Jews or Gentiles)"[2]. If a Jew comes to Christ, he/she becomes a member of the Church. At the time when Jesus spoke these words, Israel had rejected Him. It is only after the Rapture that Israel will be saved, so this is speaking about believers. The word is used some 23 times in the New Testament, and it always refers to believers. Here are but a few of the iterations used in the New Testament: Romans 8:33, Colossians 3:12, II Timothy 1:9, Titus 1:1, I Peter 1:1, I Peter 2:4.

The original language is used as an adjective and a noun in some cases. It always is referring to believers in this given context. When we compare Scripture with Scripture, we can see that the "elect" of Matthew 24 and Mark 13 is referring to believers. If this is true, then there are some important implications for the Church. The pre-tribulation position believes that these passages in both Matthew and Mark are speaking of Israel, but the language and context say otherwise. If we follow the context of the passage, we see that they have entered the 70th Week of Daniel. What pre-tribulation supporters would argue is that since the Church was not in the first 69 Weeks of Daniel's prophecy, they will not be in the 70th. There is no logical reasoning to justify this. This is simply injecting doctrine into a dispensation approach.

The elect are believers and so we see them as entering the 70th Week of Daniel according to this passage and elsewhere in Scripture. We also see in verse 15 of Matthew 24 that Jesus talks about the Abomination of Desolation, which we know starts 3 ½ years into the final seven-year period. Then and only then does the Great Tribulation start—not before. What took place before is the beginning of birth pangs. Once the Abomination of Desolation begins, we see the Antichrist causing "great tribulation", such has not occurred since the beginning of the world until now, nor ever will" (Matthew 24:21). Then, this wonderful thing takes place in verse 22. It [great tribulation] is "cut short" for the sake of the "elect"!

Who cuts the Great Tribulation short? Verse 27 tells us it is Christ ["the Son of Man"] at His coming. The phrase "Son of Man" is used in reference to Jesus Christ over 80 times in the New Testament. It speaks of His deity and His humanity. Here, in context it is also a reference back to Daniel 7:13-14, speaking of this very coming. Then we see the progression explained in detail in verses 29-31 of Matthew 24. Jesus says, "but immediately after the tribulation of those days, the Sun will be darkened and the moon will not give its light and the stars will fall from the sky, and the powers of the heavens will be shaken." The tribulation, in context, is referring back to the Great Tribulation in verse 21. So, after the Great Tribulation—after the 3 ½ years into the 70th Week of Daniel—these things happen. The Great Tribulation is cut short for the "elect" [believers] by these celestial phenomena visible in the sky.

Then Jesus continues in verses 30 and 31 as He answers His disciples question regarding *the sign* of His coming. "And then the sign of the Son of Man will appear in the sky, and then all the tribes of the earth will mourn, and they will see the Son of Man coming on the clouds of the sky with power and great glory. 31 And He will send forth His angels with a great trumpet and they will gather together His elect from the four winds; from one end of the sky to the other." A plain, literal, interpretation of this context shows that the elect are gathered sometime after the Great Tribulation starts, which is not until 3 ½ years into the 70th Week of Daniel. The same word is used of elect here. These are believers. What cuts the Great Tribulation short is His coming and the sign just described. The *sign* preceding the gathering is the sun, moon, and stars, which is consistent with the language preceding the Day of the Lord in Old Testament passages such as Joel 2:31. It is also consistent with the language contained in the sixth seal of Revelation chapter six, which speaks of the same sign preceding His wrath, which commences with the seventh seal containing the seven trumpet and seven bowl judgments and the opening of the scroll.

Some would have us believe that this passage in Matthew 24 and Mark 13 are speaking of His second coming, which they believe is separate from the Rapture. The word "coming" as used in this chapter is *parousia,* which speaks of a single coming. It is always used in the singular. There are not two separate comings. It is a coming and presence. In other words, His *parousia*, or coming, will take place along with the events associated with that coming.

Others would say that you do not find rapture language in the Olivet Discourse. It is abundantly clear that there is "rapture" language here. The classic passage on the Rapture is found in I Thessalonians 4:16-17 where we read, "For the Lord Himself will descend from heaven with a shout, with the voice of the archangel and with the *trumpet* of God, and the dead in Christ will rise first. 17 Then we who are alive and remain will be caught up together with them in the *clouds* to meet the Lord in the air, and so we shall always be with the Lord." [Emphasis mine.] Note the language in Matthew 24:30-31, "And then the sign of the Son of Man will appear in the sky, and then all the tribes of the earth will mourn, and they will see the Son of Man coming on the *clouds* of the sky with great power and great glory. 31 And He will send forth His angels with a great *trumpet* and they will gather together His elect from the four winds; from one end of the sky to the other." [Emphasis mine.] Certainly we see clouds and trumpets as similar language.

Let's take it a step further. In II Thessalonians 2:1 it states, "Now we request you, brethren, with regard to the coming of our Lord Jesus Christ and our *gathering* together to Him." [Emphasis mine.] This is clearly a reference to the Rapture. In Matthew 24:31, He [Jesus] sends forth His angels to *gather* the elect. It is the same Greek word. II Thessalonians uses the noun form and Matthew 24 uses the verb form. In John 14:1-6 we see another clear reference to the Rapture. In this text, Jesus uses the words, "receive you to Myself". In Matthew 24:40 and 41, we see where one is "taken" and another left behind. The word in both cases is *paralambanó* in the original language.

Regardless of the common language, the context is what should provide the meaning of the text, and in all cases, it is referring to the same event—the gathering, catching up, or receiving of the elect. In Luke 21, we see similar language referring to the sign of His coming beginning in verse 25. In verse 28, Jesus tells His disciples that when they see these same heavenly phenomena taking place to "lift up your heads, because your redemption is drawing near." He is speaking of deliverance. There is "rapture" language in Luke 17:24 and Luke 24:35, 36 speaking about one taken and one left behind.

In context, Jesus talks about the way it was in the time of Noah and Lot. For the unbeliever in both of those cases, sudden destruction and judgment came upon them unexpectedly, but for Noah and his family during the forty days and forty nights of rain and worldwide flooding and Lot as Sodom and Gomorrah were about to be destroyed, they were forewarned, and because they believed, they were delivered. It will be like that when the Rapture takes place. For those of us who are believers, we are forewarned and know when to look up [the sign], but for the unbeliever, the Lord will pour out His judgment upon them at a time when they do not expect it. They will hide in the caves and be terrified. His coming for the elect will not be a secret disappearance. Every eye will see when He comes, and it will be announced with a loud voice and trumpet call while incredible things take place in the sky from one end of heaven to the other.

It should also be of interest to us when individuals attempt to set times or dates regarding the Rapture. Our pre-tribulation brothers and sisters are quick to point out that no one knows the hour or day; interesting, because this is taken from Matthew 24:36, "But of that day and hour no one knows, not even the angels of heaven, nor the Son, but the Father alone." They are correct in assigning this language to the Rapture context. We can see several instances where these passages on the Olivet Discourse are speaking about His *parousia* and the Rapture.

The pre-tribulation position would state that we do not see the Church in Revelation after chapter four, and therefore the Church must have been raptured. Some would say this happens after chapter six. This also has no substance. First, the book of Revelation is to believers. It is addressed to the Church. Not just a portion of it, but the entire letter. These seven churches were literal churches that existed, and they also represent the characteristics of the Church in the future. John was taken up in Spirit in chapter four to witness the things, which were yet to come. There is no way you can refer to John as being the Church. Chapter five provides the information on a scroll and the only one who is worthy to open it. We are told that this is Jesus Christ. Chapter six addresses the seals, which align with Matthew 24 and Mark 13, which we have already demonstrated as passages that are speaking about believers being present beyond the commencement of the 70th Week of Daniel and the start of the Great Tribulation.

Another verse which is often taken out of context is found in Revelation 3:10, "Because you have kept the word of My perseverance, I also will keep you from the hour of testing, that hour which is about to come upon the whole world, to test those who dwell on the earth." This is often quoted as a verse to support the Rapture taking place before the seals are opened, therefore "pre-tribulation" in their view. There are a number of problems with this. First, the context does not support this and neither does the original language construct. Remember, there were no punctuations in the original text. The church at Philadelphia represented a good church with an open door. They kept His Word. They were absolutely faithful.

I would also suggest that the hour of testing has two different groups in mind. He will deliver those out of danger who are faithful, which is consistent with all other biblical text referring to rescue or deliverance out of the Great Tribulation by it being cut short for the sake of the elect. He will also deliver the elect from the wrath to come, according to I Thessalonians 1:10. That will be the Day of the

Lord's wrath. This is the same Day of the Lord's wrath referred to in I Thessalonians chapter five, when speaking of the times and epochs and "Day of the Lord". Couple that with II Thessalonians chapter two and you have a very telling timeline. We see the faithful and those who dwell on the earth in this passage. They appear distinct and I believe they are.

So our next question is: **Who are the earth dwellers?** We see this phrase used a number of times in Revelation. First, in Revelation 3:10, of those who are about to come into judgment. In Revelation 8:13, they are those who are subject to the Day of the Lord's wrath with the trumpet judgment beginning after the seals. In Revelation 11:10, they are referred to as "ones who were tormented by the two prophets". In Revelation 13:8, they worship the Beast and are not found written in the Lamb's book of life. In Revelation 13:14, they are the ones who are deceived and make an image to the Beast. There is no doubt that these earth dwellers are unbelievers. They are the ones who are deceived and, in Matthew 24:24, we are told that the elect will not be deceived. The language in Matthew says, "For false Christs and false prophets will arise and will show great signs and wonders, so as to mislead, *if possible,* even the elect." [Emphasis mine.] In other words, it will not be possible to deceive or mislead the elect. On the other hand, in Revelation we clearly see that the unbelievers will be deceived and will follow the Antichrist.

There are many folks who have heard the Gospel and have rejected it, believing that if all of this really does come to fruition, they will make a decision for Christ then. They want to sow their wild oats now and live worldly, getting all the world has to offer them, while holding off on making a decision to receive Christ as Lord and Savior until the last minute. What an incredibly dangerous position to put oneself in. We are told that they will be among the earth dwellers and they will be deceived. In II Thessalonians 2:10-12 Paul states, "and with all deception of wickedness for those who perish, because they did not receive the love of the truth so as to be saved. 11 For this reason God will send upon them a deluding influence so that they will believe what is false, 12 In order that they all may be judged who did not believe the truth, but took pleasure in wickedness."

There are those who sit in church every weekend and are exposed to the truth over and over again and are what Hebrews calls "enlightened and partakers" in chapter six, and yet have never made a decision for Christ. The author of Hebrews gives a strong warning and says they cannot be renewed to repentance. There is a point where a person's heart becomes hardened. If you think you can wait until these things happen and then make a decision for Christ, you are mistaken and taking a risk, which could lead to eternal separation from God. The text clearly states that you will be subject to deception and then judged. Don't be among these unbelievers and do not wait. Today is the day of salvation. Only the faithful will be rescued and delivered from the wrath that is to come.

Who are the four horseman of Revelation six? They represent the first four seals of Revelation six. They are the White Horse in 6:1-2 representing a ruler coming to power as noted with the bow and the crown. He is rising toward conquest. This appears to fit with the Olivet Discourse where we see the emergence of Antichrist in Matthew 24:4-5. The next horseman in Revelation six is the Red Horse in 6:4 representing wars, which parallels the Olivet Discourse in Matthew 24:6. The next horseman is the Black Horse in Revelation 6:5 representing the high cost of food and a full days wage for a quart of wheat and three quarts of barley. This appears to parallel the Olivet Discourse in Matthew 24:7 where Jesus speaks about famines. The next horseman is the Ashen Horse in Revelation 6:8, representing death through famine, pestilence and wild beasts. In Matthew 24:7 we see the famine and earthquakes. In Luke's account in 21:11 he mentions plagues and famines, which seem consistent with the language of the fourth horseman in Revelation.

Who is the man of lawlessness in II Thessalonians two? Who is this man, referenced as the "son of destruction", who opposes and exalts himself above every so-called god or object of worship, and so takes his seat in the temple of God, displaying himself as being God (II Thessalonians 2:4)? This is undeniably the Antichrist. We should also note for those who believe the Church will be raptured prior to the commencement of the 70th Week of Daniel (part of their reasoning being that they believe the entire seven-year period is God's wrath), that only God will be exalted on this day (referring in context to the

Day of the Lord) according to Isaiah 2:11, 17. The Lord alone will be exalted and not the Antichrist.

The Day of the Lord does not start with the commencement of the 70th Week of Daniel, but rather sometime after the Great Tribulation begins. The context within II Thessalonians describes the Antichrist's attributes and character, which clearly belong to him. He is a man of lawlessness, which speaks to his utter wickedness. He is the son of perdition, a title seen in John 17:12 given to Judas, who betrayed Christ. In context, this man of lawlessness, this son of perdition is one who opposes the Lord. He is the opposite of Christ.

There is unanimous agreement among the larger majority of Bible scholars that this passage in II Thessalonians is describing the Antichrist. I also believe this to be true. Now, when we look at the context of chapter two, we see that He [the man of lawlessness] must be revealed and sets himself up in the Temple to be exalted prior to the gathering or rapture event spoken of in verse one. Further, verse two tells us that the Day of the Lord is connected to the "gathering" and this will not happen until the man of lawlessness is revealed. We know from comparing Scripture with Scripture that the Antichrist does not reveal himself or set himself up in the Temple until the mid-point of the 70th Week of Daniel. We see this in Daniel 9:27 and in the Olivet Discourse in Matthew 24:15. These verses in II Thessalonians are critical to our understanding of the timing of the Rapture. It clearly states that the "gathering" will not take place until after the mid-point of the 70th Week of Daniel when the Antichrist [man of lawlessness] sets himself up in the Temple to be exalted. It is consistent with what Jesus taught His disciples in the Olivet Discourse, and it is consistent with the events in Revelation chapter six. The first four seals parallel what Jesus refers to as the "beginning of birth pangs". Beginning in Matthew 24:15, we see the Abomination of Desolation and the one "standing in the holy place"(verse 15), which initiates the Great Tribulation beginning in verse 21 of Matthew 24. This parallels II Thessalonians chapter two in that the elect are still present in Matthew 24 at this point, and the "gathering" has not taken place yet in II Thessalonians, indicating believers are still present.

We would expect to see the same in Revelation six, and we do. The fifth seal of Revelation 6:9-11 indicates that many will become martyrs as a result of following Christ. Who are these martyrs? Revelation 7:13-14 tells us these are believers who suddenly appear along with a great multitude in between the sixth and seventh seal. Revelation 7:14 tells us that these are the ones who came "out of the Great Tribulation". Here again, we see a full and consistent picture emerge of believers being present beyond the first half of the 70th Week of Daniel.

The author who penned the book of Revelation is John, but the words are from Jesus (Revelation 1:1-2). Paul makes an interesting statement in I Thessalonians 3:15 where he says, "For this we say to you by the *word of the Lord...*" [Emphasis mine.] All of these accounts are Jesus' words, and we would expect them to be consistent as they are.

Who will be at Armageddon? We often hear of this term and associated phrase, "Battle of Armageddon". Perhaps we should first ask what Armageddon is. We find reference to it in Revelation 16:16 as a Hebrew term, *Har-Magedon.* It means the "Mount of Meggido", which is a strategic site located at the tip of a pass, leading through the Carmel Ridge and overlooking the massive Jezreel Valley. It is the site of many ancient battles. This will be the site of the last great battle. In Revelation 16, we see that those present will be the unrepentant nations, Satan, False Prophet, the Antichrist, the 144,000 first fruits of redeemed Israel (Revelation 14:1), those who came to Christ after the *harpazó*, and Jesus Christ with His army of angels (Matthew 25:31). All are present in Revelation 19:11, 19:14, and 19:21, where we see this great battle. In Daniel 12:9-11, we see an additional 30 days during the second half of Daniel's 70th Week (1,290 days), which accounts for the 1,260 equaling 42 months, or 3 ½ years, and then an additional 30 for 1,290. At the conclusion of these 30 days, or God's swift bowl judgments, (symbolic of the shallow bowls of water used to wash hands before a meal and then the water is swiftly tossed out), we see Christ descending to earth to conduct the battle at *Har-Magedon* to crush the Antichrist's dominion (Daniel 7:26) and break him (Daniel 8:25). He [Jesus Christ] reclaims His Kingdom.

Who are the 24 Elders in Revelation? I would simply say they are 24 Elders on thrones in heaven who are worshipping the Lord. Many old and new scholars alike have assigned the 24 elders as representing the Church. Others have said they represent the combined redeemed as being one from each of the twelve tribes of Israel, combined with the twelve apostles. They make this assumption based on Revelation 21:12-14, which discusses the twelve gates with the names of the twelve tribes of Israel and the twelve foundation stones with the names of the twelve apostles on them. It does not say that these are the 24 elders, and just because those two groups add up to 24, does not mean that the 24 elders are being represented here. The word elder is not used in this passage. You might add the twelve angels who are also in this passage and are at the gates, adding up to 36; however, this is not important in identifying the 24 as elders.

We do see where Jesus, speaking to His disciples regarding rewards in Matthew 19:27-30, mentions that the twelve disciples will sit upon thrones, judging the twelve tribes of Israel when "the Son of Man will sit on His glorious throne", so perhaps there may be some truth to this observation. Again, the interpretation might be due to how nicely it might fit into a particular doctrine, but we cannot adapt the Scriptures to satisfy doctrine when there is no clear and absolute meaning. Even if these apostles and leaders of the twelve tribes of Israel were the 24, it has nothing to do with the timing of the Rapture.

One possibility Henry M. Morris mentions in his book, *The Revelation Record*[3], is that these 24 elders represent "all redeemed humanity" throughout all the ages which trace back to the "twenty-four patriarchs" listed in the line of the promised seed (Adam, Seth, Enos, Cainan, Mahalaleel, Jared, Enoch, Methuselah, Lamech, Noah, Shem, Arphaxad, Salah, Eber, Peleg, Reu, Serug, Nahor, Terah, Abraham, Isaac, Jacob, Judah, Pharez).

We all agree that these elders appear to be separate and distinct from angelic beings, so let's look at the different mentions of the 24 elders in the book of Revelation. We see a reference to them as a group of individuals speaking out some 12 times in Revelation. This is pretty significant in itself. The following are the twelve references and what is taking place when they do appear in Revelation:

(1) Revelation 4:4, "Around the throne were 24 thrones; and upon the thrones I saw twenty-four elders sitting, clothed in white garments, and golden crowns on their heads." Here is the

scene beginning to unfold as John is taken up into heaven in the Spirit (as in II Peter 1:21) to witness the unveiling which Jesus wants him to record. John sees a central throne with radiant glory. This is where the Lord God Almighty, who was and is and is to come, is seated. These elders are in the presence of four living creatures who give "glory and honor and thanks to Him who sits on the throne", but they are distinct [from the four living creatures and John] in that they have white garments, typically representative of purity, and they have crowns, or *stephanos,* typically referring to a victor's crown for the winner in ancient games. They are seen falling down before Him and worshipping, "Worthy are You, our Lord and our God, to receive glory and honor and power; for You created all things, and because of Your will they existed, and were created." They cast their crowns before the throne in verses 9-10, and refer to Him as "our God". This is really defined as being in the company of God.

(2) Revelation 4:10, "the 24 elders will fall down before Him who sits on the throne, and will worship Him who lives forever and ever, and will cast their crowns before the throne." Here we see them worshipping and falling down. So far, we have them wearing white garments and crowns, and are now able to fall down or be prostrate in the presence of one in authority or majesty. This is like bowing before the throne.

(3) Revelation 5:5, "and one of the elders said to me, "Stop weeping; behold, the Lion that is from the tribe of Judah, the Root of David, has overcome so as to open the book and its seven seals." Here we see one of the twenty-four speaking to John and declaring who is worthy to open the scroll with the seven seals. The angels had just asked the question, and the elder gives the answer. It is Jesus Christ, the Lion of the Tribe of Judah; the Root of David Who has overcome. He is worthy. John had wept prior to this revelation. We will make some observations regarding this in our summary portion of this section on the 24 elders.

(4) Revelation 5:6, "And I saw between the throne (with the four living creatures) and the elders a Lamb standing, as

if slain, having seven horns and seven eyes, which are the seven Spirits of God, sent out into all the earth." They are mentioned here only in providing proximity of the Lamb, as being gathered to witness the One Who is worthy to open the scroll. The position of these elders is one of prominence and privilege, and they fall down and worship the Lamb. Perhaps they are representative of all faithful throughout the ages, yet they are not the Church, for we do know that while the path is narrow that leads to salvation and few there are that find it, nonetheless it will be far greater than 24.

(5) <u>Revelation 5:8</u>, "When He had taken the book, the four living creatures and the 24 elders fell down before the Lamb, each one holding a harp and golden bowls full of incense, which are the prayers of the saints." What follows these prayers is a new song with the exaltation, praise, and worship of the Lord who is worthy; these are the prayers of the saints. This is a sweet verse for all who have ever believed. Beginning in Revelation chapter six, we see the seals starting to be pealed off of the scroll. There must be incredible anticipation in heaven as the title deed to earth and the culmination of human history comes to the point where the saints who have been martyred throughout the ages are vindicated, the ones who have prayed for His Kingdom to come on earth as it is in heaven will be realized, and One who alone is worthy to be exalted among all men and created heaven and earth itself. There is a beautiful verse in Psalm 141:2 where we read, "May my prayer be counted as incense before You; The lifting up of my hands as the evening offering." We know that our prayers are not perfect. They are far from it. We are sinners and at times we do not even know what to ask. Every believer can rejoice in knowing that first we can have direct access to the throne of grace to find help in a time of need, and we have unimpeded access as children who have embraced our Lord and Savior. Romans 8:26-27 states, "In the same way the Spirit also helps our weakness; for we do not know how to pray as we should, but the Spirit Himself intercedes for us with groaning's too deep for words; 27 and He who searches the hearts knows

what the mind of the Spirit is, because He intercedes for the saints according to the will of God." We can be assured that our prayers are going to be perfect when they arrive, and we are told to pray without ceasing. This is something we should take to heart. I am sure that most of us—if not all of us—could improve our prayer life. What a privilege to bring our petitions before the Creator of the universe! The seals are about to be opened and heavens hosts, angels, elders, and all anticipate what will be next. What a glorious day! Back in Matthew 24:36 we were told that no one knows the day or hour of His coming, not even the angels in heaven or the Son, but the Father alone. The scroll will unlock this long anticipated message of His coming in fulfillment of prophecy, as well as the answer to the prayers of the saints throughout the ages.

(6) Revelation 5:11, "Then I looked and I heard the voice of many angels around the throne and the living creatures and the elders; and the number of them was myriads of myriads, and thousands of thousands." Here there is rejoicing and another call to witness the opening of the scroll. It continues to result in declaring the Lamb "Worthy"!

(7) Revelation 5:14, "And the four living creatures kept saying, "Amen." And the elders fell down and worshipped." Again, more praise and worship resulting in the elders prostrating themselves before the throne of the One who is worthy to open the scroll.

(8) Revelation 7:11, "And all the angels were standing around the throne and around the elders and the four living creatures; and they fell on their face before the throne and worshiped God." The sixth seal has been removed from the scroll and then there is an interlude. The 144,000 from the 12 tribes are sealed and protected. Next there is a great multitude appearing in heaven before the throne, which no one could count, from every tribe, tongue, and nation. The scene is glorious and the elders once again prostrate themselves. Verse 12 says, "Amen, blessing and glory and wisdom and thanksgiving and honor and power and might, be to our God forever and ever Amen." The scene continues to unfold in the next occurrence with the elders.

(9) <u>Revelation 7:13</u>, "Then one of the elders answered, saying to me, "These who are clothed in the white robes, who are they, and where have they come from?" John answers in verse 14. "I said to him, "My lord, you know." And he said to me, "These are the ones who came out of the great tribulation, and they have washed their robes and made them white in the blood of the Lamb." This is a very important text in our study. This great multitude, which suddenly appears before the throne is from every tribe, tongue, and nation. They are more than can be counted. Israel is still unsaved, but for the remnant which is securely sealed and remains on earth. This multitude came out of the Great Tribulation. This is the Church. These are the raptured saints. Coupling the idea, which some have proposed, that John's witness to these things in heaven is representative of the Church with the interpretation that the elders are representative of the Church seems very illogical at this point in the text, for this is the first time we see this great multitude appear in heaven. The elders were already there and so they are not the Church. John sees himself as distinct from this group and so do the elders, yet we do know that John himself will be among the raptured saints when that day comes, for the dead in Christ shall rise first, then we who are alive and remain will be caught up together with them in the clouds to meet the Lord in the air. This might explain John's response to the elder. This occurs just prior to the opening of the final seal, the seventh seal, which will contain the trumpet and bowl judgments. We will not see these 24 elders mentioned again until the seventh trumpet and Christ's reign being imminent.

(10) <u>Revelation 11:16</u>, "And the twenty-four elders, who sit on their thrones before God, fell on their faces and worshipped God." The seventh trumpet has sounded, there is a loud voice in heaven saying, "The kingdom of the world has become the kingdom of our Lord and of His Christ; and He will reign forever and ever" (verse 15). This is what the elders respond to. The final vindication is coming. The Kingdom is coming. The saints have already been raptured. The Day of the Lord's

wrath is nearing the end with the seventh trumpet initiating the seven swift bowl judgments. Christ is about to reclaim the earth and set up His Kingdom. They proceed to give thanks.

(11) Revelation 14:3, "And they sang a new song before the throne and before the four living creatures and the elders; and no one could learn the song except the one hundred and forty-four thousand who had been purchased from the earth." These were the ones sealed in Revelation chapter seven. These are now the first fruits of the promised covenant with Israel. This is a special song for them only. They did not succumb to the mark of the beast or worship him after the Church was raptured. They endured and remained faithful.

(12) Revelation 19:4, "And the twenty-four elders and the four living creatures fell down and worshipped God who sits on the throne saying, "Amen. Hallelujah!" This is the last time we see the 24 elders mentioned in Revelation. It is important to understand a little about the construct of the book of Revelation. It is not sequential from chapter one to twenty-two. It can be thought of in two parts. The first ends at Revelation 11:15, where we read, "Then the seventh angel sounded; and there were loud voices in heaven, saying, The kingdom of the world has become the kingdom of our Lord and of His Christ; and He will reign forever and ever." Chapter 12 starts it all over. When we look at Revelation, it is really narrowing in on the second half of the 70th Week of Daniel with little in the first half. Even as we see the elders in these later chapters it is with the detail and culmination that we saw in Revelation 11:15. John was told to repeat what he saw when we come to the end of Revelation chapter 10, where we read, "And they said to me, "You must prophesy *again* concerning many peoples and nations and tongues and kings." [Emphasis mine.] He is told to repeat the prophecy. Chapter 12 will start it over again.

To conclude our assessment of who the 24 elders are, we can simply say that they are 24 elders. They are not angels or creatures, but elders. They have prominence and privilege before the throne, and they are present to give honor, praise, and worship to the Lamb along with angelic beings and four living creatures. They hold the golden bowls representing the prayers of the saints, rejoice in the final vindication of the martyred believers, and witness the seals, trumpets, and bowls leading to the final Kingdom. There are a lot of theories as to who they are specifically, but while they rejoice over the redeemed and raptured saints, they are not the Church. John is also distinct from them, and as he weeps over the question of who is worthy to open the scroll, it is one of these elders who provides the answer, which also indicates distinction from John or the Church. We will have to wait to find out for sure, but the fact that God could have 24 elders around His throne is something He has chosen, and that is what the text provides. We should exercise caution in attempting to make more out of it than what exists in Scripture. Here I would agree with John F. Walvoord when he said, "This is an issue that most scholars agree cannot be finally determined"[4].

Who are the 144,000? We read of this group in Revelation 7:4-8, "And I heard the number of those who were sealed, one hundred and forty-four thousand sealed from every tribe of the sons of Israel:" Verses five through eight name those tribes and state that twelve thousand are sealed from each, adding up to the 144,000. One could do a lengthy study on the twelve tribes of Israel. We will devote a little space here in an attempt to bring some clarity with regard to the names. The twelve tribes by name are not always the direct sons of Jacob. For instance, Ephraim and Manasseh were sons of Joseph, not Jacob. They were, however, adopted by Jacob and included in the tribes of Reuben and Simeon. Joseph was given double honor as a result of saving the family during the famine (Genesis 47:11-12 and Genesis 48:9-22).

During the different periods of Israel's history, the tribes were scattered. Originally they were given parts of the Canaan, which was portioned among the tribes. The eastern portion was given to Judah, Issachar, and Zebulun. The northern portion was given to Dan, Asher, and Naphtali. The southern portion was given to Reuben, Simeon, and Gad. Dan was also given a southern portion originally, which is why you hear the phrase "from Dan to Beersheba", Dan being in the north and south originally, and Beersheba to the south. The western portion was given to Manasseh, Ephraim, and Benjamin. Levi was assigned the priesthood and did not receive a portion of the land. Joseph, while not directly receiving a portion of the land, is doubly blessed with Ephraim and Manasseh receiving land, both of who were his sons.

As you start to compare lists of names from both sons and tribes of Jacob (Israel), you can easily get confused. Part of the key is understanding there is a division of land for purposes of governing tribes, as well as the blessings for Israel, purposes for preserving the priesthood, and the times of scattering and impacts related to God's commands to Moses to share with the sons of Israel during the covenant in Moab, found in Deuteronomy 29. There is also the promise to save a remnant (Romans 9:27), which is a quote from Isaiah 10:22. All of these things have bearing on the names given in Revelation 7:4-8.

When we come to the list in Revelation chapter seven, we see that Dan and Ephraim are not listed, but Levi and Manasseh are. It still contains 12 tribes of Israel, but why are Dan and Ephraim not in the list and Levi and Manasseh are? There are two reasons for this. God is always faithful to His word, so let's look at Deuteronomy 29:16-21, "for you know how we lived in the land of Egypt, and how we came through the midst of the nations through which you passed; 17 moreover, you have seen their abominations and their idols of wood, stone, silver, and gold, which they had with them; 18 so that there will not be among you a man or woman, or family or tribe, whose heart turns away today from the Lord our God, to go and serve the gods of those nations; that there will not be among you a root bearing poisonous fruit and wormwood. 19 It shall be when he hears the words of this curse, that he will boast saying, 'I have peace though I walk in the stubbornness of my heart in order to destroy the watered land with the dry.' 20 The Lord shall never be willing to forgive him, but rather the anger of the Lord and His jealousy will burn against that man, and every curse which is written in this book will rest on him, and *the Lord will blot out his name from under heaven.* 21 Then the Lord will single him out from adversity from all the tribes of Israel, according to all the curses of the covenant which are written in this book of the law." [Emphasis mine.]

Both Dan and Ephraim were joined to idols. We see that in I Kings 12:25-30 in the case of Dan. In Hosea 4:17, we see the same thing with respect to Ephraim. They were joined to idols and, according to the instruction given by God to Moses, their names were to be blotted out. In Numbers 18:6, we see where the tribe of Levi is given as a gift for the Lord and to do the service of the tabernacle of the congregation. We can see why they would be included in the Revelation list where there will be a new Temple and a new tabernacle among the remnant. These then become the twelve tribes from which a remnant is preserved.

These 144,000 are also mentioned in Revelation chapter 14, verses one and three. There they are standing on Mt Zion with the Lamb. His name and the name of His Father are written on their foreheads. This is consistent with the sealing in Revelation seven. The seal speaks of ownership. The same Greek word is used of believers in Ephesians 1:13, "In Him, you also, after listening to the message of the truth, the gospel of your salvation-having also believed, you were sealed in Him with the Holy Spirit of promise, 14 who is given as a pledge of our inheritance, with a view to the redemption of God's own possession, to the praise of His glory." In the same manner, once the Church is raptured, these 144,000 are sealed as ownership of God, also preserved as a remnant in keeping with the covenant to redeem Israel. They sing a new song, which only they can learn. They are the first fruits of redeemed Israel.

Who is the "one who restrains"? Many have reasoned in the past that the "restrainer" spoken of by the Apostle Paul in II Thessalonians 2:6-7 is either the Church or the Holy Spirit. This author does not believe that the restrainer is either. Here again, it will be important to look at context. In this case, we have some indications from the immediate context—and certainly within the overall biblical context—as to who the restrainer might be.

In II Thessalonians 2:1, we see that Paul is specifically referring to the Rapture of the Church with language such as, "the coming of our Lord Jesus Christ" and "our gathering together to Him." He goes on and describes to the church at Thessalonica that this event [the Rapture] will not take place until a few things first occur. Paul speaks about the apostasy and the revealing of the Antichrist, or "man of lawlessness". He then goes on to describe what appears to be an individual who is keeping this man of lawlessness from being empowered and revealing himself in the Temple. We know that this does not happen until the mid-point of Daniel's 70th Week. This is also when Satan himself indwells and empowers the Antichrist and then begins his reign of terror known as the Great Tribulation or the "Times of Jacob's Trouble". There are a few reasons why we can eliminate the one who restrains as the Church. First, the Church is present and enduring this period of time. We can see this from the passages in Revelation chapter six and within the Olivet Discourse passages in Matthew 24 and Mark 13, where the "elect" are still present once the Great Tribulation commences. Secondly, while the Church can and should have an impact on the darkness of this world and set the tone for moral and ethical values, we are not holding back or restraining Satan from coming and indwelling the Antichrist, which is what is happening in context. Thirdly, the Church is always referred to in the feminine where the restrainer here is in the masculine.

We also believe that the one who restrains is not the Holy Spirit. Some believe that if the Church or the Holy Spirit were removed or "taken out of the way", that Satan will have full, unrestrained authority and power to conduct his reign of terror unimpeded. The Holy Spirit does not necessarily restrain as it is being used in context.

According to *Vine's Expository Dictionary of New Testament Words, unabridged edition*, the Greek word in II Thessalonians 2:6-7 is *katechó*, which means to "hold fast or down", and is translated "restraineth" in 2 Thessalonians 2:6-7. In verse 6, lawlessness is spoken of as being restrained in its development: in verse 7, "one that restraineth" is, lit., 'the restrainer' (the article with the present participle, 'the restraining one'); this may refer to an individual, as in the similar construction in I Thess. 3:5, "the tempter"..."[5].

While the Holy Spirit is a person of the Triune God-Head, He typically convicts, guides, directs, teaches, and indwells the believer, but is not the restrainer spoken of here in context. We also know that individuals will come to Christ even after the Rapture occurs, and they will be indwelt with the Holy Spirit when they believe.

The restrainer spoken of here is most likely the Archangel Michael. He is the angel who protects Israel. Notice in context the restrainer is keeping something from happening, described for us in II Thessalonians 2:7-10. It is the empowering of the Antichrist by Satan. We said that the act of the restrainer as defined above is to "hold fast or down". The restrainer, therefore, is holding down Satan from being able to empower the Antichrist up to a certain point.

In Daniel 10:21, we see Michael's protection over Israel. The verb used here is *chazaq*, meaning "to be strong and uphold, restrain or conquer". This is the idea of being strong so as to hold, cling, and restrain something or someone. In Daniel 11, we see the rise of the Antichrist, and then something very interesting takes place in Daniel 12:1: "Now at that time Michael, the great prince who *stands* guard over the sons of your people, will *arise*, And there will be a time of distress such as never occurred since there was a nation until that time; and at that time your people, everyone who is found written in the book, will be rescued." [Emphasis mine.]

The moment Michael arises, the Great Tribulation starts. Now let's look at Revelation 12:7-10, "And there was war in heaven, Michael and his angels waging war with the dragon. The dragon and his angels waged war, 8 and they were not strong enough, and there was no longer a place found for them in heaven. 9 And the great dragon was thrown down to the earth, and his angels were thrown down with him 10 Then I heard a loud voice in heaven saying. "Now the salvation, and the power and the kingdom of our God and the authority of His Christ have come, for the accuser of our brethren has been thrown down, he who accuses them before our God day and night."

Michael arises, the one who has historically restrained the accuser, the dragon, which is Satan. Michael casts Satan [the devil] to earth. At this point, Satan is enraged and goes on to empower the Antichrist in a last ditch effort (Revelation 12:12). This initiates the Great Tribulation or the Time of Jacob's Troubles. Note that he only has a short time of his [Satan's] wrath. This is consistent with the Olivet Discourse where we are told that the Great Tribulation will be cut short. He persecutes Israel and then goes after her offspring, which is the Church (Revelation 12:13-17).

The overall biblical context leans toward the one who restrains as being the Archangel Michael. This also has some implications for those who support the pre-tribulation, imminent rapture position. If the restrainer is the Archangel Michael and not the Church or the Holy Spirit, then this removes a facet of the pre-tribulation, imminent rapture position. As we have learned from the immediate context, this begins at the middle of the 70th Week of Daniel, not prior to it. Those who hold to the pre-tribulation position claim that the restrainer is removed from the earth unexpectedly and almost secretly during the Rapture before the 70th Week of Daniel begins, leaving the world in chaos and nothing to keep it from going into its darkest hour. They would also hold to the position that this could happen at any moment, and that essentially no Scripture or prophecy has to be fulfilled before this event takes place.

We have already seen that this is in stark contrast to what is taught in II Thessalonians 2:1-7. Further, His [Jesus Christ's] coming will not be sign-less or secret. The entire world will see Him coming in all of His Glory. There will be signs in the heavens just prior to and before the announcing of His *parousia*. When Michael stands and Satan is cast to earth, then the Antichrist will be empowered to go after Israel and her offspring, which is the Church. He [the Antichrist] will only have a short while to pour out his wrath, because it will be cut short by the sign in the sun, moon, and stars as the trumpet sounds and Christ returns for His bride.

Who is the "False Prophet"? This is the third party of the unholy trinity. You have these powerfully satanic imitators of God that come on the scene: Satan, the Antichrist and the False Prophet. This is the beast from the earth. This indicates a human being. He is found in Revelation 13:11-15. He is described as the one representing the first beast, which is the Antichrist. He is, therefore, the right-hand man of the Antichrist, doing his evil bidding. This beast will make those who dwell on the earth worship the Antichrist. These uninformed unbelievers will be highly persuaded, deceived, misled, misguided, and directed to take the mark of the beast and worship the Antichrist. "He performs great signs, so that he even makes fire come down out of heaven to the earth in the presence of men." He tells those who dwell on the earth [unbelievers] to make an image to the Antichrist and they do. He is also found in Revelation 19:20, "And the beast was seized, and with him the false prophet who performed the signs in his presence, by which he deceived those who had received the mark of the beast and those who worshipped his image; these two were thrown alive into the lake of fire which burns with brimstone."

Here we see the demise of the Antichrist and the False Prophet. This happens at the end of the 70th Week of Daniel at the conclusion of the trumpet and bowl judgments. Satan is bound for 1,000 years. This false prophet, the right-hand of the Antichrist will be responsible for the deception spoken of by Jesus in the Olivet Discourse. In Matthew 24:23-25 we read, "Then if anyone says to you, 'Behold, here is the Christ,' or 'There He is,' do not believe him. 24 For false Christs and false prophets will arise and will show great signs and wonders, so as to mislead, if possible, even the elect. 25 Behold, I have told you in advance."

There are people who have rejected Christ and the saving message of the Gospel since the beginning of time. There are those who claim that they will believe when that time comes and not before. Here again, the warning is clear; "Behold, I have told you in advance". This period of time will be like none other. This master of deception will take in those who dwell on the earth and are not saved. He will be more persuasive than anyone in human history. He will ensure that if you do not take the mark and worship the Antichrist, that you will not be able to purchase food or the basic necessities of life. This will cause those who are not true believers to cave in because they love themselves more than Christ—or because they have chosen to remain ignorant and do not know of these things to come.

It is just the opposite for believers during this time. They will be well grounded and rooted in their faith. They will not be deceived. They will recognize this individual as well as the Antichrist, and will know not to take the mark. They will take heed to the warning Jesus gave in advance. They may lose their life, but they will not take the mark. If they heed the warnings, they may even be spared their life and be raptured.

Note in Revelation 7:16-17, speaking about this great multitude from every tribe and nation who appears in heaven suddenly (raptured saints) comes out of the Great Tribulation, "They will hunger no longer, nor thirst anymore; nor will the sun beat down on them, nor any heat; 17 for the Lamb in the center of the throne will be their shepherd, and will guide them to springs of the water of life; and God will wipe every tear from their eyes." There is a definite parallel here. Those who do not take the mark will not be able to buy food. Many Christians may starve during the Great Tribulation, but they will love the Lord more than themselves and they will know that one day they will hunger no more.

The last time we see a reference to the False Prophet is in Revelation 20:10. After Satan is bound for one thousand years, he is released for the final battle. He is conquered. We read, "And the devil who deceived them was thrown into the lake of fire and brimstone, where the beast and the false prophet are also; and they will be tormented day and night forever and ever." He is the loser. He and all those who followed him will suffer everlasting destruction from the presence of the Lord for eternity. This is too important to just pass over. Are you a true believer? If you are not sure, read the last chapter of this book. Right now. If the Holy Spirit is speaking to your heart, do not hesitate. This is not a science fiction discourse; this is the truth from the Word of God. The False Prophet will be far too cunning for those who have not placed their trust in Jesus Christ as Savior and Lord. The Lord Himself will also send a strong delusion during this time (II Thessalonians 2:11-12). Do not gamble with your eternal state.

Who is Antichrist? He is the second party of the unholy trinity. He is a man who comes to power as a world ruler. He is no ordinary man, for at some point he is empowered by Satan, the devil himself, when cast out of heaven down to earth. He is referred to by many names; Antichrist, beast, man of lawlessness, man of sin, son of perdition, and his number is calculated to be 666. He is found as a beast in Daniel 7:7-8 as "dreadful and terrifying and extremely strong". Here we see the parallel of the 10 nations found also in Revelation chapter 17. In Daniel 9:27, he is the one who makes a covenant with Israel during the 70th Week of Daniel and then breaks that covenant 3 ½ years into it.

The Bible uses typology. Types are pre-figures in the Old Testament of the antitypes in the New Testament. Antiochus IV (Epiphanies) was a real ruler of the Seleucid Empire/based in Syria. He attacked Israel and set himself up in the Temple, where he placed a statue of Zeus on the altar, and then on Kislev 25, 168 B.C., he slaughtered a pig in the Temple, which was an abomination. Many in Jerusalem fled and hid in order to not cave into the Hellenistic ways and demands of this wild beast ruler. He was murderous and vicious. Those who did not bow down to this ruler were killed. A small band of Maccabees led by Judas Maccabeus revolted against Antiochus IV and were victorious. They reclaimed Jerusalem and then rededicated the Temple after cleansing it. The Jewish Feast of Dedication, or Hanukkah, resulted from this. The menorah with eight candles, and one raised in the center as a ninth to light the others, is used in the celebration, and one candle is lit each night. This symbolizes the rededication of the Temple when there was only enough pure oil used by the high priest to light the golden lampstand for one day; tradition says, however, that it burned miraculously for eight days until they could have more consecrated oil on hand. This Antiochus IV is a type of the Antichrist who will rise to power during the 70th Week of Daniel. He will have similar attributes, and will make an abomination of desolation in the Temple while demanding worship and allegiance.

He is referred to by many names and in many ways within the New Testament. Here are but a few: Matthew 24:5—he comes in Christ's name to mislead many; Matthew 24:24 and parallel passage in Mark 13:22—he is a false Christ who performs signs and wonders to mislead many; Luke 21:8—he comes in Christ's name saying that he is Christ; I John 2:18—he is referred to as the Antichrist who is coming; I John 2:22—he is the Antichrist who denies that Jesus is the Christ, and denies the Father and the Son; I John 4:3—we see the spirit of the Antichrist as not only characteristic of him, but of anyone who does not confess Christ; II John 1:7—we see many deceivers who do not acknowledge Jesus Christ as coming in the flesh; Revelation 13:—he is the beast.

The title "beast" is figurative, giving us an indication of his character. This word beast carries with it the idea of a wild animal or a ferocious, wild, violent, evil, corruptive ruler. In Revelation 13:3, we see he has an apparent fatal head wound from which he comes back to life, and in Revelation 13:14, he is the beast who the False Prophet supports, and we see the supposed miraculous coming to life from the fatal wound. Revelation 13:18 states that he has a number of 666. In Revelation 17:7-13, we see the seven heads and ten horns described. The seven heads are the seven beast empires of the past, which align with the statue in Daniel, chapter two. We also learned of the beast nations and his coming out of a revived empire in Daniel chapter seven. During the 70th Week of Daniel, he will rule from an emerged eighth beast empire. The ten horns are ten nations from which he will have dominion over. Many believe this is the European ten-nation confederacy, or European Economic Union. Revelation 19:19-21 tells us that he is doomed, conquered, and cast into the lake of fire, burning with brimstone along with the False Prophet.

A great deal has been said over the centuries regarding the Antichrist. We know about his attributes, character, and actions, but we do not know who he is specifically. Many have speculated. Some thought Nero, some thought Hitler, and even some presidents, but we will not know until he sets himself up in the Temple to be worshipped and exalted. We may see an individual rise to power with all the attributes, but until this evil beast truly unveils himself, we will only be guessing as to his identity. We do know that he will be a charismatic ruler who will deceive the world and gain authority over it. He will make a covenant of peace with Israel, which Isaiah refers to as a "covenant with death" (Isaiah, 28:15, and 18). This will initiate the final seven-year period known as the 70th Week of Daniel and in the middle of that "week", or seven years, he will break that covenant, set himself up in the Temple to be exalted, and will demand worship and his mark. Those who do not take the mark or worship him will be martyred. He will be the most vile person the world has ever experienced, and his time will mark a time of trouble unequaled in history. He will pour out his wrath, empowered by Satan [the devil] himself, but it will be for a short while (Revelation 12:12). The Antichrist's wrath is cut short by Christ's coming (Matthew 24:22).

In summary, there are three beasts: Satan, the Antichrist, and the False Prophet. Satan is often referred to as the serpent, dragon, or devil. He will be cast out of heaven to earth and will be enraged. He will empower the Antichrist and he, along with the False Prophet, will deceive many. In the middle of the 70th Week of Daniel, this empowered Antichrist will break the covenant with Israel, will set himself up in the Temple to be exalted and worshipped, demanding allegiance through a mark, and then will begin the Great Tribulation. His wrath will be cut short during the second half of the 70th Week of Daniel, and then the Lord will pour out His wrath. In that day (the Day of the Lord), Jesus Christ alone will be exalted. Satan, the Antichrist, and the False Prophet will eventually be cast into the lake of fire, burning with brimstone for eternity. Those who have not placed their trust in Christ and are not found written in the Lamb's book of life, will be cast into the lake of fire as well when judged at the Great White Throne judgment (Revelation 20:11-15).

Let's go on and consider some of the **"what"** questions in section two.

SECTION 2 WHAT?

What are the basic tenets of each position on the timing of the Rapture? Since we have talked about this briefly in previous chapters, we will spend our time with simple diagrams and descriptions of each. We will not address the "partial rapture" position, which basically states that some believers will be raptured and others will not. The Scriptures clearly teach in I Thessalonians 4:16-17 that "the dead in Christ will rise first and we who are alive and remain will be caught up together with them..." in other words, all believers in Christ will be raptured at the time of His *parousia*.

We will briefly describe the following views, what they have in common, and what their basic premises are: 1) Pre-Tribulation, 2) Mid-Tribulation, 3) Pre-Wrath, and 4) Post-Tribulation. For the purpose of this study, we will be referring to the 70th Week of Daniel from time-to-time as the "tribulation period", but there is no place in Scripture where the entire 70th Week of Daniel is identified as such.

Let's start by drawing a simple horizontal line, which will represent the final seven-year period known as the 70th Week of Daniel. We will then place a vertical line, indicating approximately where the various positions believe the Rapture will take place.

70th Week of Daniel (seven years)

1) The "Pre-Tribulation" Position

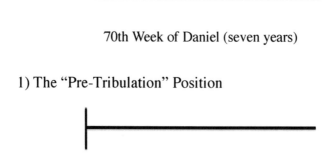

This position believes that the Rapture of the Church will take place prior to the commencement of the 70th Week of Daniel. They believe that the entire seven years is the "Tribulation" and the wrath of God, and therefore, since the Church is "not destined to wrath", they must be raptured prior to it commencing.

2) The "Mid-Tribulation" Position

As you can probably guess by the title, those who hold this position believe that the Church will be raptured at the mid-point, 3 ½ years, or 42 months, into the seven-year period. They would say that the Great Tribulation does not start until the mid-point, and they would identify that as the beginning period of God's wrath, and therefore the Church would be raptured just prior to that.

3) The "Pre-Wrath" Position

This position believes that the Rapture takes place some time in the second half of the 70th Week of Daniel, and that it is preceded by the sign in the sun, moon, and stars, placing it somewhere between the sixth and seventh seal of Revelation. There is no specific time within the second half, however it is wherever the Day of the Lord starts.

4) The "Post-Tribulation" Position

This position states that the Rapture will take place at the end of the seven-year period or at the sounding of the seventh trumpet of Revelation, which begins the bowl judgments.

What do these views have in common? All of these views believe that the Lord will return prior to the establishment of the millennial kingdom. This is the one-thousand-year period when Christ sets up His earthly kingdom and Satan is bound. There are views that do not believe in a literal millennial kingdom, which we have addressed in earlier chapters. The following are just a few of the things that these pre-millennial rapture views have in common:

- All believe in a literal, one-thousand-year reign of Christ taking place after the 70th Week of Daniel. In other words, Christ will rapture His Church prior to the one thousand-year period.
- All believe that just prior to the one-thousand-year reign on earth, there will be a seven-year period of trouble, beginning with the signing of a covenant between the Antichrist and Israel.
- All believe that this seven-year period is referred to as the 70th Week of Daniel, however some refer to it erroneously as the "tribulation period".
- All believe that this seven-year period has a subdivision of two halves, each being 3 ½ years in duration and dominated by a real person known as the Antichrist.
- All believe that the covenant between the Antichrist and Israel is broken at the mid-point by the Antichrist.
- All believe that the Antichrist will set himself up in the Temple to be worshipped at the mid-point and demand that people take a mark in order to buy or sell goods and services; those who do not take the mark may be martyred.
- All believe that the Great Tribulation begins at the mid-point just after the Antichrist commits an abomination of desolation in the Temple, spoken of by the prophet Daniel.
- All believe that the mark of the beast is 666.
- All believe that the 144,000 represent the first fruits of Israel, and that they are a sum of the 12,000 from each of the 12 tribes.
- All believe that there will be two witnesses who come on the scene, are slain in the streets, and come back to life.
- All believe that there is an Antichrist, a false prophet, and Satan on the scene at some point during the 70th Week of Daniel.
- Most believe in the general timing of Armageddon.
- All believe that the Church will be raptured prior to the wrath of God being poured out. This is perhaps the most important

aspect on their agreement. This is why we have devoted an entire chapter to this topic. The line drawings depicting the various positions all contain the vertical representing the Rapture of the Church prior to what they believe is the wrath of God.

These are but a few of the key elements each has in common. The point being made is that there is a great deal in common. What they do not have in common is the timing of the Rapture.

What are the major tenets of each position?

1) "Pre-Tribulation": As depicted on our simple diagram, the Rapture of His Church, the bride of Christ will take place just prior to the start of the 70th Week of Daniel at a day and hour that no one knows. Some of the key Scriptures cited to support this view are: I Thessalonians 5:9, where we read, "For God has not destined us for wrath, but for obtaining salvation through our Lord Jesus Christ." In order for this to be correct, those who hold this position claim that the entire seven years are God's wrath. Revelation 3:10 is another Scripture they would cite. "Because you have kept the word of My perseverance, I also will keep you from the hour of testing, that hour which is about to come upon the whole world, to test those who dwell on the earth." They maintain that this verse, along with verses in I Corinthians 15 and I Thessalonians 1:10, are clear indications that the Church is rescued from the "coming wrath". Again, ascribing the "coming wrath" as being the entire seven-year period, or that period as being the "Day of the Lord's wrath".

Because all these references lend to a "snatching" and suddenness like a "thief in the night", they would also reason that the Rapture must therefore take place at any moment. This is known as the "imminent return of Christ". In other words, they would have us believe that there are no prophecies yet to be fulfilled before the *parousia* of Christ. They would also contend, for the most part, that this has been true since the day of Pentecost. Some proponents of the pre-tribulation rapture position believe that the "restrainer" of II Thessalonians 2:6-7 is either the Church or the Holy Spirit, and therefore once removed, the Antichrist will have unrestrained control over evil corruption to carry out his evil plan.

Most who hold to the pre-tribulation position would also be in the dispensational camp. That is to say, they are fairly strict dispensationalists in their theology. They would reason that since the Church was not mentioned in the first 69 weeks of Daniel's prophecy, that it is therefore not in the 70th Week of Daniel. They would conclude that the Church Age, or Age of Grace, is concluded prior to that final seven-year period, and that God then reconvenes His plan, promises, and purpose for Israel. From this perspective, they would also divide the Olivet Discourse into near and future prophetic statements and conditions, leaving the Church out. Furthermore, they would hold the same view with regard to their interpretations of Mark 13 and Luke 21.

This position believes in two distinct halves of the 70th Week of Daniel, marked at the halfway point by the Abomination of Desolation of the Antichrist in the Temple at 1,260 days, or 42 months, into the final seven-year period. They would agree that this period is marked by seal, trumpet, and bowl judgments, and that *all* belong to the Lord's wrath. Most in this camp also believe that you do not see the Church mentioned in the book of Revelation after the first four chapters until chapter 22 and therefore, they conclude, it must have been raptured. Some would also assign Revelation 4:1-2 as a picture of the Church being raptured, as opposed to John alone being taken up in Spirit to witness the revelation of Christ. Others would assign the 24 elders of Revelation chapter five as a picture of the Church and Old Testament Saints being represented by the twelve apostles and twelve leaders of the tribes of Israel. This position would also see two separate comings, one for the Rapture just prior to the 70th Week of Daniel, and one when the Lord returns with His Saints (raptured saints, in their view) for the establishment of the earthly kingdom at the end of the seven-year period.

The pre-tribulation rapture position found its origin in the early to mid 1800s. Men like John Darby, who was a major figure in the Plymouth Brethren movement, built it into a systematic approach to eschatology amidst much controversy. It reached America in the mid to late 1800s and was further popularized by the second edition of the *Scofield Study Bible* in 1917, published by Oxford University Press. The first edition containing his notes was published in 1909, but he revised the notes in 1917[1].

Cyrus I. Schofield, DD was a dispensationalist who lived from 1843 to 1921. He was born in Michigan. Scofield is an interesting character to look up. Like all of us, he was a sinner and had what appears to be a pretty shady past. In the late 1800s, he came to Christ. His writings became extremely popular, and his Bible with study notes found their way into nearly every fundamental Bible College of that time. It would contain the pre-tribulation position. This view is still taught at major seminaries across America today. Great teachers and Bible scholars still hold to this view. We will discuss some of the key individuals of that time period who would challenge men like Darby and Schofield on the pre-tribulation teaching when we come to the pre-wrath position.

I should note here that there are many books published on various positions regarding the timing of the Rapture. Many contain information on who held to the view being presented and who did not from historical records and whatnot. It is not our intent to list who was for or against a particular view with that level of detail, because our contention from the beginning is that God's Word is the plumb line for truth, not what one individual or another may have said, regardless of credentials or popularity within Christian circles. I am reminded of the exhortation by the Apostle Paul to the church at Corinth in I Corinthians chapter one where he is calling for unity within the body. There were apparent disagreements causing division. In I Corinthians 1:10-13 he says; "Now I exhort you, brethren, by the name of our Lord Jesus Christ, that you all agree and that there be no divisions among you, but that you be in the same judgment. 11 For I have been informed concerning you, my brethren, by Chloe's people, that there are quarrels among you. 12 Now I mean this, that each of you is saying, "I am of Paul, " and "I am of Apollos, " and "I am of Cephas," and "I am of Christ." 13 Has Christ been divided? Paul was not crucified for you, was he? Or were you baptized in the name of Paul?" His point is clear. Unity in the body is crucial, and we should not become divisive on issues because one man or another teaches something that we may agree or disagree with. We should be like the Bereans who searched the Scriptures to see if these things are so.

2) "Mid-Tribulation": This position has become far less popular in recent years, however it had some strong proponents during the World War II period. It gained some following in 1941 with the publication of Norman Harrison's book, *The End: Rethinking the Revelation*[2], published by Harrison Service, 1941. A revised publication came out in 1948. Gleason Leonard Archer, Jr. also supported this position.

As depicted on our simple diagram, this position states that the Rapture occurs at the mid-point of the 70th Week of Daniel. One of the primary reasons for this position losing popularity is the fact that we could know the day. We know that the 70th Week of Daniel will last seven years with two halves equally divided into 1,260 days, or 42 months. There is an additional 30 days at the end of the seven years as well as an additional 45 days, but the seven years are divided in half. Those who hold this position believe that the "wrath of God" does not start until the mid-point when the Great Tribulation begins. They say that the first 3 ½ years are not part of God's divine wrath, and so the Church must endure this portion.

There is also some confusion over the sounding of trumpets and the "catching up" of the two witnesses. They believe in two separate comings, just as those in the pre-tribulation camp do. Most who hold to this position would say that the restrainer is the Holy Spirit. They would agree with pre-tribulation position in that the Church is promised deliverance from wrath. They do not teach an imminent return of Christ, however, and do believe the Church is present after Revelation, chapter four. Most in this camp deny the basic premises of dispensationalism and keep a strict distinction between Israel and the Church.

3) "Pre-Wrath": As depicted on the simple diagram, this position believes the Rapture will take place sometime within the second half of the 70th Week of Daniel. This is the position that this author believes most aligns with the whole of Scripture. This view may be amongst the oldest in substance, but was recently introduced under this title. Marvin J. Rosenthal wrote *The Pre-Wrath Rapture of the Church*, subtitle *A new understanding of the Rapture, the Tribulation, and the Second Coming*, in 1990[3], which popularized the name and gained acceptance among a number of critics. Robert Van Kampen

is credited by Marvin Rosenthal as the one who "planted the seed of this book", referring to *The Pre-Wrath Rapture of the Church*. Marvin Rosenthal, *The Pre-wrath Rapture of the Church* (Nashville, Tennessee: Nelson Publishing, 1990), xiv[4]. Robert Van Kampen also authored books on this position, including *The Sign*[5], as well as *The Rapture Question Answered Plain & Simple*[6]. Since these publications, a number of scholars have written on the topic from a pre-wrath perspective. Again, it is not important who wrote about it as much as it is important to study the Scriptures and arrive at one's own conclusion.

Those who espouse to the pre-wrath position hold to the following tenets: They believe the Church is not raptured until after the mid-point of the 70th Week of Daniel. The Church will endure the first six seals of Revelation. They believe that the same signs given in the book of Revelation 6:12-17 and the Olivet Discourse found in Matthew 24:29-31, Mark 13:24-27, and Luke 21:25-28 give a clear key to unlocking the general timing of His return. They are consistent with Old Testament passages such as Isaiah 2:10-21; 13:10, Joel 2:30-31; 3:14-15, Amos 5:18-20 and Zephaniah 1:14-16, where the Day of the Lord's wrath is preceded by the same clear signs in the sun, moon, and stars.

Here you see the sign in the celestial heavens just prior to the Day of the Lord's wrath and then the gathering of the elect between the sixth and seventh seal. They do not believe that the entire seven-year period is the "tribulation period". They would contend that you would not find it defined as such anywhere in Scripture. They believe that the first four seals of Revelation, chapter six align with what the Lord Jesus Christ refers to as the "beginning of birth pangs" in the Olivet Discourse, Matthew 24:8. They believe that the Great Tribulation begins at the mid-point as do the other positions, but that it is still a portion of the Antichrist's wrath and not the Lord's.

This [Great Tribulation] would be consistent with the fifth seal of Revelation where we see saints martyred. This is crucial because Isaiah two tells us that the Lord alone will be exalted on that day, referring to the Day of the Lord. During the Great Tribulation, which everyone agrees starts at the mid-point, the Antichrist sets himself up in the Temple to be exalted (II Thessalonians 2:4). They believe that the Great Tribulation is being referenced in Matthew 24:29, where Jesus says; "But immediately after the tribulation of those days the sun will be darkened, and the moon will not give its light, and the stars will fall from the sky, and the powers of the heavens will be shaken." They believe that this is what "cuts short" the Great Tribulation referred to in Matthew 24:22. They believe that believers who are alive during this time will endure the Great Tribulation, but will be rescued out of it as it is cut short by the *parousia* of Christ, consistent with I Thessalonians 1:10. They would also contend that the Day of the Lord's wrath is within the context of I Thessalonians 5:9, which is what believers are not destined to. In other words, the Church is not destined to receive the Lord's wrath. Where you place the Lord's wrath is critical to the argument. They believe that the Lord's wrath is not until the seventh seal, sometime after the Great Tribulation starts. They believe that the restrainer is the Archangel Michael based on Daniel 12:1, II Thessalonians 2:6-7, and Revelation 12:7-17. They believe that the Church is present after Revelation chapter four and the great multitude appearing in heaven suddenly between the sixth and seventh seal in Revelation 7:13-14, that specifically mentions they are the ones who came out of the Great Tribulation.

This passage is speaking of a number, which no man could count, from every tribe, tongue, and nation. This is the Church. They believe that the "kept from the hour of testing" is based on the faithful, and that the earth dwellers being separate has nothing to do with the timing, but when observed in the original language, supports the fact that the Church will be present.

Those who accept the pre-wrath view believe that the whole world will witness Christ's *parousia*, and it will not be without signs. It will be like a thief in the night for those who are not prepared, which includes unbelievers following the Antichrist. Believers, however, are not in darkness, and this day should not overtake them with surprise. His glory will shine from one end of the heavens to the other. Men will hide in the caves for fear. They believe that the Olivet Discourse is being addressed to believers as well as Israel, and that they can occupy the same period of time, contrary to strict dispensationalist teaching. They believe that the Day of the Lord is key to the timing of the Rapture, which we will discuss in greater detail in the next chapter.

They also believe in one coming, not two. They believe His coming [*parousia*] is always in the singular and includes all the elements of His coming, which is to say that, while each are distinct events, His coming for the elect, the Day of the Lord's wrath, and His return to set up His earthly kingdom, are all part of His coming. This would be analogous to His first coming, which included His birth, life, death, and resurrection.

The major elements of this position were found in early writings as far as the Church going through the Great Tribulation, and are found in such documents as the *Didache*, which is a very early Church teaching. It is the teaching of the twelve apostles and dates back to sometime between A.D. 50-120. In this early teaching, Christians believed that persecution would increase, and that the man of lawlessness [deceiver of the world] would appear before the Church would be raptured. (See *Didache*, chapter 16).

Believers in the early Church were to heed the warnings and not be deceived. This is consistent with the warnings given by Jesus, the Apostle Paul, and John wherever the end-times are mentioned in Scripture. There appears to be complete harmony throughout Scripture to support this position without compromising a proper hermeneutic. It is this pre-wrath position, in this author's humble opinion, that fits the plain and literal interpretation of Scripture.

When we discussed the pre-tribulation position, we said that one of the early proponents who had a great influence on the establishment of this position was a man named John Darby of the Plymouth Brethren. One of his contemporaries was a man named Benjamin Wills Newton. He did not agree with Darby. Newton was a well-respected scholar, and he would go on to write *The Prophecy of the Lord Jesus as Contained in Matthew XXIV. & XXV*[1]. He believed that the Church would encounter the Antichrist and the Great Tribulation prior to the Rapture. He writes concerning the Great Tribulation, "Fearful as that hour of tribulation will be (so fearful, that all whom Jesus acknowledges as His, are bidden to flee from the spot on which it is to fall), yet the wrath and utterly destroying judgment which immediately follows it on the appearing of the Son of Man in His glory, will be infinitely more terrible." He goes on to say that the Great Tribulation "precedes the advent of the Lord: it describes the appearing of the

Lord in glory and the mission of the angels to gather together His elect (that is, His own believing people) from the four winds"[8].

Benjamin Newton would find support for his theology on the subject from men like Charles Spurgeon and George Mueller. He was in good company, however, we only mention this for contrast with the pre-tribulation position. It is imperative that we search the Scriptures to determine truth.

4) "Post-Tribulation": As depicted on the simple diagram, this position believes that the Rapture takes place at the end of the 70th Week of Daniel. This is perhaps the oldest view and is still taught today in many foreign countries. Those who hold this position believe that the Church and Israel will suffer during the entire seven-year period. Most proponents of this view deny a distinction between the Church and Israel. They believe that the wrath of God does not occur until the bowl judgments of Revelation, which begin at the seventh trumpet and start the 30-day period following the last half of the 70th Week of Daniel. These 30 additional days are biblical and are found in Daniel 12:11. They believe the Church will endure all the previous trumpet judgments and base this on I Corinthians 15:52, where the Apostle Paul writes, "at the last trumpet; for the trumpet will sound, and the dead will be raised imperishable, and we will be changed."

Some of the early beliefs claim that all of this has already happened and that Daniel nine is not talking about the future, but is an allegorical approach to interpreting Scripture; this is *Preterist* teaching, which spiritualizes the truth and is not based on a proper hermeneutic. They do believe, as the others, that the Church is exempt from the Day of the Lord's wrath, but contend that this day does not begin until the last, or seventh trumpet, initiating the bowl judgments.

We have only touched lightly on each of these positions. It will be up to the reader to search the Scriptures and come to one's own conclusion. One thing I would suggest as you begin your study is to take careful consideration into what is common amongst the views. While they differ in a great many ways, the one thing that they all agree upon is that the Church is exempt from the Lord's wrath. Having said that, it will be imperative to learn as much as you can about the Lord's wrath and where it begins. Once you determine the Day of the Lord's wrath is different from the wrath of the Antichrist and see the signs preceding the Day of the Lord's wrath, I believe you will arrive at a firm conviction, which you will be able to defend. I will provide some brief information on the Day of the Lord's wrath in the next chapter to help point you to some Scripture that might help your journey in search of truth.

What is the 70th Week of Daniel? The book of Daniel was written in the sixth Century B.C. in Babylon and Persia. It is an interesting book in that it was written during the Babylonian captivity (Jews of the Kingdom of Judah were exiled to Babylon) and was written in Aramaic and Hebrew. Chapter one is written in Hebrew, chapters two through seven in Aramaic, and chapters eight through twelve in Hebrew. It is often referred to as the "Apocalypse of the Old Testament". The 70th Week of Daniel is a reference to Daniel 9:24, where it states, "Seventy weeks have been decreed for your people and your holy city, to finish the transgression, to make an end of sin, to make atonement for iniquity, to bring in everlasting righteousness, to seal up vision and prophecy and to anoint the most holy place." The "seventy weeks" here are really seventy times seven years each, or a total of 490 years.

The prophecy given in Daniel chapter nine goes on to define the periods. In verse 25, we see a period of 7 weeks (49 years) and 62 weeks (434 years). These combined 69 weeks total 483 prophetic years. The key is the issuing of a decree to restore and rebuild Jerusalem until Messiah the Prince (483 prophetic years). When you attempt to look at these prophetic years with our modern Gregorian calendar system, it can be rather confusing. There were a few different calendar systems in use during the captivity. One thing that will help is to think of the Jewish calendar as having 360 days, with each month having 30 days. This would not be a purely lunar calendar, but more of a modified Egyptian calendar. As we start to calculate times based on what evidence we have in Scripture, the 30-day month and the 360-day year will make more sense. We know from Genesis 29:26-28 that a biblical week can be seven years.

The starting point for the first 69 weeks was to begin with a decree to restore and rebuild Jerusalem (Daniel 9:25). We go to Nehemiah 2:1-4 to see when the decree was issued. From these verses we learn that it was in the 20th year of the reign of Artaxerxes Longimanus who ruled Persia from 464 B.C. to 424 B.C. It was in the month of Nisan, which some would say corresponds with 14 March 445 B.C. We see where the work did begin, and the decree was also referenced in Ezra 4:11-13.

The walls were built. There was fear that they would not pay tribute once the city was restored. The building of the Temple was delayed, and it was King Darius (most likely the same as Cyrus) who issued a decree to rebuild the Temple based on the earlier decree (Ezra 6:1-5). We know that the first 49 years, or seven weeks, of Daniel 9:25 was fulfilled by Nehemiah in Nehemiah 6:15. The next 434 years take us to Messiah the Prince.

Let me just pause here for a moment. There is a lot of debate over the dates and times and calendars. Most scholars teach what I am about to present, but I am not dogmatic on this approach. The prophecy of Daniel, chapter nine really has three parts: (1) the building of the walls (49 years, or seven weeks), (2) until Messiah the Prince (434 years, or 62 weeks), (3) and the sanctuary and city destroyed *after* 62 weeks, which took place in A.D. 70. Some scholars will use a dating system, which begins with the day of Creation and moves forward based on the noted genealogies provided. I would encourage readers to research this approach as well. For our study, we will refer to the widely held view that converts the days from the ancient calendar of days and months into the modern Gregorian calendar. So, if we start with March 14, 445 B.C. as the beginning of the first 69 weeks, we should be able to move 483 prophetic years of 360 days each (totaling 173,880 days) from the starting point to the time Messiah the Prince comes, and it *does*—right to the very day. Here is how one can calculate it:

The Passover is in the month of Nisan on the Jewish calendar. On the 14th day of Nisan, the sacrifice lamb is slain, (Leviticus 23:5). Jesus was crucified on the 14th Nisan in the year A.D. 32. Jesus' earthly ministry started during the 15th year of Tiberious Caesar. His reign started on August 19 A.D. 14, placing the 15th year at A.D. 29 (Luke 3:1-23). Jesus ate at Martha's house on the ninth Nisan in the year A.D. 32 (John 11:55; 12:1). The following day, 10th Nisan A.D. 32, He made his triumphal entry into Jerusalem through the East Gate in fulfillment of Zechariah 9:9. This would have been April 6, A.D. 32 (Luke 19:28-44).

The length of time between the issuing of the decree to rebuild Jerusalem and the event of Messiah the Prince entering Jerusalem is 173,880 days *to the day.* If we strictly look at the Gregorian calendar, it would be 476 years and 24 days. In this case, you take 476 times 365 days and you end up with 173,740 days. Add the intervening days between March 14 and April 6 and you have 24 additional days for 173,764. There are 116 days of leap years between March 14, 445 B.C. and April 6, A.D. 32. Add the 116 to 173,764 and you have exactly 173,880 days. This would account for the second portion of the prophecy in Daniel, chapter nine. Now the language in Daniel 9:26 says, "Then after sixty-two weeks the Messiah will be cut off and have nothing, and the people of the prince who is to come will destroy the city and sanctuary." The key phrase here is *"then after".* Messiah was crucified after the 173,880 days and the city and sanctuary was destroyed after the 173,880 days in A.D. 70.

The first 69 Weeks of Daniel's prophecy have been fulfilled. Israel rejected their Messiah as was prophesied, and there remains the final week, or what we refer to as the "70th Week of Daniel". This final week, or 70th Week, is described in Daniel 9:27, "And he will make a firm covenant with the many for one week, but in the middle of the week he will put a stop to sacrifice and grain offering; and on the wing of abomination will come one who makes desolate, even until a complete destruction, one that is decreed, is poured out on the one who makes desolate."

Notice that the final week begins with a covenant. A week is seven years and thus 2,520 days. Notice he breaks the covenant in "the middle of the week". The middle of seven years equals 1,260 days, or 3 ½ years, or 42 months. Notice that during this final week at the mid-point he commits the Abomination of Desolation. We can be sure of these numbers because we find them in the New Testament as well.

For instance, Revelation 11:2 speaks of the 42 months as does Revelation 13:5 when referring to that final half. Revelation 11:3 and Revelation 12:6 speak about the 1,260 days being that same period, and Daniel uses an interesting description in Daniel 7:25 and Daniel 12:7, when he uses the phrase, "time, times, and a half a time" referring to that same period. A "time" equals one year, "times" equals two years, and "a half a time" equals a half-year, for a total of 3 ½ years.

The same period is described by these words in Revelation 12:14, where the remnant is hid in the wilderness for that period of time. In Daniel 12, we see two other numbers also used. They are 1,290 days and 1,335 days. The 1,290 days is the 30 additional days at the conclusion of the 70th Week, which starts the bowl judgments and concludes with the battle at Har-Magedon, or "Armageddon (Revelation 16:16).

There are a number of other things that happen during this period and after as well. For example, believers' works will be judged at the judgment seat of Christ, often referred to as the bema seat. It comes from the Greek word *béma*, found in II Corinthians 5:10 for "judgment". Here the believer is not judged, but rather his or her works are. The Greek word goes back to the early games, and it speaks of a raised platform where the victor would be taken by a judge to receive a reward. It is the same idea for the believer; they will be rewarded according to their works. Paul also mentions this in Romans 14:10-12. The believer is not condemned (John 3:18, Romans 5:1, I Corinthians 11:32). The believer is not judged, only his or her deeds.

During this period will be the marriage of the Lamb (Revelation 19:7-8). Christ, the Lamb appears at Mt Zion with the 144,000 who were the sealed remnant and first fruits of redeemed Israel (Revelation 14:1-5). At the end of the 30 days, the Antichrist and the False Prophet are cast into the lake of fire, which burns with brimstone (Revelation 19:20-21). The 1,335 days are the reclaiming of the earth and the ushering in of the New Jerusalem coming down from heaven, followed by the marriage supper of the Lamb (Revelation 19:6-9).

Israel is re-gathered and restored in accordance with the promise found in Jeremiah 30. Again, many other things happening during the 30-day and 45-day periods and those mentioned are not necessarily in sequential order, but for a beginner's guide to end-times eschatology, we will keep it simple. Once the 1,335 days are complete, Satan is bound for one thousand years, and at the end of the one thousand years, he is loosed to battle one last time and then cast into the lake of fire for eternity. At the end of the one thousand years, there will be the Great White Throne judgment where all unbelievers will be judged, and the righteous Judge will cast them into the lake of fire also for eternity (Revelation 20:11-15).

Note the books the Lord will use. There is more than one book. There is the Lamb's book of life, where all believers are listed. If you are found in this book, you will not be judged. It will be used to show unbelievers that their name is not listed. The other books will include every word, thought, and deed, which will condemn them. The difference between the unbeliever and the believer is not a result of works. The believer would be just as guilty as the unbeliever if it were based on works. As a matter of fact, there are unbelievers who may appear to have better works than a believer, but God, the righteous Judge, does not grade on a curve (James 2:10, Titus 3:5-7). The believer is not condemned and found in the Lamb's book of life only because he or she placed their trust in Jesus Christ alone for salvation and accepted the finished work Jesus Christ did at Calvary to bear all sin. Have you placed your trust in this magnificent Savior? Will you be found in the Lamb's book of life? Will you be partakers of His Glory or recipients of His wrath?

The main take away is that there is a yet future time, often referred to as the 70th Week of Daniel, which will be seven years in duration and will be divided into two halves of 42 months each. It starts with the covenant between the Antichrist and Israel. The middle is defined by the Antichrist setting himself up in the Temple in the middle of the week and committing an abomination of desolation. The second half begins with the Great Tribulation, which is cut short by the Day of the Lord. Note that the Great Tribulation is cut short, not the last 3 ½ years, or the 1,260 days. This period [70th Week of Daniel] is often erroneously referred to as the "tribulation period".

The Coming Prince by Sir Robert Anderson[9] has been a standard for outlining the dates and times of the 70th Week of Daniel. I would also suggest reading *God's Elect and the Great Tribulation, An Interpretation of Matthew 24:1-31 and Daniel 9* by Charles Cooper[10]. The 70th Week as explained here follows more of Sir Robert Anderson's explanation, however Charles Cooper does a great job of defining the period using the dates from Creation as well as defining explicit terms within Daniel. His work is very compelling and should be considered.

What is the Abomination of Desolation? With regard to the topic of eschatology, the "Abomination of Desolation" is a direct reference to an event, which will take place during that final 70th Week of Daniel. We know this from Daniel 9:27 where we read, "And he will make a *firm covenant with the many for one week*, but in the *middle of the week* he will put a stop to sacrifice and grain offering; and on the *wing of abominations will come one who makes desolate*, even until a complete destruction, one that is decreed, is poured out on the one who makes desolate." [Emphasis mine.] From our earlier discussion, we learned that a biblical "week" in this context refers to seven years. We also said that the seven years is divided into two halves, each having 3 ½ years, or 1,260 days. The "middle of the week" would be 3 ½ years into the seven-year period, or 1,260 days from the time the "firm covenant" is made. In Isaiah 28:15-18, this covenant is referred to as a "covenant with death".

We can learn about this individual by comparing Scripture with Scripture as we did previously in the "who" section. Daniel 11:31-32 states, "Forces from him will arise, desecrate the sanctuary fortress, and do away with the regular sacrifice. And they will set up the abomination of desolation. 32 By smooth words he will turn to godlessness those who act wickedly toward the covenant, but the people who know their God will display strength and take action". In verse 36 of that same chapter it goes on to say, "Then the king will do as he pleases, and he will exalt and magnify himself above every god and will speak monstrous things against the God of gods; and he will prosper until the indignation is finished, for that which is decreed will be done." This smooth talking, arrogant world ruler will continue to gain power and will bring forces against Israel and God's elect. He will break the agreement at the mid-point of the seven years and will stop the sacrifice.

This is also consistent with II Thessalonians 2:4 where we read, "who opposes and exalts himself above every so-called god or object of worship, so that he takes his seat in the Temple of God, displaying himself as being God." According to Daniel, this happens 3 ½ years into the seven-year period. When the Antichrist breaks the agreement (covenant), he will make an abomination of desolation in the holy place, or Temple. The Hebrew word for abomination is *shiqquts*, which means "abominable, detestable" according to *Young's Analytical Concordance to the Bible*[11]. *Wilson's Old Testament Word Studies*, unabridged edition defines it this way: "To detest; to be abominable, unclean, chiefly used of idolatry, and of things that one may not touch, eat, or worship"[12]. The Hebrew word "desolate" in Daniel 9:27 is *shamem*. *Wilson's Old Testament Word Studies*, unabridged edition defines it this way: "To be laid waste or ruined by a sudden tumultuous overthrow, which beareth down all before it"[13].

So, this world ruler breaks the agreement at the mid-point of the week and takes it by force, committing a detestable act in the Temple, which will cause it to be laid to waste. This will happen suddenly, and what follows in Daniel 12 is a "time of distress such as never occurred since there was a nation until that time: and at that time your people, everyone who is found written in the book, will be rescued." This starts a period of "great distress". In Jeremiah 30:7 it is referred to as the time of "Jacob's troubles". This starts what is also referred to as the "Great Tribulation". This is absolutely consistent with the language in the New Testament Olivet Discourse given by Jesus to His disciples at the Mount of Olives in Matthew 24:15-21, "Therefore when you see the Abomination of Desolation which was spoken of through Daniel the prophet standing in the holy place (let the reader understand). 16 then those who are in Judea must flee to the mountains, 17 Whoever is on the housetop must not go down to get the things out that are in his house. 18 Whoever is in the field must not turn back to get his cloak. 19 But woe to those who are pregnant and to those who are nursing babies in those days! 20 But pray that your flight will not be in the winter, or on the Sabbath. 21 For *then* there will be *great tribulation* such as has not occurred since the beginning of the world until now, nor ever will." [Emphasis mine.]

Note the urgency in the warning given by Jesus as He speaks about this time. It matches the suddenness described in the Hebrew text. Also note that in verse 21 the word *"then"* is used, causing us to look at what precedes it, which is the Abomination of Desolation. In other words, the "Great Tribulation" starts after the Abomination of Desolation. Jesus uses Greek words for Abomination and Desolation.

The word Abomination in the Greek is *bdelugma*, and according to *Vine's expository dictionary of New Testament words,* unabridged edition, it "denotes an object of disgust, an abomination. This is said of the image to be set up by Antichrist"[14].

The Greek word used by Jesus for desolation is *"erēmōsis"*, which *Young's* defines as "making desolate or desert"[15]. *Vine's* says this about the word, "The genitive is objective; the abomination that makes desolate; (b) with stress upon the effect of the process"[16]. Jesus is telling us that when this agreement is broken, 3 ½ years into the seven-year, it will happen along with an Abomination of Desolation and then there will be great tribulation like never before. His elect are warned to flee suddenly and with determination. This is also consistent with the beginning of the fifth seal of Revelation chapter six. Here we see the ruler's power and many being martyred by his forces (verses 9-11). They are martyred during the Great Tribulation. We know this because we follow the context in Revelation 7:13-14, "Then one of the elders answered, saying to me, "These who are clothed in the white robes, who are they, and where have they come from?" 14 I said to him, "My lord, you know." And he said to me, "These are the ones who come out of the *great tribulation,* and they have washed their robes and made them white in the blood of the Lamb." [Emphasis mine.] He is referring here to the raptured saints who have come out of the Great Tribulation. In other words, those who are alive when the Antichrist commits this detestable act will experience the Great Tribulation.

The Abomination of Desolation is a very important event to mark for the believer. If you come to the conviction that we will experience a portion of the 70th Week of Daniel as this author believes, you will want to know when the Great Tribulation starts and when the man of lawlessness is going to reveal himself. There will be no need to speculate at this point. 3 ½ years into the 70th Week of Daniel, the Antichrist will break the agreement and will make an abomination of desolation in the Temple. This Antichrist, or beast as he is sometimes called, will deceive many along with his cohort, the False Prophet who will tell those who dwell on the earth to "make an image to the beast". He will demand that many worship the image or be killed, and will also demand that they take his mark (Revelation 13:11-18). There will be no question about this if you are alive when this happens. Antiochus IV was a type of antichrist and he, too, committed an abomination by slaughtering a pig on the altar and setting up a statue of Zeus to be worshipped. The Antichrist will reveal himself 3 ½ years into the 70th Week of Daniel and will do a similar thing, in that he will make an abomination, which causes desolation. When this happens, we are warned by Jesus to flee immediately.

What is tribulation? The Greek word for "tribulation" is *thlipsis*. It is translated as, "anguish, burdened, distress, persecution, tribulation, trouble, and affliction"[17] by *Vine's*. It is the idea of extreme pressure, like that of a wine press. In John 16:33, Jesus tells us, "These things I have spoken to you, so that in Me you may have peace. In the world you have tribulation, but take courage; I have overcome the world."

Over and over again in Scripture, we are told that we will suffer tribulation. Jesus said that if the world hated Him, they would hate us also. Paul uses the word three times in I Thessalonians, chapter three to describe the affliction they were experiencing. Paul also uses the word in II Thessalonians 1:7 where he states, "and to give relief to you who are afflicted and to us as well when the Lord Jesus will be revealed from heaven with His mighty angels in flaming fire."

The word "afflicted" here is *thlipsis*. Note that Paul says that there will be relief for those who are afflicted, indicating that they can expect to be afflicted prior to that relief. It is also used in Matthew 24:29 where Jesus says, "But immediately after the tribulation of those days the sun will be darkened and the moon will not give its light, and the stars will fall from the sky, and the powers of the heavens will be shaken." What was He referring to in context? It is found in Matthew 24:21 where He said, "For then there will be great tribulation, such as has not occurred since the beginning of the world until now, nor ever will."

The point here is that you will never find the word tribulation in reference to the entire 70th Week of Daniel, or what some erroneously refer to as the "tribulation period". When used in context of the Olivet Discourse, it is referring back to the Great Tribulation, not the entire seven years. I will give some relief here in that the entire period could be characterized in some sense as trouble or distress, but on the other hand, we know that the deceiver will initiate the period with peace and an appearance of peace.

Paul would also share with us in I Thessalonians that the unbelieving people, or the earth dwellers, at that time will be saying "peace and safety!" (I Thessalonians 5:3). This will be the deceptive climate just prior to the Lord pouring out His wrath during the Day of the Lord. It will be anything but peace and safety for the believer during that time period, but for the unexpected unbeliever, it will appear as such. For the believer, they can expect great tribulation and even martyrdom. We are told over and over again that we will suffer affliction and tribulation as believers in this world. We are never exempt from it, nor will we be in that final seven-year period, more rightly referred to as the 70th Week of Daniel.

What is the Great Tribulation? The Great Tribulation is a biblical reference to the time that commences just after the Antichrist commits the Abomination of Desolation, spoken of by the prophet Daniel. We said this is also the "Time of Jacob's Troubles", indicating extreme persecution against the Jews as well. Revelation 12:17 says "So the dragon was enraged with the woman, and went off to make war with the rest of her children, who keep the commandments of God and hold to the testimony of Jesus." The "rest of her children" are Christians. Sometimes they are referred to as the "rest of her offspring". The "woman" is Israel. This happens when Satan is cast to earth and empowers the Antichrist to wage war "for a time and times and half time" (Revelation 12:14). The Antichrist will demand worship and a mark, and those who do not submit to him will be martyred.

The Great Tribulation starts 3 ½ years into the 70th Week of Daniel, but it is cut short by the *parousia* of Christ and the Day of the Lord. We see this in Matthew 24:22 and 29-31. We also see martyred saints appear in heaven "from every nation and all tribes and peoples and tongues" (Revelation 7:9), which are the saints who have come out of the Great Tribulation. Also note that the Great Tribulation is cut short, not the 3 ½ remaining years of the second half of the 70th Week of Daniel.

The entire seven-year period is *not* the Great Tribulation. The first 3 ½ years are what the Bible refers to as the "beginning of birth pangs". I would also submit that the first 3 ½ years are the first four seals of Revelation, chapter six. The Great Tribulation should not be confused with what some are calling the "tribulation period", or more correctly the 70th Week of Daniel. It is part of the 70th Week of Daniel, but does not commence until 3 ½ years into the final seven-year period. It begins when the Abomination of Desolation takes place and Satan empowers the Antichrist.

This is also the wrath of Satan, not Christ. Notice that Revelation 12:12 states, "For this reason, rejoice, O heavens and you who dwell in them. Woe to the earth and the sea, because the devil has come down to you, having great wrath, knowing that he has only a short time." He only has a short time because the Lord will come and cut it short. Remember that the Lord alone will be exalted on that day. This wrath of Satan through the Antichrist during the Great Tribulation is not the wrath spoken of by Paul in I Thessalonians, chapter five that we are not destined to. I Thessalonians 5:9 is speaking of the Day of the Lord's wrath in context, which is quite different.

We are not destined to the Day of the Lord's wrath, but nowhere are we exempt from the wrath of the Antichrist. In this life we will have tribulation. James 1:2-4 tells us to "Consider it all joy, my brethren, when you encounter various trials, 3 knowing that the testing of your faith produces endurance. 4 And let endurance have its perfect result, so that you may be perfect and complete, lacking in nothing."

We should expect trials and tribulation if we are Christians. I Peter 4:12 says, "Beloved, do not be surprised at the fiery ordeal among you, which comes upon you for your testing, as though some strange thing were happening to you; 13 but to the degree that you share the sufferings of Christ, keep on rejoicing, so that also at the revelation of His glory you may rejoice with exultation." We should count it an honor and blessing to endure hardship and even great tribulation if we are that generation who will experience it.

What is the Olivet Discourse? This is where Jesus answers His disciples' questions regarding the time of His coming and the end of the age, as recorded in Matthew 24, Mark 13, and Luke 21. This is just not reference, they *specifically* ask Him when these things that He has spoken of will happen, and when will be the end of the age. The question has two parts, His coming and the end of the age. Jesus just came from the Temple and the city of Jerusalem where He was rejected. He crosses the Kidron Valley and walks up a hill, called the "Mount of Olives". It is a ridge east of Jerusalem's old city, named for an Olive Grove. It is also a site of an ancient Jewish cemetery, dating over 3000 years back and holds over 150,000 graves. From the Mount of Olives, the city of Jerusalem and the Temple were in clear view.

My wife and I had the wonderful privilege to visit this site in 2000 and imagined what it must have been like as Jesus gave this most important discourse to His disciples. He was teaching eschatology just before the Passover, His betrayal, arrest in the Garden of Gethsemane, mock trial, crucifixion, resurrection, and issuing of the Great Commission. All this happened in a short time frame. These were His important last words of hope, not only for them, but a reminder of His own soon coming victory, followed by incredible suffering and Him taking on the sins of the world. He is teaching about His *parousia*, and His language is consistent with the rapture of the saints after enduring hardship and suffering at the hands of the Antichrist.

He taught a "near and far prophecy" regarding the destruction of the Temple, which still existed as He was sharing with His disciples about the future 70th Week of Daniel. One event would take place in A.D. 70, the destruction of the Temple and Jerusalem; it would lead to the *diaspora*, or dispersion, of Israel among many nations. In order for the second part, or the "far prophetic" event, to take place, they would need to be back in the land. This did not take place until May 14, 1948, when they became a recognized sovereign State.

The Olivet Discourse is for the elect. It is for the generation that will experience the future 70th Week of Daniel. It is full of warnings and promises for the believer and Israel.

What is the coming, *parousia*, revelation, and appearing of Christ? These are all referring to the same thing: His coming. This is the singular use of the term "*parousia*", meaning "arrival and consequent presence with"[18]. His revelation is His unveiling and coming. His appearing is also a reference to when He comes in the clouds with great glory for His saints, the elect. Throughout Scripture, you will see these various terms used when speaking about the return of Jesus. Coming, or *parousia*, is used a number of times in Scripture, including I Thessalonians 4:15 and Matthew 24:27, which both refer to the same event.

Revelation, or *apokalypsis*, is used in I Corinthians 1:7 in the same context. The word "appearing" is found in Titus 2:13 in reference to this same event. Appearing with the angels in I Thessalonians 3:13, II Thessalonians 1:7, and Matthew 16:27. A shout, voice of the archangel, and trumpet will sound in I Thessalonians 4:16 announcing His coming. All of these words are referring to the return of Jesus Christ.

What is the Rapture? We have talked about this term before, but if you have a Latin Bible, you will find a very similar word used in I Thessalonians 4:17 where we read "caught up" in our English Bible. The Lord Jesus Christ will come one day and cut short the Great Tribulation with His coming in the clouds. At that moment, He will rapture, or catch up, His saints. He will deliver them out of the midst of trouble. "For the Lord Himself will descend from heaven with a shout, with the voice of the archangel and with the trumpet of God, and the dead in Christ will rise first. 17 Then we who are alive and remain will be caught up together with them in the clouds to meet the Lord in the air, and so we shall always be with the Lord."

This is the blessed hope of every believer spoken of by Paul in Titus 2:13. If you were to look up the word "rapture" in your English Bible, you would not find it, but the fact of the rapture is real and true. It is when we are "caught up", which *is* in our English Bible. The word "rapture" is a Latin transliteration of those words. In that one moment we will be changed at the twinkling of an eye (I Corinthians 15:51-52).

This is the most important event to look forward to for every believer. We should not only know that it will happen, but we should understand the teaching on this most important subject. I am personally thrilled that you are reading this book and have an interest in learning more about this subject. It is our blessed hope, and we should learn as much as we can about it.

What is the sign of His coming? We have said that His coming is always in the singular, so we should not expect two comings. The disciples asked Jesus what the sign of His coming would be. His coming is closely associated with the Day of the Lord. Nobody knows the hour or the day of His coming; this is clear in Matthew

24:36. However, to say that His coming is without a sign would not be accurate. Matthew 24:29-30 gives us the answer, "But immediately after the tribulation of those days the sun will be darkened and the moon will not give its light, and the stars will fall from the sky, and the powers of the heavens will be shaken. 30 And then the sign of the Son of Man will appear in the sky, and then all the tribes of the earth, will mourn, and they will see the Son of man coming on the clouds of the sky with power and great glory."

This same language appears in Mark 13:24-26, Luke 21:25-28, Revelation 6:12-14, Isaiah 13:10, Joel 2:30-31, and Zephaniah 1:14-16. The sign will be in the sun, moon, and stars. At the moment just preceding the Day of the Lord when He returns, the lights will go out. There will be utter darkness. This will be an unimaginable time. You will look up into the heavens and it will be completely dark. It will be frightening for all the inhabitants who are alive at this time, but for the believer who is forewarned, he or she is told to look up "for your redemption is drawing near" (Luke 21:28).

The darkness will be replaced by His glorious coming. His glory will light up the heavens in a spectacular display like never seen before, and all the earth will see it. There will be the trumpet sound and the voice of the archangel. This will not be a secret coming. He will come and it will be a visible coming. So magnificent will this glorious coming be that those who have not believed will run to hide in the caves for fear—as if they could hide from God.

What are the seals, trumpets, and bowls of Revelation? There are seven of each. The seven seals are on the outside of the scroll, which only Jesus Christ can open. As each seal is removed, we are told of events that are associated with each in Revelation, chapters six and seven. The first four seals align with the "beginning of birth pangs" in the Olivet Discourse. The fifth seal is consistent with the beginning of the Great Tribulation where saints are martyred. The sixth seal is consistent with the sign in the sun, moon, and stars preceding the Day of the Lord's wrath, and the seventh seal is the last of the seals before the scroll is opened, and it contains the seven trumpet judgments that follow.

The seventh trumpet contains the seven swift bowl judgments (Revelation 16:1) and the wrath of God. These trumpet judgments begin right after the Church is raptured and continue to the end of the second half of the week. The bowl judgments are within the 30-day period, or what make up the additional days between 1,260 and 1,290. At the conclusion of the bowl judgments is the Battle of Armageddon, which then leads to the restoration period of 45 days, or the difference between 1,290 and 1,335 spoken of by Daniel in chapter 12.

What is kept from the "hour of testing"? This is a reference often quoted from Revelation 3:10 where Jesus says, "Because you have kept the word of My perseverance, I also will keep you from the hour of testing, that hour which is about to come upon the whole world, to test those who dwell on the earth." As previously stated, this is referring to two groups: one is the faithful who have kept His word and persevered, and the other is the unfaithful "earth dwellers". The faithful will be rescued from danger and removed from the midst of trouble, but not so for the others. The faithful rescued out of danger is, in my view, a picture of the Church being rescued when the Great Tribulation is cut short. Many will be martyred before Jesus' return, but many will remain until they are raptured.

This is not talking about a "pre-tribulation rapture". Again, it is very important to look at the original language and understand the passage as it relates to all context—immediate, book, and Bible. There will be some who will endure the Day of the Lord and will come to faith along with the first fruits of Israel after the Rapture takes place. They will endure the most difficult time of all, but the faithful Church will be raptured prior to the Day of the Lord's wrath being poured out.

These who and what questions have provided some necessary, detailed information, and so we spent some time with each. As we move on to the remaining questions, we will be brief with our answers, since they are more pointed and specific.

We will now move on to the **"when"** questions in section three.

SECTION 3 WHEN?

When was the fulfillment of the first 69 Weeks of Daniel? We covered this in our discussion on the 70th Week of Daniel. It started with the decree to rebuild Jerusalem according to Daniel 9:25. Most scholars believe that this happened in 445 B.C. It would continue from that point until Messiah the Prince would come, which took place on 06 April, A.D. 32, when Jesus entered Jerusalem. Verse 26 goes on to describe the subsequent events that would complete the prophecy, "Then after the sixty-two weeks the Messiah will be cut off and have nothing, and the people of the prince who is to come will destroy the city and the sanctuary". This did happen in A.D. 70 when Titus destroyed the Temple and the holy city. At this time a great dispersion, also referred to as the *diaspora*, took place when the Israelites were banished from the land. Israel would not have claim to the land as a sovereign State until May 14, 1948.

When does the 70th Week of Daniel begin? Obviously, there remains a large gap in time between the 69th Week of Daniel and the final 70th Week. There are some who feel this was fulfilled in A.D. 70, but there is not a consistent, harmonious biblical construct for such. The characteristics of this final seven-year period have too many details that are yet to be fulfilled. We have not seen a rebuilt Temple or even a tabernacle where the daily sacrifices could be re-instituted. We only recently saw Israel back in the land. We have not seen the rise of the Antichrist, the False Prophet or the empowering by Satan. We have yet to see the Great Tribulation. We have not seen the glorious coming of our Lord and Savior Jesus Christ.

This 70th Week of Daniel will be initiated with a covenant according to Daniel 9:27. The covenant will be broken 3 ½ years into the seven-year period. Will we know when the covenant happens or who the Antichrist will be? This is hard to say. We know that a world ruler will make this agreement, and there is a chance that we will be aware of it due to the massive media coverage over anything resembling peace processes or talks involving Israel. On the other hand, it might be very covert. We may or may not know who this Antichrist is. We do know that he will reveal himself in the Temple 3 ½ years into the seven-year period and set himself up to be exalted and worshipped. At this point we will know that the 70th Week of Daniel started exactly 1,260 days prior to this occurrence. We will also know who he is at this time, but might not before. Could this happen in our lifetime? I guess that depends on whose lifetime you are talking about. I am 62 at the time of this writing, and so I may not see it. There are so many things taking place, which appear to be setting the stage for this final week, but we need to always avoid sensationalism and not speculate. All I can tell you is that we will know when he breaks the covenant in the middle of the week.

When will the Abomination of Desolation take place? By now, you can probably answer this. It will happen 3 ½ years into the 70th Week of Daniel. We know this from Daniel 9:27.

When is the Great Tribulation? The Great Tribulation starts right after the Antichrist commits the Abomination of Desolation. We know this from Matthew 24:15-21. This is 3 ½ years into the final seven-year period.

When is the coming of the Lord? As previously discussed, His *parousia*, or coming, involves the events associated with it. Matthew 24:29-31 tells us that He will come sometime after the Great Tribulation starts. In verse 22, the Great Tribulation is cut short by His coming. We do not know the hour or day (Matthew 24:36). We do know from our study, however, that it is in connection with the Day of the Lord, which is preceded by a sign in the sun, moon, and stars and does not take place until after the middle of the 70th Week of Daniel, but before the pouring out of His wrath. From this, we can conclude that it will be sometime during the second half of the 70th Week of Daniel.

Understanding that "wrath" is a reference to the Day of the Lord's wrath, we conclude that we are not destined to wrath when viewed in its proper context (I Thessalonians 5:9). We have consistently said that the key to understanding the timing of the Rapture is having a clear hermeneutic on the Day of the Lord's wrath. It is preceded by a sign in the sun, moon, and stars, which also lines up with the Olivet Discourse accounts in Matthew 24, Mark 13, and Luke 21, as well as in Revelation and the Old Testament books of Isaiah, Joel, Amos, and Zephaniah.

When does the Day of the Lord's wrath begin? Joel tells us that it takes place just after the heavenly phenomena, "Before them the earth quakes, the heavens tremble, the sun and the moon grow dark and the stars lose their brightness" (Joel 2:10). "The sun will be turned into darkness and the moon into blood before the great and awesome day of the Lord comes" (Joel 2:31). This is consistent with Revelation 6:12-13, "I looked when He broke the sixth seal, and there was a great earthquake; and the sun became black as sackcloth made of hair, and the whole moon became like blood; 13 and the stars of the sky fell to the earth, as a fig tree casts its unripe figs when shaken by a great wind." Verse 16 continues the context with, "and they said to the mountains and to the rocks, "Fall on us and hide us from the presence of Him who sits on the throne, and from the wrath of the Lamb."

Jesus said the same thing in Matthew 24:29, "But immediately after the tribulation of those days the sun will be darkened, and the moon will not give its light, and the stars will fall from the sky, and the powers of the heavens will be shaken." What follows is His appearing in the clouds to rapture the Church and then pour out His wrath.

When do the seals, trumpets, and bowls of Revelation take place? The seals as recorded in Revelation, chapter six begin at the start of the 70th Week of Daniel. It starts with the four horsemen, representing a ruler rising to power, war, famines, and pestilence. These are all within the natural phenomena. These, along with the fifth seal, are the wrath of the Antichrist, not the Day of the Lord's wrath.

The fifth seal starts in the middle of the week with the Abomination of Desolation and the start of the Great Tribulation, where many are martyred. The sixth seal takes place with the heavenly phenomena in the sun, moon, and stars. There is a brief interlude as the Lamb breaks the seventh seal: "When the Lamb broke the seventh seal, there was silence in heaven for about half an hour" (Revelation 8:1). The Church has been raptured in between the sixth and the seventh seal, and there is great rejoicing around the throne when this happens; but all of a sudden, complete silence falls upon the heavens as the Lamb breaks the seventh seal.

This is the last seal on the scroll. All heaven waits in anticipation as the Lamb opens it. His day has come. The Day of the Lord's wrath has come. The trumpets begin to sound, and one by one there are signs of His assembling to take His rightful possession of the earth and pour out His wrath on the ungodly. This begins sometime after the mid-point of the 70th Week of Daniel, and the trumpet judgments (seven of them) will continue to the end of the second half of the week.

The first trumpet judgment contains "hail and fire, mixed with blood, and they were thrown to the earth; and a third of the earth was burned up, and all the green grass was burned up" (Revelation 8:7). The second is "like a great mountain burning with fire was thrown into the sea; and a third of the sea became blood, and a third of the creatures which were in the sea and had life, died; and a third of the ships were destroyed" (Revelation 8:8-9). The third trumpet sounds and "a great star fell from heaven, burning like a torch, and it fell on a third of the rivers, and on the springs of waters" (Revelation 8:10). Many will die from the polluted water. The forth trumpet sounds and there is another phenomena in the heavens among the sun, moon, and stars.

The remaining three trumpets carry with them the woe judgments. Locusts come out of a bottomless pit; so much so that the sun and the air are darkened by them. These locusts go after the men who do not have the seal of the Lord on their foreheads. For five months they are tormented so much that they will seek death. The sixth trumpet sounds and four angels kill a third of mankind with a two hundred million army. The two witnesses are on the scene and they are murdered at the end of the second 1,260 days. They will come to life at the end of the week. Many are killed during this second woe.

The last trumpet carries the third woe, and the Lord begins to take ownership of the earth. The heavenly scene is incredible. The bowl judgments start, which are contained within the seventh trumpet. These take place during the 30-day period immediately following the second 1,260 days and the seven bowl judgments discussed in section 2 of Chapter 8,

The judgments are swift wrath: Bowl one, malignant sores on those who took the mark. Bowl two, every living thing in the sea dies. Bowl three, rivers contaminated. Bowl four; the sun scorches men with fire. Bowl five, extreme pain for all within the kingdom of the beast and they gnaw their tongues. Bowl six; the river Euphrates is dried up for the final battle to come, which is Armageddon. Bowl seven, a loud voice from the Temple and the throne saying, 'It is done", resulting in final destruction and victory of the Lamb. There is the marriage supper of the Lamb and the false prophet and Antichrist are cast into the pit burning with fire and brimstone.

When is the man of lawlessness revealed? II Thessalonians, chapter two tells us that it will be before the gathering (verse 1-2). It also goes on in verse four to say that he will come in conjunction with the apostasy, and when he "opposes and exalts himself above every so-called god or object of worship, so that he takes his seat in the Temple of God, displaying himself as being God." Daniel 9:27 indicates that this will take place in the middle of the week. In other words, 3 ½ years into that final seven-year period.

We also know that this man of lawlessness is the same person referred to as the Antichrist, the son of perdition, the man of sin, and the beast. He will come to power as a world ruler who will engage in a peace process with Israel. He is highly deceptive and his smooth talking and cunningness will deceive many. It is possible with today's worldwide media coverage that we could get a glimpse of who this individual is prior to this time, but we cannot be certain. Israel would not purposely enter into a covenant with one whom the world would openly identify as the Antichrist, and so we believe that we may not know his true identity until the mid-point of the final seven-year period.

When will the apostasy take place? In order for II Thessalonians 2:3 to be fulfilled, the apostasy must come before the gathering at the Rapture. The word "apostasy" is better translated as "defection" or "rebellion". *Vine's* defines it as "a defection, revolt, apostasy, is used in the N.T. of religious apostasy"[1]. Those who hold to the "pre-tribulation" position would have you believe that "apostasy" is translated as "depart", the physical act of departing; they are using "depart" as a verb, however, when it is only used as a noun in II Thessalonians 2:3.

In both the historical and classical Greek, this word is defection, not physical departure. You can think of this like the Soviet pilot who defected with the fighter jet. He was once perceived as a dedicated member of the Soviet Air Force, but then "defected" to another country to gain freedom. In this case, those who have been exposed to the faith, but are not truly grounded or sincere believers, will defect and capitulate to the desires of this one-world ruler. They are in the company of believers and have what appears to be faith, but they are not true believers. They will be deceived.

In II Thessalonians 2:3, the word "and" appears as a conjunction, connecting the apostasy with the man of lawlessness being revealed in the Temple. This apostasy will be quite evident 3 ½ years into the 70th Week of Daniel. Jesus talks about this in the Olivet Discourse in Matthew 24:10-12, "At that time many will fall away and will betray one another and hate on another. 11 Many false prophets will arise and will mislead many. 12 Because lawlessness is increased, most people's love will grow cold." This falling away (different Greek) is translated "offended" in the KJV.

Here the meaning is to have something occur that causes one's perceived love to grow cold. This defection, this abandonment of perceived faith is a direct result of deception on the part of the Antichrist and insincerity on the part of the one with perceived faith. These are not true believers. We are called to be imitators of God. During this time, these unregenerate imposters will come to light. They will do whatever it takes to seek comfort and self-preservation. Ephesians 5:6 provides a strong warning for those who are not sincere believers. The idea of falling away during the end-times is also seen in I Timothy 4:1, "But the Spirit explicitly says that in later times some will fall away from the faith, paying attention to deceitful spirits and doctrines of demons." II Timothy 3:5 describe these individuals as "holding to a form of godliness, although they have denied its power." II Peter 2:17-22 describes these individuals as well.

As we come closer and closer to the beginning of the 70th Week of Daniel, we can expect to see the false church compromising more and more. This lawlessness is not necessarily civil law, but more importantly a departure from the biblical precepts and principles. There will be a growing spirit of lawlessness. We are seeing signs of that in the Church today. In addition to the religious institutions departing from true biblical precepts and principles, individuals who have faithfully attended church and perhaps even served in the church and been baptized have not truly made a genuine commitment to receive Christ as Lord and Savior; these are the individuals who will fall away and eventually defect from the Church and embrace the man of lawlessness. This will take place leading up to the mid-point of the 70th Week of Daniel, and we will see its full fruition when the Antichrist demands their allegiance. This is so, so serious. Once an individual submits to the demands of the Antichrist, that person is destined to receive the wrath of God and will be lost for all eternity. We need to examine ourselves and see if we are in the faith. For the true believer, there will be no question. They will deny the Antichrist even if it costs them their life. They will not take his mark.

When are the 144,000 sealed? This happens between the sixth and seventh seal of Revelation. After the sign of the sixth seal in the sun, moon, and stars and the Rapture of the Church (sometime after the mid-point of the seven-year period), there is a brief interlude. During this time God will seal the 144,000 on their foreheads and will protect them throughout the coming wrath (Revelation 7:3-8).

When does the great multitude appear in heaven? This also takes place between the sixth and seventh seal. Just after the heavenly phenomena in the sun, moon, and stars, the Lord sends His angels to gather the elect from the four winds; from one end of the sky to the other according to Matthew 24:31. Right after the sixth seal, which describes the same phenomena recorded in Matthew 24 preceding the gathering, we see a "great multitude which no one could count, from every nation and all tribes and peoples and tongues, standing before the throne and before the Lamb, clothed in white robes, and palm branches were in their hands; and they cry out with a loud voice, saying, "Salvation to our God who sits on the throne, and to the Lamb" (Revelation 7:9-10). This is the raptured Church. This happens after the Great Tribulation starts, and in verse 14 of that same text, we see that these are the ones who have come out of the Great Tribulation. This is also just prior to the seventh seal in Revelation, chapter eight, which contains the trumpet judgments and the beginning of the Day of the Lord.

We will now move on to some **"where"** questions in section four.

SECTION 4 WHERE?

Where is the Church during the 70th Week of Daniel? It is this author's opinion that the Church will experience a portion of the 70th Week of Daniel. Most fundamental, Bible-believing churches would still hold to what we have described as a pre-tribulation rapture position. They would believe that the Church will be raptured prior to the commencement of the 70th Week of Daniel. From our study, I would conclude that the Church will endure the first six seals of Revelation. The Olivet Discourse teaching is consistent with this.

I believe that we are the "elect" of Matthew 24:22. This would place the Church in a position to enter not only the 70th Week of Daniel, but the Great Tribulation as well. Paul seems to agree with this teaching in II Thessalonians 2:1-4. We also see this teaching in the book of Revelation, chapter six, in addition to Mark 13 and Luke 21. While the Church will experience the "beginning of birth pangs", the *Great* Tribulation, and the first six seals of Revelation, chapter six, they will be rescued from the coming wrath. They may endure the wrath of the Antichrist, but his wrath during the Great Tribulation will be cut short by the coming of the Lord. When we see the sign in the sun, moon, and stars, we are told to "*look up for our redemption is drawing near*" (Luke 21:25-28). This will take place sometime during the second half of the seven-year period known as the 70th Week of Daniel.

Where does the Abomination of Desolation take place? In II Thessalonians, chapter two and Daniel 9:27, as well as Matthew 24:15, we are told that this will take place in the Temple or "*holy place*". This one-world ruler known as the Antichrist will set himself up in Jerusalem in the place where the daily sacrifices are resumed, display himself as an exalted one, and commit a detestable act, causing desolation. This is assumed to be in a rebuilt Temple. This will take place as the Antichrist breaks the covenant he made with Israel just 1,260 days prior. This is the mid-point, or 3 ½ years into the seven-year period.

Today there is no Temple in Jerusalem. There is a lot of talk about rebuilding one, and even recently, members of the tribe of Levi have been holding mock Passover ceremonies in preparation and anticipation of the rebuilding of the Temple. They have done this adjacent to the place believed to be the ancient site. Even with opposition from animal activist groups, the courts in Israel have given permission for this sacred ceremonial ritual. Many have spent years of research and work to replicate the very utensils used in the Temple by the High Priests. There is much anticipation of a rebuilt Temple. Whether it becomes a magnificent structure or a tabernacle, one day the Antichrist will announce his authority and demand worship in that place. Any news related to the rebuilding of a Temple in Jerusalem should get the attention of any serious Christian and Jew alike. I believe that it is very near.

Where is the sign of His coming taught? For many years we were taught that His coming would be without a sign. We have been taught in literature, movies, and periodicals that He will come silently and that Christians will be whisked away without a sign. We see clothes falling to the ground, airplanes falling out of the sky without their Christian pilots, cars crashing on the roads, et cetera. It all makes wonderful theatre and has been used to teach believers that He could come at any moment, so you better get your life in order, but is this accurate? Does it align with God's Word? I do not believe it does.

In Genesis 1:14 we read, "Then God said, "Let there be lights in the expanse of the heavens to separate the day from the night, and let them be for signs and for seasons and for days and years." I find this verse to be interesting when we look at the signs given by Jesus in the Olivet Discourse. There we read, "But immediately after the tribulation of those days, the sun will be darkened, and the moon will not give its light, and the stars will fall from the sky, and the powers of the heavens will be shaken. And then the *sign* of the Son of Man will appear in the sky, and then all the tribes of the earth will mourn, and *they will see* the Son of Man coming on the clouds of the sky with power and great glory. And He will send forth His angels with a *great trumpet* and they will gather together His elect from the four winds, from one end of the sky to the other" (Matthew 24:29-31). [Emphasis mine.]

Jesus said there will be a sign. He said all the tribes of the earth will see Him when he comes. There will be a great trumpet. It is preceded by total darkness and replaced with His Shekinah Glory.

196

It will not just be daylight in one portion of the earth where the sun rises. It will be a glorious light, which the entire world will see at the same time. Revelation 6:12-17 puts it this way: "I looked when He broke the sixth seal, and there was a great earthquake; and the sun became black as sackcloth made of hair, and the whole moon became like blood; 13 and the stars of the sky fell to the earth, as a fig tree casts its unripe figs when shaken by a great wind. 14 The sky was split apart like a scroll when it is rolled up, and every mountain and island were moved out of their places. 15 Then the kings of the earth and the great men and the commanders and the rich and the strong and every slave and free man hid themselves in the caves and among the rocks of the mountains; 16 and they said to the mountains and to the rocks, "Fall on us and hide us from the presence of Him who sits on the throne, and from the wrath of the Lamb; 17 for the great day of their wrath has come, and who is able to stand?"

This is hardly sign-less. Joel 2:30-31 puts it this way: "I will display wonders in the sky and on the earth, Blood, fire and columns of smoke. 31 The sun will be turned into darkness and the moon into blood before the great and awesome day of the Lord comes." Even in the classic rapture passage of I Thessalonians 4:16-17 we read, "For the Lord Himself will descend from heaven with a *shout*, with the *voice of the archangel* and with the *trumpet of God*, and the dead in Christ will rise first. 17 Then we who are alive and remain will be caught up together with them *in the clouds* to meet the Lord *in the air*, and so we shall always be with the Lord." [Emphasis mine.]

When He comes it will be with a shout, with the voice of the archangel, and with a loud trumpet. We will meet Him in the clouds in the air. This is hardly secret or silent. When Jesus comes, it will be the most glorious wonder the world has ever seen. In Acts 1:11 an angel says this to His disciples just after His ascension: "They also said, "Men of Galilee, why do you stand looking into the sky? This Jesus, who has been taken up from you into heaven, will come *in just the same way as you have watched Him go into heaven*." [Emphasis mine.]

In other words, you will see Him return just as you saw Him depart. We said that *parousia*, or coming, is always in the singular. It will be one coming with the subsequent events that follow. The sign of His coming will be when the lights go out and are replaced by His glorious light in the heavens. Every eye will see, and it will come with a loud shout and trumpet call.

Where does the Day of the Lord's wrath start? The Day of the Lord and the Day of the Lord's wrath are connected, but not the same. In other words, the Day of the Lord's wrath is contained within the Day of the Lord, but so are other things. First, Jesus comes for His bride, the Church by cutting short the Great Tribulation, and then the seventh seal is opened, which contain the trumpet judgments. The Day of the Lord's wrath has begun against the "earth dwellers" and all the ungodly.

The last trumpet, or seventh trumpet contains the bowl judgments, which are the outpouring of His most fierce wrath. These bowl judgments take place in the 30-day period following the second half of the week, and then the remaining additional 45-day period is the reclamation and restored promises to Israel. All of this is part of the Day of the Lord, or "His day", but the wrath period is specific to the last seal, trumpet, and bowl judgments.

Where is the man of sin/Antichrist revealed? The passages we have studied have indicated that he will be revealed in Jerusalem, in the holy place or rebuilt Temple. Again, there is much speculation over who the Antichrist might be, or whether this individual is alive today or not. We will not speculate here. There is enough biblical evidence to allow the watchful believer to know who he is when he does reveal himself in the Temple and sets himself up to be exalted and worshipped. He will demand that those living at the time pay tribute and full allegiance to him, and he will demand that they take a mark that identifies them as his followers.

For the believer, we are warned ahead of time. This Antichrist will come from men. The real Christ will come from heaven with the incredible phenomena occurring in the sky. This Antichrist will be a world ruler and represent lawlessness. The real Christ will reclaim the earth and will pour out His wrath against ungodliness and lawlessness.

The Antichrist will cause an abomination and desolate the Temple of God. The real Christ will reclaim His throne; establish a new Temple, and the throne of David. The Antichrist will have limited power and perform mock miracles. The real Christ will come as King of kings and Lord of lords with infinite power, great glory, and will astound the world with His miraculous display of glory and power. The Antichrist will cause many to take a mark through deceit. The real Christ has sealed all true believers, and will seal the 144,000 with His mark of ownership based on truth and divinely protect them. The Antichrist is part of the false trinity. The real Christ is one with the Father and the Holy Spirit. The Antichrist will exalt himself for a short while in the Temple and world, but the real Christ alone will be exalted when He comes, and every knee will bow and every tongue will confess Him as King of kings and Lord of lords.

The Antichrist will battle and destroy life. The real Christ will win victoriously and is the way the truth and the life. The Antichrist will be cast into the lake of fire burning with brimstone for eternity. The real Christ will cast him there and will set up an everlasting Kingdom as King of kings and Lord of lords. The Antichrist will bash and destroy hope. The real Christ is our blessed hope!

Where do the saints cry out? Revelation 6:9-10 says, "When the Lamb broke the fifth seal, I saw underneath the altar the souls of those who had been slain because of the testimony which they had maintained; 10 and they cried out with a loud voice, saying, "How long, O Lord, holy and true, will You refrain from judging and avenging our blood on those who dwell on the earth?" Jesus said we will be "delivered to the courts, flogged in the synagogues, and stand before governors and kings" (Mark 13:9). We are warned that it will start in Jerusalem, but it will not be isolated to Jerusalem alone.

The first seal of Revelation six tells us that the Antichrist will take peace from the earth. He will be a world ruler bent on conquest. The immediate intensity of his wrath will be experienced in Jerusalem and Israel, but it will spread to the world. He will make war not only with Israel, but also with her offspring, the Church (Revelation 12:17). These saints crying out are those who have been martyred during the terror of this diabolical leader. It begins 3 ½ years into the seven-year period, and it starts in the holy place, Jerusalem. It will eventually reach believers throughout the world who have not taken the mark. Those from every tribe, tongue, and nation will be impacted by his terror.

Where is Israel during the 70th Week of Daniel? They will have made a covenant with death. They will have an appearance of their longed for peace in the beginning, which may last for 42 months or 3 ½ years, but in the middle of the week that peace will be taken from them. The Antichrist will break his agreement and pursue Israel. Jesus warns that when they see the Abomination of Desolation, they must to flee immediately to the mountains. Many in Israel will be martyred. They are not believers at this point.

The False Prophet and the Antichrist will deceive many. Once the Great Tribulation starts, some *will* understand and flee. The Great Tribulation will be cut short by the coming of Christ, and the eventual promise in Zechariah 12:10 will be fulfilled where we read, "I will pour out on the house of David and on the inhabitants of Jerusalem, the Spirit of grace and of supplication, so that they will look on Me whom they have pierced; and they will mourn for Him, as one mourns for an only son, and they will weep bitterly over Him like the bitter weeping over a firstborn." It starts with the first fruits of Israel being sealed as the 144,000. Eventually all Israel will be saved (Romans 11:25-29).

Where are the 144,000 after the Rapture? They are sealed by God and divinely protected during the Day of the Lord's wrath. They will emerge alive and be with Christ when He physically goes to Mt Zion (Revelation 14:1).

Where will the Battle of Armageddon take place? This battle will take place at the end of the 30-day period following the second half of the 70th Week of Daniel. Revelation 16:16 says, "And they gathered them together to the place which in Hebrew is called Har-Magedon." It is the mountain of Megiddo, about 25 miles west-south-west of the southern tip of the Sea of Galilee in the Kishon River area, where the massive Jezreel Valley is located.

Where is the millennium with respect to the 70th Week of Daniel? We said that we hold to the "futurist" view and believe in a pre-millennium position. This means that we believe that the one thousand year period will take place after the return of Christ. The Rapture will occur before the one thousand year reign. The one thousand year kingdom will take place after the 70th Week of Daniel. We believe this is a literal one thousand years as indicated by the use of the phrase six times in Revelation 20. Satan is bound for these one thousand years. In verse seven, he is released and there is a last ditch effort by him and those whom he will deceive. He is conquered and "cast into the lake of fire and brimstone, where the beast and the false prophet are; and they will be tormented day and night forever and ever" (Revelation 20:10).

Where is the Great White Throne of God? We read about this in Revelation 20:11-15. This takes place at the end of the one thousand years and after Satan is cast into the lake of fire. This takes place before the throne of God. It is a place of judgment. Those who have rejected the saving message of Jesus Christ and/or did not look forward to His redemption from the ancient past will stand before this throne of judgment. It will be a righteous judgment. This is a place for unbelievers throughout the time of man. Books will be opened and they will be judged not only according to their deeds, but also because they are not found in the Lamb's book of life. They will be judged rightly and will be cast into the lake of fire for eternity, separated from God.

This is a horrifying proposition. Hell is a real place and not everyone goes to heaven. Those who have rejected Christ will be doomed. Jesus, speaking about His return, said, "I am the way, and the truth, and the life; no one comes to the Father but through Me" (John 14:6). Acts 4:12, "And there is salvation in no one else; for there is no other name under heaven that has been given among men by which we must be saved."

Not all roads lead to heaven and eternal life with God. It is a narrow road. In that day, many will mourn, but it will be too late. This is not a place that believers will have to experience, for their judgment fell upon Jesus Christ at the cross, and they accept the fact that they cannot save themselves.

This is so, so important. We will talk more about this in the last chapter, but do not wait to receive Him. Do it now while you still can. He is a righteous judge and a holy God. He does not, nor ever will grade on a curve. While your good deeds are probably less than your bad, just one bad deed can condemn you for eternity. James 2:10, "For whoever keeps the whole law and yet stumbles in one point, he has become guilty of all."

Where is the United States in prophecy? This is one of those mysteries that we just do not know. There is a lot of speculation, but there is nothing that I can find in Scriptures with reference to the United States. You would think that this powerful nation would have mention in the Scriptures regarding the last days, however we are still a relatively young nation. Whether the critics want to acknowledge it or not, our nation was established on moral ethics and principles found in the Bible. This nation has been blessed since she gained her independence based on her predominate faith. Today, this nation is beginning to experience a departure from those early Judeo-Christian values and moral teachings.

At the time of this writing, the United States is experiencing over 16 trillion dollars in debt and it continues to mount daily. Much of the national debt is owed to China. There is no approved budget, and a thing called "sequestration" has come into effect that institutes funding cut-backs on critical support items like our military defense. Many parts of the country have embraced gay marriage and abortion, and yet there is still a large remnant who still believe that the Bible is the final authority and should be taken seriously with regard to these issues.

Some churches have embraced the culture to define their moral ethics, and believe that the teaching of God's Word is old and out of date, and therefore no longer relevant. School shootings and suicide among young people are on the rise. There is a spirit of lawlessness. Some might question the leadership's support for Israel, which is critical to our blessing as a nation. It is hard to imagine that we will not have a significant role to play during the last days, but we just cannot say.

There is increasing persecution of the Church. Our economy is lower than it has been in many years. While we are cutting our own defense budgets, we are providing advanced weapons to foreign countries like Egypt, who may not have our best interest or that of Israel in mind. Just recently North Korea threatened to attack the United States with nuclear weapons, causing the deployment of our missile defenses. The P-5 Plus One is attempting to negotiate with Iran to halt their development of nuclear weapons with little success. The Arab Spring has led to violence and instability in the

Arab countries of the world. Civil war is being fought in countries, which surround Israel and pose a threat to her security. We live in a world that is becoming more and more rebellious, and it is becoming a more and more dangerous place to live and raise a family. Christians are being martyred around the world. I do believe that technology and the current world crisis could lead to the emergence of the Antichrist within our lifetime. The United States needs to be the light to the world that it once was.

The United States should heed the words found in II Chronicles 7:14, "and My people who are called by My name humble themselves and pray and seek My face and turn from their wicked ways, then I will hear from heaven, will forgive their sin and will heal their land." This is a great nation, founded on biblical principles. We need to repent and return to our Judeo-Christian heritage, values, and morals or we will be judged.

We now move on to the **"why"** questions in section five.

SECTION 5 WHY?

Why are the seals of Revelation relevant? The entire book of Revelation is significant. It is the New Testament prophecy book. The emphasis is on the second half of the 70th Week of Daniel, but it is not without mention of the first half. The book starts off with, "The Revelation of Jesus Christ, which God gave Him to show to His bond-servants, the things which must soon take place;" (Revelation1:1a). In verse 19, we are told that John is to write the things that he has seen, the things that are, and the things that will come after.

The message continues with a warning to the seven churches, which were real churches [things which are], and then moves on to the scroll with seven seals in chapter five [things that will come after], which would also include the Church in the future, with some of the characteristics and warnings from the ancient ones. As the seals are removed from the scroll, events take place, which directly parallel the events described by Jesus in the Olivet Discourse; the rise to power of a world ruler, wars, famine, and pestilence.

These first four seals align with the "beginning of birth pangs". As the fifth seal is opened, we see a parallel with the Abomination of Desolation and the beginning of the Great Tribulation and martyrdom. The sixth seal aligns with the sign in the sun, moon, and stars spoken of in the Olivet Discourse as the sign preceding His coming for His Church. Just prior to the seventh seal we see the 144,000 from the twelve tribes of Israel sealed, and this great multitude from every tribe, tongue, and nation appear before the throne and before the Lamb. This is a result of the Rapture of the Church. The seventh seal provides the chronology of the outpouring of the Day of the Lord's wrath upon the ungodly.

These seals are often overlooked and yet provide a clear, consistent picture of the events associated with the 70th Week of Daniel and also harmonize Old and New Testament teaching on the last days.

Why is II Thessalonians, chapter two significant? If we approach the Scripture and take it at face value for what it is saying, this passage becomes critical in understanding the timing of the Rapture. There is no question that Paul is speaking about the Rapture when he refers to the "gathering". He then goes on to tell the church at Thessalonica that this *will not* take place [the gathering and Day of the Lord] until the apostasy comes first and the man of lawlessness sets himself up in the Temple to be exalted. [Emphasis mine.]

I said before that this is the text that I cannot reconcile with the pre-tribulation rapture teaching that I had held to for many years. It clearly states that the gathering will not take place at the beginning or before the beginning of the 70th Week of Daniel. It clearly states that it will not take place until after the mid-point of the 70th Week of Daniel. When taken in all contexts, it harmonizes well. I Thessalonians 5:9 is speaking about the Day of the Lord's wrath, not Satan's wrath. Yes, we are not destined to the Day of the Lord's wrath, but we can clearly see throughout Scripture that the Day of the Lord is preceded by these heavenly phenomena in the sun, moon, and stars. This does not happen until the sixth seal, which is consistent with His teaching found in the Olivet Discourse. His wrath does not start until the seventh seal is removed and the scroll is opened.

I find this passage in II Thessalonians to be one of the clearest passages in all of Scripture that defines the timing of His return and the Rapture. There will be an apostasy [defection of non-sincere followers], and the man of lawlessness will set himself up in the Temple to be exalted prior to the gathering. Scripture further informs us that the man of lawlessness will not only set himself up in the Temple to be exalted, but will demand that people worship him and receive his mark. Those who do not will be the subjects of his great tribulation. The Church will be present, but the Great Tribulation will be cut short at His [Christ's] *parousia*.

Why is "kept from the hour" significant? Those who are kept from the hour of testing, which is about to come on all the earth dwellers, are the "faithful". Revelation 3:10 has been used as a "proof text" for pre-tribulation, but the hour of testing is taken out of context. There are two groups in mind here, the faithful Church and the earth dwellers. The faithful will be delivered out of the midst of danger as suggested in I Thessalonians 1:10 in the original language, as well as delivered from the "wrath to come". The "wrath to come" is a reference to the Day of the Lord's wrath. The earth dwellers will endure this, but those faithful believers, the true Church, will not. I would recommend a pamphlet by Charles Cooper entitled *Revelation 3:10 A Bombshell*[1] for a thorough explanation of this verse.

Why is the Day of the Lord and Day of the Lord's wrath so significant? As previously stated, most positions agree that the Church is not destined to wrath. Virtually every position on the timing of the Rapture is built around this premise. It is therefore of utmost importance to determine, if possible, when the Day of the Lord and His wrath begin. It is also important to define what this is—and what it is *not*. We will do that in the next chapter.

The Lord's wrath is not the same as the wrath of the Antichrist. The Lord's wrath is never referred to as the Lord's tribulation. I believe that the pre-wrath position is the most accurate way of stating that the Lord will return for His Church at the Rapture prior to the pouring out of His wrath. This is the wrath that we are not destined to as stated in I Thessalonians 5:9. The "Day of the Lord" phrase is used numerous times in whole or part within Scripture, but the Day of the Lord in reference to His return—and more specifically—the Day of the Lord's wrath is always in reference to a future time within the 70th Week of Daniel.

The Day of the Lord in this context provides a sign which precedes it, according to Joel 2:30-31. This sign is consistent with the Olivet Discourse in all accounts, as well as with the book of Revelation. It is also consistent with the language found in I Thessalonians, chapter five and II Thessalonians, chapter two when looking at the timing of the "gathering". This wrath that the Church is not destined to does not occur until after the Great Tribulation begins, sometime within the second half of the final seven-year period.

Why is Matthew 24 significant? Matthew 24 and the Olivet Discourse are significant because they provide the answer to the questions the disciples ask, as well as those questions that Christians of future generation will ask. It has often been referred to as strictly for Israel and the future fulfillment of the covenants previously made with them. A portion of this thinking resulted from the book of Matthew itself, in that its primary audience was Jewish in nature.

When it comes to the return of Christ and understanding the harmony throughout the whole of Scripture, some problems start to emerge. While the language and sequence appear to be consistent with other text, which certainly refer to the Rapture, this has been largely assigned to a separate "advent" of Christ. Many good arguments have been given to support this conclusion, however when taking the text at face value and applying normal methods of hermeneutics, the argument begins to break down. Furthermore, those who would rightly advise us that nobody knows the hour or day of His coming (referring to the Rapture), often quote Matthew 24:36. They are right in assigning this text to this discussion, but you cannot have it both ways, meaning that one cannot use Matthew 24:36 to both reference a second coming *and* the immediate context of the Rapture. This verse cannot support two different interpretations simultaneously, and it is illogical to attempt to do so.

It is my personal belief that while the text contains the future promises and hopes for Israel, it also contains hope for the Church, or who Jesus refers to as the "elect". We have to remember that the early Church was comprised mostly of Jews and certainly these disciples were Jewish, therefore it would make sense to assume an audience of Jewish heritage. Additionally, we should remember the commandment given by Jesus in Acts 1:8 after His resurrection and just prior to His ascent, "but you will receive power when the Holy Spirit has come upon you; and you shall be My witnesses both in Jerusalem, and in all Judea and Samaria, and even to the remotest part of the earth."

These early disciples who heard the words of Jesus at the Olivet Discourse were the instruments used by Jesus to fulfill this commandment. To isolate this discourse to Israel only presents a number of problems. First, as we have said before, Matthew is not the only Gospel to include language on the Olivet Discourse. We see the same language in Mark and Luke. Mark presents Jesus as the servant and has a Gentile audience in mind, perhaps Romans of the time. Luke provides the longest of the Gospels, and is the most detailed and chronological. He writes to the Gentiles as well, perhaps the Greek audience. Luke was probably a Gentile physician, not Jewish. These small facts mean little aside from driving home the point that all of God's Word is given to everyone, not just a targeted audience. The Gospel accounts are not just for the predominate reader of that day, but for all generations.

207

Secondly, as we have noted before, there are not two separate comings. To refer to the Olivet Discourse as the "second coming or advent" and the Rapture as a previous event would call for two comings. The word for "coming" in both the Olivet Discourse and elsewhere in the New Testament is *parousia*. It is always used in the singular, and it refers to His coming and the subsequent presence and events associated with that coming.

Thirdly, and perhaps most important, the Olivet Discourse aligns perfectly with Revelation, chapters six and seven. The question the disciples asked Jesus was, "Tell us, when will these things happen, and what will be the sign of Your coming, and of the end of the age?" (Matthew 24:3). Jesus gave a chronology of events that match Revelation seals in a remarkable way. He also refers back to the prophecy of Daniel in Matthew 24:15, further tying it to a timeline consistent throughout Scripture. Jesus certainly knew what persecution and fate lay ahead for these first disciples, but He answered their questions to provide courage and hope, just as He has for all generations.

His return *is* referred to as "the blessed hope" (Titus 2:13). He promised to send the Holy Spirit; He was not going to leave them uninformed, which is why Paul uses this phrase when he refers to Christ's return in I Thessalonians 4:13. In I Thessalonians 4:15 Paul gives the authority by which he is about to present the hope and that is, "by the word of the Lord". Paul was not present at the Olivet Discourse, but he could reference that teaching and hope, which Jesus gave to His disciples and to all generations to follow. It is this author's humble opinion that the Olivet Discourse provides a perfect harmony throughout Scripture on the subject and timing sequence of our Lord's return. To assign it as separate causes confusion and biblical gymnastics that does not make sense. Remember the "golden rule for interpreting Scripture", "When the plain sense of Scripture makes common sense, seek no other sense"[2].

Why do the Old Testament books of Isaiah, Joel, Amos, and Zephaniah hold significance with regard to the timing of the Rapture? We must remember that the sum of God's Word is truth. We must also remember that over one-fourth of the Bible is prophetic. You cannot fully understand the New Testament apart from the Old

208

Testament. The Old Testament books in particular provide some clarifying information with regard to the Day of the Lord.

When comparing Scripture with Scripture, we find that there is a preceding sign given in these Old Testament passages regarding the Day of the Lord. The Day of the Lord references look forward to the future in these Old Testament passages, a future that would be the *parousia* of Christ. In these passages, we are told that there will be a sign in the sun, moon, and stars preceding the Day of the Lord. When we look at New Testament passages regarding the timing of the Lord's return, we see the same thing in Matthew, Mark, Luke, Acts, and Revelation. As we look at the placement of the passages referring to the same heavenly phenomena, we discover something about the timing of the Rapture. The language is the same and it is consistent throughout Scripture. The parallels are stunning. While we will not know the hour or the day, we do have a feel for the general timing and what will precede it.

Why is the book of Revelation significant? For many in the modern Church, the book of Revelation remains the least studied and least understood of all the books in the Bible. Many will not study it believing that all of the symbolism and construct is far too hard to grasp. It is probably the least taught of all the New Testament books, but it is the key to our understanding of the greatest event and hope for every believer since the first coming of Christ. Part of the reason for all the confusion is the biblical gymnastics that scholars have done to make it fit the pre-tribulation position. In all fairness to them, I, too, believed this position for many years and still hold the highest regard for the wonderful biblical scholars who gave us that position. The problem with this approach, however, is the harmony of Scripture. Many texts seem to provide reasonable arguments for this position when isolated to the immediate context of the verse being quoted, but when viewed in the book and Bible context, things start to come unglued. If we understand the book of Revelation in light of comparing Scripture with Scripture, a beautiful, uncomplicated picture comes to light.

The book of Revelation is not as difficult to understand as many make it out to be. It is not a book of chronology from chapter one to twenty-two. This belief is where some of the confusion comes from. The first eleven chapters provide sequence, and then John repeats with greater detail from chapter twelve through twenty-two. Revelation 10:11 says, "And they said to me, "You must prophesy again concerning many peoples and nations and tongues and kings." In Revelation 11:15, we see the culmination of the events as the seventh trumpet is sounded.

Revelation is the key to understanding end-times prophecy. Revelation 1:3 provides us the answer to the significance, "Blessed is he who reads and those who hear the words of the prophecy, and heed the things which are written in it; for the time is near." We need to read it, hear it, and heed it. It is to the Church. Revelation chapter six, when viewed in an overall biblical context, tells us so much about the future and the hope of the Church. It parallels the Olivet Discourse, as we would expect, since these are the words of Jesus. It is also consistent with the sign given in Old Testament books regarding the Day of the Lord.

The Apostle Paul said that we should not be uninformed regarding the coming of our Lord. Revelation is the key to being informed.

Why is Israel a key to future prophecy? Israel has been the nation that God has chosen to bless all the nations of the world. One day the throne of David will be re-established in Israel. Jesus will stand on Mt Zion once again. One day the Temple and daily sacrifice will be re-established. One day, the Antichrist will make a covenant with Israel and then will break it at the mid-point, 3 ½ years later. One day there will be an incredible battle at the site of Mount Megiddo. One day the King of kings and Lord of lords will return to Israel and will reclaim His rightful title deed to this earth.

Jesus exhorted us that we have been told ahead of time to watch for certain things. Israel is the key. We may or may not know when that covenant of peace will be made, but we will know when the Antichrist breaks it. Jesus warns His elect to flee in haste when this takes place. There are many things taking place in Israel today, and there are many promises yet to be fulfilled for Israel.

One of the most exciting prophecy fulfillments in the 20th Century was when Israel became a recognized independent state on May 14, 1948. Even more recently there was the famed six-day war from June 5-10 of 1967, where in just six days, Israel defeated the foes of Egypt,

Jordan, and Syria to gain the Gaza Strip, the Sinai Peninsula, the West Bank, East Jerusalem, and the Golan Heights. They have been in a near state of war since their independence. Today, they continue to be threatened by radicals calling for their demise, but God will keep His promises to these descendants of Abraham, and will one day return as their Messiah. He will be recognized this time and they will have mourning mixed with rejoicing. Every Bible-believing Christian should keep their eye on the developments in Israel and pray for them.

Why would God allow Christians to suffer at the hands of the Antichrist? This is not just a question that is posed with regard to the end-times. People ask this question daily when they lose a loved one, especially in the case of little children. Since beginning this chapter, I have lost two more friends who were fairly young. We have to remember that we are in a fallen world. It is really only because God has mercy and is long-suffering towards us that we exist at all. I cannot begin to explain to you why a child would suffer or why young parents would experience the death of an innocent child. The heart breaks in ways that only they can understand. The earth and mankind will suffer the curse as a result of the sin of Adam and Eve in Genesis chapter three. Nobody can give a good answer as to why we suffer apart from the fact that we have an all-knowing God who has also been acquainted with our grief and suffering.

Jesus certainly knew suffering and He was without sin. He was crucified unjustly in order to take upon Himself the sins of the world. There are times when suffering takes place or the loss of a loved one in order for God to display His majesty and glory. We saw this when Lazarus died. We have heard of heroic stories of those whom have died horrible deaths in the past and what has been accomplished because of it. It also reminds us of our mortal existence and that life is but a breath.

More Christians have been martyred since 1900 than in all of the history of the Church. In America we have been so blessed to be able to worship as we please, but there may come a day when that will not be the case. If we suffer for Christ, we are blessed. Peter put it this way in I Peter 1:6-7, "In this you greatly rejoice, even though now for a little while, if necessary, you have been distressed by various trials, 7 so that the proof of your faith, being more precious than gold which is perishable, even though tested by fire, may be found to result in praise and glory and honor at the revelation of Jesus Christ." I Peter 4:12-13 says, "Beloved, do not be surprised at the fiery ordeal among you, which comes upon you for your testing, as though some strange thing were happening to you; 13 but to the degree that you share the sufferings of Christ, keep on rejoicing, so that also at the revelation of His glory you may rejoice with exultation."

Paul said, "and to give relief to you who are afflicted and to us as well when the Lord Jesus will be revealed from heaven with His mighty angels in flaming fire" (II Thessalonians 1:7). Jesus said that in this life we would have tribulation (John 16:33). Today, many Christians are suffering and being afflicted for Christ. We are not exempt from it today, and we certainly will not be exempt from it during the 70th Week of Daniel. The blessed hope is not found in the absence of suffering for Christ, it is found in our *deliverance* out of the midst of trouble and our reunion with the One who paid it all for our eternal salvation which, we need to remember, we did not deserve. If we are counted among the saints who have suffered with Him, then we are blessed and privileged.

Let's now move on to our final "**how**" questions in section six.

SECTION 6 HOW?

How do the seals of Revelation, chapter six relate to Matthew 24? By now you should be able to answer this question. Pastors sometimes use a method called "blinking". It is saying the same thing in different ways over and over again in order to drive home a point. In this book, we have said the same thing in different ways in order to achieve the same goal. Take some time to read Revelation, chapter six and Matthew 24. Look at each one as a sequence of events. While there are some slight language differences between what Jesus refers to as the "beginning of birth pangs" and the first four horsemen of Revelation (the first four seals), the parallels are undeniable. This is especially true when you look at Mark and Luke. You see the rise to power, the wars, the famines, and pestilence in all passages.

As Jesus shares about the Abomination of Desolation in verse 15 and describes the Great Tribulation and the subsequent martyrs, we see the exact same thing in Revelation with seal number five. Jesus goes on to explain that the Great Tribulation is cut short for the sake of the elect, and then He describes the sign in the sun, moon, and stars. This perfectly parallels Revelation with the sixth seal. The next event is His coming to gather the elect from the four winds. This takes place during the interlude between the sixth and seventh seal of Revelation where we see a great multitude appear before the throne from every tribe, tongue, and nation. The relationship is in the teaching contained in both accounts. We would expect this since both are the revelation of Jesus Christ.

How do First and Second Thessalonians relate? These are the classic New Testament books on the subject of the Rapture. These, along with I Corinthians, describe the blessed hope. I Thessalonians 4:16-17 are the classic rapture verses. In I Thessalonians chapter five, Paul states, "Now as to the times and the epochs, brethren, you have no need of anything to be written to you. 2 For you yourselves know full well that the day of the Lord will come just like a thief in the night." Note here that Paul is equating the Rapture with the Day of the Lord. He goes on to explain that we are not destined to wrath, which is a direct tie to his previous immediate context. In other words, He is referring to the Day of the Lord's wrath.

We know from our reading of Revelation that it does not start until the seventh seal is opened and the trumpet judgments begin. In II Thessalonians, chapter two we are told that the "gathering" is in connection with the Day of the Lord in verses one and two. We are also told that both will not happen [the gathering and Day of the Lord] until the apostasy comes first and the man of lawlessness is revealed in the Temple. This compares well with the Olivet Discourse and Revelation in that we are told that the love of many will grow cold. We are told that the Abomination of Desolation and the Great Tribulation precede the Day of the Lord in those texts as well.

How do the writings of I and II Peter fit in? I Peter one talks about a "living hope" and the perseverance of the power of faith "resulting in praise and glory and honor". We are told to prepare our minds, keep sober in spirit, and fix our hope on His return. We are exhorted to live godly lives. In chapter three we are told to be ready to defend this hope by giving an account. This will be tough if we do not understand it.

In chapter four we are told that the end is near and that we need to "be of sound judgment and sober spirit for the purpose of prayer" (verse seven). We are told we should expect suffering and that we are blessed if we experience it for Christ. In II Peter, we are told that God's Word is just that. Not a result of man. We are warned in chapter two of the false teaching. In chapter three we are told about the Day of the Lord and the relationship to His coming (verse 10), and how mockers will come. Just as in I Thessalonians, we are exhorted to be blameless.

If we were going to be raptured before any of the real suffering and persecution takes place under the wrath of the Antichrist, then much of the New Testament, including these Epistles, would not make sense.

How do the Church and Israel relate? For the strict dispensationalists, this may pose a problem as they see Israel and the Church so distinctly as having no overlap whatsoever. When Israel rejected their Messiah at His first coming, Jesus was deeply saddened even though He knew this would happen. There are many promises yet to be fulfilled in Israel. In the Olivet Discourse, Jesus begins to speak about the hope for the elect. At that time, there was no Church. His disciples were the first to preach Jesus Christ as the Savior to the Jew first and then to the Gentile. The Church was formed on the day of Pentecost, but God was not done with Israel. Romans, chapter 11 clearly tells us that God is not finished with Israel. Some would contend that when the Church Age began, that He stopped reaching and working out His plan with Israel, but Scripture reveals that this simply is not true. The God of Abraham, Isaac, and Jacob is *still* the God of Abraham, Isaac, and Jacob, and He still blesses Israel today.

I believe with all my heart that the battles Israel has been involved in since her rebirth as an independent sovereign State have had the hand of God participating and preserving them. I believe that He has blessed the return of many Jews to the land of Israel, and that they are rich in resources and provision because of the hand of God. I believe He is preserving a people for His possession with whom He will fulfill all the promises of Ezekiel and Jeremiah. Just because we have entered into the Church Age does not mean that the Church Age must cease before God can return to work out His plan for the restoration of Israel. Romans 11:11, "I say then, they did not stumble so as to fall, did they? May it never be! But by their transgression salvation has come to the Gentiles, to make them jealous."

God is not done with Israel, and He can work with both the Church and Israel simultaneously. One of the things that will happen in the last days is the Church will be raptured and then 144,000 Jews—12,000 from each of the 12 tribes—will be sealed and divinely protected as the first fruits of Israel. The prophecy of Zechariah 12 will come to pass in these later days.

How does this time compare in history? I suppose that all generations have had the hope of His return. The early Church must have thought that A.D. 70 with the destruction of Herod's Temple and the desolation of Jerusalem was it. You can imagine what Christians were thinking during World War I. The world was at war, there were famines and, at the time, no cure for diseases. Many would die from plagues and diseases, which antibiotics can cure today. Then World War II came along. There was a world ruler who emerged with a vengeance against the Jewish people and Christians who supported them. He murdered in the millions. The persecution was unimaginable. They must have thought Hitler was the Antichrist.

While there was some early movement and progress by Zionists, such as Dr. Theodore Herzl and the eventual Balfour Declaration of 1917, there was no restoration of a State of Israel. What makes our time unique is the continued Zionist movement, which gained support from President Truman. When Israel became an independent sovereign State on May 14, 1948, everything changed. As Jews by the thousands returned to Israel from the diaspora, a nation was coming alive. The six-day war gained the East Jerusalem area in 1967. Incredible amounts of research has been taking place ever since to link genealogies and descendants. The lines of the twelve tribes are becoming clearer today. The Levites are working on the ancient rituals and preparing every day for a rebuilt Temple. Israel is in a position today like never before.

There has been talk even among our recent presidents of a "one-world order". This should cause the hair on the back of your neck to rise. The European Economic Union has been formed. The Arab states are becoming more fused. There is growing anti-Semitism among radicals who are calling for the demise of Israel. The world economic system is in peril. There are wars and unrest throughout the world. There are new strains of disease and incurable discoveries. There is technology like never before that makes a world system more feasible and the means for a world ruler to track everyone on the planet. We are seeing more natural disasters with greater intensity than ever before.

Persecution of Christians is growing. The Church, in many areas, is compromising and caving in to the demands of its modern, immoral culture. The Gospel is reaching parts of the world where people have never been exposed to the Gospel. Bibles are being printed in nearly every language on the planet. The electronic media and Internet have connected the world socially and technically. There are more books on this subject then ever before, and the Scriptures regarding prophecy are becoming clearer. There is a spirit of lawlessness and the beginnings of apostasy. The idea of people taking a mark not so long ago would have sounded absurd, but today people are marking their bodies and paying to do so. This future mark of the beast will be made so appealing that unbelievers will most likely wait in long lines looking forward to it, not realizing that they will be forever lost and subject to the wrath of God.

We live in a unique time in history. The stage is being set like never before.

How is there any hope in a pre-wrath eschatology? I believe that the pre-wrath eschatology is the only hope. *Vine's* defines the word "hope" this way: "favorable and confident expectation. It has to do with the unseen and the future (Romans 8:24, 25). Hope describes (a) the happy anticipation of good (the most frequent significance)"[1]. We are saved, looking forward to the blessed hope of His return.

When the U.S. soldiers were being overwhelmed in the Philippines during the beginning of World War II, General MacArthur was reportedly ordered by President Roosevelt to depart. As the story goes, he left in the night on PT boats. He transferred to a B-17 and eventually got to Australia. It was there on March of 1942 that he said his famous line, "I came through and I shall return". To those soldiers who were left behind, it was hope. They waited as prisoners of war in great expectation of their leader's return to rescue them. Eventually, he did return and it was General MacArthur who was our representative on the Battleship Missouri when the Japanese signed the conditions of surrender at the conclusion of the war.

When soldiers experience the suffering and difficulty associated with combat, they look forward to coming home or being rescued. As an Infantry Soldier in Vietnam, I looked forward with anticipation to the sound of the helicopters coming to take us for a break from the jungle to a safer place where we could get a warm meal, medical attention, and clean clothes. How much more we all appreciated our country and the blessing of our homes and surroundings when compared to the struggles associated with combat zones! It was with expectation that we looked forward to this with great hope. Soldiers keep "short time calendars" and mark off the days as they get close to going home. When that day arrives, it is the sweetest expression of hope that you can imagine. We referred to the aircraft that would transfer us home as "freedom birds".

It is not any different with the pre-wrath eschatology. The deliverance comes with expectation as we see the signs. We may have momentary affliction, and many will lose their lives but we look forward to His coming and the deliverance out of the Great

Tribulation and from the coming wrath. How much sweeter the arrival and deliverance will be after having gone through such difficulty.

How will I know when the time is near? Scripture tells us that the apostasy and the revealing of the man of lawlessness will take place prior to the gathering. We know that this man of lawlessness reveals himself in the Temple to be exalted and worshipped at the mid-point of the final seven-year period. Once this happens, the time of His coming will be near.

The Great Tribulation will start and it will be like no other time in history. We are told to flee to the mountains. Thankfully, this time of great tribulation will be cut short. When we see the heavenly phenomena take place, where the sun, moon, and stars go black, we can look up because our redemption is near. This will be some time during the second half of the 70th Week of Daniel.

How should I prepare? I have a dear friend who has asked that very question of Bible scholars. The answer varies. Jesus tells us that those who are in Judea at the time the Antichrist commits the Abomination of Desolation are to flee to the mountains. He also tells us that we will be brought before courts and that brother and sister, mother and father, and son and daughter will turn against each other.

Ultimately, the answer to this question should be a result of personal prayer. Each of us has to ask in prayer: "Lord, what would you have me to do?" Some have said that they want to be among those who will provide the warning to people and point out that the Antichrist is not who he claims to be. They want to warn against taking the mark, they want to share the Gospel, and shelter those who are being persecuted as long as they can.

Others will go to great lengths to store up provisions for a future time when they will not be able to buy or sell. There are people today who are investing large amounts of their life savings to build underground shelters and fortresses and hidden places in the wilderness. They are stockpiling huge caches of food and supplies. Some have even purchased space in renovated, old, and hardened missile silos. Many are buying arms to defend themselves. Many are taking classes in survival as to how to live off of the land.

While it may not be unwise to flee and have provision to do so, it would be unwise to stand and fight. It will be a battle that you cannot win. To stay, warn, and share truth comes with both risks and possible divine protection. To pray and to take care of your Christian loved ones is acceptable too. This is something each individual believer will have to determine. I personally believe that we should continue to be ambassadors for Christ and share in His glory in making disciples and fulfilling the Great Commission, while we still have breath, regardless of the personal cost.

The "six serving men" have helped us to be somewhat specific in determining answers to questions regarding that final week. As you have seen, we have repeated a lot of the earlier chapters' material within a number of our answers, but it serves to validate these conclusions. You can and should ask many more than these basic samplings which we have provided in the short span of this book.

PART V

KEY ELEMENTS AND SELF-EXAMINATION

9

THE DAY OF THE LORD'S WRATH

This is a key phrase within Scripture regarding the return of Christ. Up to this point, we have discussed the elements contained within the 70th Week of Daniel. There is the initial covenant between the Antichrist and Israel, often referred to as a "covenant with death". Then there are the first four seals of Revelation chapter six with the four horsemen, representing essentially the same elements contained within what Jesus refers to as the "beginning of birth pangs". This would be the rise of a world ruler, wars, famines, pestilence, and the rise in persecution. Then at the mid-point, the Antichrist breaks the covenant and commits the Abomination of Desolation in the Temple, demanding worship and a mark, paralleling the fifth seal. This begins what is referred to as the Great Tribulation, or time of Jacob's trouble.

These events all surround three individuals. They are the Antichrist, the False Prophet, and Satan (the devil cast down to earth). The Great Tribulation is an unparalleled time in all of history. During this time, one figure is prominent and bent on destruction, persecution, and death to all who will not capitulate to his demands and desires. This Antichrist demands to be exalted above all else. This time will only last for a short while. We do not know how long, but we do know what cuts it short. Enter the Day of the Lord.

The Day of the Lord is just that, His day. It is not a shared day. We are told in Revelation and Isaiah that when He comes, the earth dwellers will enter the caves and wish for the rocks to fall on them. The proud will be humbled. Isaiah 2:12 says, "For the Lord of hosts will have a day of reckoning against everyone who is proud and lofty and against everyone who is lifted up, that he may be abased." Isaiah 2:17 states, "The pride of man will be humbled and the loftiness of men will be abased; and the *Lord alone will be exalted in that day.*" [Emphasis mine.] Prior to this, the Antichrist is exalted among the earth dwellers. This is a very important point. When the Lord comes at His *parousia*, at the day of the Lord, He alone will be exalted. The tables turn. He will humble this Antichrist and his false prophet, along with those who have embraced these evil cohorts. The Day of the Lord marks the beginning of His plan to redeem the earth and His bride (the Church). Just as the *parousia*, or coming, indicates His coming and the subsequent events associated with this coming, the Day of the Lord will include His coming, wrath, redemption of the Church, and the restoration of Israel and a future kingdom.

The Day of the Lord's wrath is a specific set of events associated with His coming. We have talked about this quite a bit, but it is critical to understand the Day of the Lord's wrath as separate and distinct from the wrath of the Antichrist. The wrath of the devil through the Antichrist will only last a short time beginning at the mid-point of the 70th Week of Daniel (Revelation 12:12). This wrath is being poured out against the elect, which we have previously determined are believers. During His wrath, He is exalted. The Day of the Lord's wrath will cut short the wrath, or Great Tribulation of the Antichrist. When Christ comes, He will pour out His wrath on the ungodly, the unbelievers, and the darkness of this world. When Christ comes, He alone will be exalted.

The word for "wrath" as it is used in Revelation 12:12 relating to the devil's wrath, is *thumos* in the Greek. The word often associated with the Day of the Lord's wrath in the New Testament in places such as I Thessalonians 1:10, I Thessalonians 2:16, I Thessalonians 5:9, Revelation 6:16,17, Revelation 11:18, Revelation 16:19, and Revelation 19:15 is *orgē*.

There is an important difference between the two. *Vine's* explains: "(1) *Thumos*, wrath (not translated "anger"), is to be distinguished from *orgē*, in this respect, that *thumos* indicates a more agitated condition of the feelings, an outburst of wrath from inward indignation, while *orgē* suggests a more settled or abiding condition of mind, frequently with a view to taking revenge. *Orgē* is less sudden in its rise than *thumos*, but more lasting in its nature"[1]. In other words, the Antichrist will have an agitated condition, and his sudden outburst of anger will result in the martyrdom of the saints, whereas the wrath of the Lamb will be more lasting and takes vengeance on those who have rejected Him, as well as putting down the darkness and ungodliness of this world.

The Day of the Lord's wrath will result in the culmination of human history and vindication of His martyred saints (Revelation 6:10-17). I have often said that this world is on a collision course with its Creator. One day He will come and judge the ungodly and will abase the proud. He will rebel against evil and will dispel the darkness with His glorious light at His coming. He will reclaim and restore righteousness. He will take His place as King of kings and Lord of lords. He will come as a Lion this time, and He will pour out His wrath on the earth dwellers who have rejected Him. He will cast the Antichrist and the false prophet into the lake of fire burning with brimstone.

There is a clear difference between the object of wrath with the Antichrist and the object of wrath with the true Christ. The Antichrist will pour out his wrath on the elect and Israel for a short while. The real Christ will pour out His wrath on the unbelievers of this dark world. It is the *orgē* that believers, or the elect, are not destined to. We will experience only the *thumos* of the Antichrist.

We have contended from the beginning of this book that if you can find the Day of the Lord's wrath, you will have a better exegetical reference for the timing of the Rapture. Here is where we compare Scripture with Scripture to identify some fascinating parallels. We believe that His *parousia* is not without signs. The reason we believe this, is because of the Day of the Lord reference. Let's look at a few of these to discover what they have in common.

Look at Isaiah 13:10, "For the stars of heaven and their constellations will not flash forth their light; The sun will be dark when it rises and the moon will not shed its light." Verse one of that chapter provides the context, "Wail, for the day of the Lord is near," so we see these heavenly phenomena in the sun, moon, and stars associated with the Day of the Lord. Now, Joel 1:15 states, "Alas for the day! For the day of the Lord is near, and it will come as destruction from the Almighty." The Day of the Lord is destruction from the Almighty, not the devil. In other words, the entire 70th Week of Daniel cannot be the Day of the Lord.

Joel 2:30-31 states, "I will display wonders in the sky and on the earth, blood, fire, and columns of smoke. The sun will be turned to darkness and the moon into blood before the great and awesome day of the Lord comes." This is an important text in that it states that these heavenly phenomena in the sun, moon, and stars occur before the Day of the Lord comes. Amos 5:18, "Alas, you who are longing for the day of the Lord, for what purpose will the day of the Lord be to you? It will be darkness and not light;" The Day of the Lord is a day of darkness, which is what you would expect when the sun does not give its light. Zephaniah 1:14-15 states, "Near is the great day of the Lord, near and coming very quickly; Listen, the day of the Lord! In it the warrior cries out bitterly. 15 A day of wrath is that day, a day of trouble and distress, a day of destruction and desolation, a day of darkness and gloom, a day of clouds and thick darkness."

The sign preceding the Day of the Lord in all these Old Testament references is found in the sun, moon, and stars not giving their light. The lights go out for a moment. Now let's look at the New Testament. Matthew 24: 29-30, "But immediately after the tribulation of those days the sun will be darkened and the moon will not give its light and the stars will fall from the sky, and the powers of the heavens will be shaken. 30 And then the sign of the Son of Man will appear in the sky, and then all the tribes of the earth will mourn, and they will see the Son of Man coming on the clouds of the sky with power and great glory."

"After the tribulation of those days" is a reference to the Great Tribulation, which is cut short by this sign. It is the same sign as the Old Testament references preceding the Day of the Lord. Mark 13:24-26 states, "But in those days, after that tribulation, the sun will be darkened and the moon will not give its light, 25 and the stars will be falling from heaven, and the powers that are in the heavens will be shaken. 26 Then they will see the Son of Man coming in the clouds with great power and glory." Luke 21:25-28, "There will be signs in sun and moon and stars, and on the earth dismay among nations, in perplexity at the roaring of the sea and the waves, 26 men fainting from fear and the expectation of the things which are coming upon the world; for the powers of the heavens will be shaken. 27 Then they will see the Son of Man coming in a cloud with power and great glory. 28 But when these things begin to take place, straighten up and lift up your heads, because your redemption is drawing near."

Luke adds the element of the Rapture to this sign. Peter refers to this same sign as he quotes the book of Joel during his sermon on the day of Pentecost in Acts 2:17-20. In I Thessalonians, it is the Day of the Lord's wrath that we will not experience. Revelation 6:12, "I looked when He broke the sixth seal, and there was a great earthquake; and the sun became black as sackcloth made of hair, and the whole moon became like blood; 13 and the stars of the sky fell to the earth, as a fig tree casts its unripe figs when shaken by a great wind."

In every one of these New Testament references to the Day of the Lord, the very next verses describe His coming for His saints. We see this in Revelation chapter seven, following the sixth seal and just prior to the opening of the seventh seal in chapter eight. The opening of the seventh seal begins the Day of the Lord's wrath as the scroll is opened and the trumpet judgments and bowl judgments come. We would conclude from these verses that the Day of the Lord has a direct correlation to the Rapture of the Church at His *parousia*. The Apostle Paul tells us in I Thessalonians 5:1-3, "Now as to the times and the epochs, brethren, you have no need of anything to be written to you. 2 For you yourselves know full well that the day of the Lord will come just like a thief in the night. 3 While they are saying, "Peace and safety!" then destruction will come upon them suddenly like labor pains upon a woman with child, and they will not escape." The "*they*" are the un-expecting unbelievers. Paul goes on to discuss the believer while stating, "*but you, brethren* are not in darkness, that the day would overtake you like a thief;" II Thessalonians 2:2-3, "*that you* not be quickly shaken from your composure or be disturbed either by a spirit or a message or a letter as if from us, to the effect that the day of the Lord has come. 3 *Let no one in any way deceive*

227

you, for it will not come unless the apostasy comes first, and the man of lawlessness is revealed, the son of destruction." [Emphasis mine.]

The Day of the Lord is what cuts short the Great Tribulation of the Antichrist. The Day of the Lord is preceded by the sign in the sun, moon, and stars when the lights go out and those on the earth who are not looking forward to the appearing will hide in the caves for fear. The Day of the Lord is connected to the Rapture of the Church, and in all these instances, the language declares this to be so. In II Thessalonians chapter two, we see that the "gathering" does not take place until the apostasy and man of lawlessness is revealed in the Temple, exalting himself. This does not happen until 3 ½ years into the 70th Week of Daniel. Then the Great Tribulation starts.

On the Day of the Lord, He [Christ] alone will be exalted. The Lord Jesus Christ will descend from heaven with a shout and with the trumpet of God, and the darkness will be displaced by His Shekinah glory. Every eye will see Him. For the elect who are alive and remain and have not been martyred by the Antichrist, they will look up and be raptured. For the ungodly unbelievers, they will be subject to the wrath of God. For the 144,000 remnant and first fruits of redeemed Israel, they will be divinely sealed and protected, but will be present. The Day of the Lord will culminate in a new heaven and a new earth after the cleansing judgment, reclamation, and restoration of a thousand-year earthly kingdom and final victorious battle over Satan, who will be cast into the lake of fire where the Antichrist and false prophet were cast at the end of the battle of Armageddon. Satan is bound during the thousand-year reign of Christ, but is loosed at the end for the final showdown, where he will be defeated for the last time and cast forever into the lake of fire. The great white throne judgment will take place, and those who are not found in the Lamb's book of life will also spend eternity in the lake of fire. It is the Day of the Lord!

10

SUMMARY-ARE YOU READY?

I started this book talking about a sunny morning walk with my then nine-year old Boxer dog, Abby. Today as I write this final chapter, the sun is starting to shine, but yesterday was one of the windiest days we have ever experienced. It was a day of destruction for many, where fires broke out, trees fell on cars, telephone poles toppled, and collisions occurred due to lack of visibility caused by the dry, desert dirt whirling everywhere. No walks on that day. Some days are like that. They come with difficulty and disappointment, yet in the midst of it we can still find ways to give thanks.

My wife made it home safely from work, and we had the shelter of a home, which also provided shelter for the night for one of our daughters and granddaughter who could not make it to their home. I prayed with two friends on the phone; one who was entering a medical exam to see if her cancer treatments were conquering the disease, and the other with a friend who had lost his dad that evening. The first resulted in good news, but the other with sadness. In this life you will have tribulation, but we have the hope of Jesus Christ, and greater is He that is in us than he that is in the world.

Abby is 10-years-old now and starting to fade rapidly. I still take her for short walks, but she has a hereditary disease known as degenerative myelopathy and can only stand for a short while. About all she can handle is a ten to fifteen minute slow walk. Even while I watch my faithful four-legged companion struggle, she still gets excited and looks forward to the short walks. She has provided a life example for me that no matter what the circumstance we find ourselves in, we can have passion, hope, and joy in the midst of it.

When I come with the leash, Abby gets excited. She looks forward to it with hope. When I think about the Lord coming, I get excited. Hard decisions will face me in this upcoming year with Abby, but I will forever be thankful for the joy she has brought me. If you have a pet whom you love, you can identify with me here. We also have a little Boxer puppy now, who is just five-months old as I write this final chapter. He has learned from Abby, and experiences the same joy and anticipation of an outdoor adventure when he hears the sound of the leash being picked up. Abby taught him a lot. We named him Teddy, after a Boxer I grew up with who was there when I went to war and waited until I came home to greet me, even though he was fading himself. I get attached to my pets, and yet they are only here for a short while.

Life is short. The Bible tells us that it is like a vapor or breath. Over and over again we are reminded of how short life really is. Look at these verses: James 4:14, Job 7:7, Psalm 39:5, Psalm 78:39, Psalm 102:3, Psalm 144:4, and on and on. What is your passion? What are you looking forward to in this short life? What brings you joy in the midst of sorrow and disappointment? Whom or what are you trusting in to sustain you and fulfill your life?

My wife likes to get her hair cut from time-to-time and she goes to a young Christian lady. She has engaged her in conversation on the topic of Christ's return and the teaching I provide at seminars. This young lady's comment is not uncommon. She said something to the effect of, "He doesn't tell the scary version does he?" One of the reasons for writing this book is to provide a warning. Over and over again we are told to be alert and sober, vigilant, and not uninformed. In Matthew 24:25, Jesus said, "Behold, I have told you in advance." I do not consider this the "scary version". It is not the popular version. Yet there is but one version of truth, and "it is what it is."

Our study of eschatology in this book attempted to share all the end-times positions that are being taught, but with a particular emphasis on the cohesive, biblical truths that support and clearly demonstrate the accuracy of the pre-wrath position. I suppose that the pre-tribulation position that espouses the imminent return of Christ would be the "not-so-scary" position, in that it contends we are whisked away before this diabolical man of lawlessness comes on the scene, but this simply is not biblical. Those who find comfort in the belief that life simply goes on day-to-day until the Lord unexpectedly raptures the Church before the real trouble begins (during what they refer to as the "tribulation period") have been misled.

I, too, believed the pre-tribulation position for a long time, but after many years of searching the Scriptures, I became convinced that all the tenets of this position were not truly biblical. The Scriptures state very clearly that Christians *will* experience the first 3 ½ years and the Great Tribulation, which aligns with the pre-wrath position.

Testing Scripture against Scripture, the Bible clearly tells us that Christians will face trouble while the Antichrist rises to power and persecutes Israel and the Church. It is a reality that many do not want to face yet, in my humble opinion; I do not consider this to be the "scary" position. As I have stated before, I believe the deliverance is that much sweeter when it is a deliverance from something or someone. In this case, it will be both.

We, as believers, will be delivered (if still alive) from the trouble associated with the Antichrist during his reign of terror when the Great Tribulation is cut short. We may face very difficult circumstances and family members may even have to give their life, but there is hope. Many faithful believers have passed before us and still do every day, but they, too, have a hope. Jesus said it this way, "Do not let your heart be troubled; believe in God, believe also in Me; 2 In My Father's house are many dwelling places; if it were not so, I would have told you; for I go to prepare a place for you" (John 14:1-2). Here is the hope, "If I go and prepare a place for you, I will come again and receive you to Myself, that where I am, there you may be also" (John 14:3). Paul refers to the Rapture as our blessed hope. It is our hope for those who have fallen asleep (died) in the past, and it is our hope for those who might enter the 70th Week of Daniel. Do you have that hope? Are you looking forward to His return with expectation?

The world is on a downward spiral. The economy is toppling, and there is instability in many nations of the world. There is a spirit of lawlessness and a decline in moral and ethical values. Christians are being persecuted and even martyred in many places around the globe today. Natural disasters seem to be on the rise. More children and adults are taking mind-altering medication for depression, attention deficit disorder, bipolar disorder, and anxiety than ever before.

We are part of the "me" generation that has been convinced that life evolves around one's self, and that whatever makes one "feel good" is okay. It is no wonder that a "feel good" theology has become necessary to accommodate such mindsets. It is contrary to what the Bible teaches, which is a Christ centered life. The institution of marriage between a man and a woman has come under assault. Divorce is nearly as common among Christians as it is with unbelievers. Marriage itself is being viewed as irrelevant for many who choose to live in sin. School and workplace shootings are in the news every month. There is the threat of nuclear war once again. I believe that we are facing an unparalleled time in world history. I believe that we may see the emergence of the man of lawlessness within a short time. II Timothy 3:12, "Indeed, all who desire to live godly in Christ Jesus will be persecuted". Are you experiencing persecution today? Will you be ready for it and, more importantly, for what is to come with the return of Christ?

There are a lot of programs on television showing people building elaborate bunkers and fortresses. They are stockpiling food, water, weapons, and ammunition. Some do it because of the economy, some do it because of fear of war, some do it because of forecasts of food shortages, and some do it because of solar flare potentials, natural disaster scenarios, and on and on. I suppose there are some doing it in anticipation of the rise of the Antichrist. Whatever their motives, without Christ, there is no hope.

You can buy all the gold and silver you want. You can build up your stock portfolio or work till you drop, saving for a "secure" retirement. You can run on a treadmill for hours a day, ride your bicycle, pump iron, take every vitamin known to man, and you still are going to die one day, unless you are among the true believers at the Rapture when it occurs. Even then, your mortal body will be changed, becoming immortal in the twinkling of an eye.

If you are a young person, you probably do not want to hear this. After all, you have your whole life ahead of you. There is college, a long awaited career, marriage, and children. Jesus said that if you are the generation present when the Antichrist commits the Abomination of Desolation that you better flee to the mountains. He said you better hope you are not a nursing mother. This may sound harsh, but His point is that when the real difficulty comes, the believer will have to flee or face possible martyrdom. Fleeing with a baby is difficult. I am not saying that you should not have children or plan for college or careers, but make sure that as you do, Christ is at the center of your life.

You can expect mockers to come saying, "Where is the promise of His coming?" (II Peter 3:4). When the difficult times come we are told "they will not endure sound doctrine; but wanting to have their ears tickled, they will accumulate for themselves teachers in accordance to their own desires" (II Timothy 4:3). Where are you? Are you ready? Will you listen to sound doctrine?

Here are the most important questions. Let me repeat myself. Here are *the most* important questions. Are you trusting in Jesus Christ alone for your salvation? Have you placed your absolute trust in Him alone? Are you sure without a shadow of a doubt that when you die you are going to heaven? Are you living for Jesus Christ and desiring to glorify Him with your life—empowered by the Holy Spirit residing within you? If you said no to any of these questions, you need to pray that the Lord will open your mind and heart to His message of salvation.

If you are reading this book and have the television on or a distraction in the background, move to a quiet place. The writings of this book and the author of this book cannot save you. Only the Lord can save you. Only He can cause you to be one of His elect. I can only plant a seed and pray for you. John 3:35-36, "The Father loves the Son and has given all things into His hand. 36 He who believes in the Son has eternal life; but he who does not obey the Son will not see life, but the wrath of God abides on him." You can know that you have eternal life. You can know that when He comes, He will deliver you from the wrath to come. I John 5:12-13, "He who has the Son has the life; he who does not have the Son of God does not have the life. 13 These things I have written to you who believe in the name of the Son of God, so that you may know that you have eternal life." Do you have the Son?

There are a number of those whom we might refer to as "good people" in this world, based on some subjective standard we might evaluate as being "good". On the other hand, God said that there is not one righteous or good person (Romans 3:10). All have sinned (Romans 3:23). Even one sin (missing the mark) could condemn us to hell for eternity (James 2:10). What is God's standard? Jesus said you must be perfect (Matthew 5:48). We would all agree that none of us is perfect. Would you agree that you have probably sinned at least once? The Bible tells us that what we deserve (our wages) for sin is death (Romans 6:23). This is eternal separation from God.

Think of your life. Have you ever told a lie? Have you ever taken anything that did not belong to you? Have you ever lusted after someone? Have you ever had a bad thought? Have you ever felt hatred toward someone? Have you ever used the Lord's name in vain? Have you ever disobeyed civil law? Do you exceed the speed limit? If you said yes to any of these questions, you are a sinner and deserve eternal separation from God. I am without a doubt a sinner. How about you? Romans 6:23 "For the wages of sin is death, but the free gift of God is eternal life in Christ Jesus our Lord." Eternal life is a free gift. Hard as that may be to comprehend, it is a free gift to us, but cost the Father His Son, and in that case, the cost was immeasurable. To not accept the Son would be to dishonor the Father, and as a result, He will not allow you into His heaven.

You might be tempted to say, "Well, even still, I *am* a pretty good person." God does not grade on a curve. One sin is too much, and you have already established that you are a sinner. It is not our good works that save us. Paul said it this way in Titus 3:5-7, "He saved us, not on the basis of deeds which we have done in righteousness, but according to His mercy, by the washing of regeneration and renewing by the Holy Spirit, 6 whom He poured out upon us richly through Jesus Christ our Savior, 7 so that being justified by His grace we would be made heirs according to the hope of eternal life." Ephesians 2:8-9, "For by grace you have been saved through faith; and that not of yourselves, it is the gift of God; 9 not as a result of works, so that no one may boast."

God must and will punish sin. Will you be found at the judgment seat of Christ where only your works are judged, and you, as a believer, are not, or will you be one of the unbelievers found at the Great White Throne where both you and your works will be judged? Will you enter the clouds with the Lord in the air with all the saints, or will you stand before the throne one day only to have a righteous God show you that your name is not written in the Lamb's book of life?

God loves you and has made a provision for your sin. He poured out His wrath on His Son in order that you might be saved. You must receive Jesus Christ alone for your salvation. You must receive the free gift of His grace in order to be saved. You must believe. Romans 10:9-10, "that if you confess with your mouth Jesus as Lord, and believe in your heart that God raised Him from the dead, you will be saved; 10 for with the heart a person believes, resulting in righteousness, and with the mouth he confesses, resulting in salvation." Do not think that a mere belief in God will save you (James 2:19).

Trusting involves a full reliance. In other words, true faith will result in the realization that apart from Christ, you can do nothing. Saving faith places Him at the center of your life, and subsequently everything you do revolves around Him. You will *hunger* to know Him and make Him known to others. Saving faith is not a casual Christian experience. It is dynamic. Your priorities in life will change, and you will have the Holy Spirit within you to guide, direct, teach, and empower you to live a fruitful life. You will work for *Him* at your occupation—not for the boss—and yet you will be rewarded because Christ will bless your obedience. You will change. A person, who becomes a believer by faith, changes (Galatians 2:20). Nothing will bring you more joy than serving Him. You will desire the company and fellowship of other believers. Your life will have evidence of the fruit of the spirit (Galatians 5:22). You will long for and desire to see His glory in everything and so look forward to His appearing. You will recognize that He is our blessed hope.

You cannot do this on your own. Jesus Christ is the only way to eternal life. There is no other way. In that same passage where Jesus spoke of the many dwelling places and His promise to return for His own, He said, "I am the way, and the truth, and the life; no one comes to the Father but through Me" (John 14:6). Acts 4:12 puts it this way, "And there is salvation in no one else, for there is no other name under heaven that has been given among men by which we must be saved."

235

Have you received Jesus Christ as your Lord and Savior? He must be your Lord as well as your Savior. The Lordship of Jesus Christ in your life means that He is in control, not you. You must confess your sins, ask His forgiveness, and turn from them. He alone can help you do that. If you feel the Lord is speaking to your heart at this moment, I would encourage you to stop and pray. Ask the Lord Jesus Christ to forgive you of your sins and to come into your life and make you new. The Bible says we become a new creation in Christ. Pray that prayer in faith and tell Him you cannot do it on your own—that you need Him and will place your trust in Him as your Lord and Savior. If you prayed that prayer and accepted Christ, then you will need to grow and be in the company of other believers who will encourage you in your walk of faith (Hebrews 10:23-25).

Perhaps you have read this book out of interest for the subject and have been a believer for many years, but you have not been walking with Him as you should. Maybe you have backslidden to a place where you wonder if there is any hope for you. Some have made you feel that you just do not belong to the Church anymore, and you feel you have gone too far. Nothing could be farther from the truth. Only God knows the heart. The Bible tells us it is desperately wicked, so you will sin from time-to-time while you occupy this mortal body. It should not dominate your life, however, and if it is, then you need to examine yourself to see if you are truly saved.

Paul talks about his struggle in Romans seven. In Romans 8:16 it says, "The Spirit Himself testifies with our spirit that we are children of God." One of the ways that takes place in the believer's life is in the area of conviction of sin. If you are a believer, you will feel all the weight and heaviness that comes from a disobedient life. We will all sin at one time or another. I John 1:8-10, "If we say that we have no sin, we are deceiving ourselves and the truth is not in us. 9 If we confess our sins, He is faithful and righteous to forgive us our sins and to cleanse us from all unrighteousness. 10 If we say that we have not sinned, we make Him a liar and His word is not in us." Confess your sin and He will forgive and restore you. I do not believe that a true believer can lose their salvation. Too many verses in the Bible state otherwise. Here are some you can look up: Ephesians 1:13-14; Romans 8:38-39; John 10:27-30; Philippians 1:6.

In summary, we believe that the Church will experience the wrath of the Antichrist during the 70th Week of Daniel, but that it will be cut short by the *parousia* of Christ. The Day of the Lord will begin with the Rapture and then the pouring out of His wrath on the ungodly who remain.

My prayer is that you have pondered what has been presented in this book. Ample Scripture has been provided to emphasize that these truths about the end-times are not just the opinion of man. Ultimately, it is up to you as a believer to study the Word of God and arrive at truth. Most importantly, you must first receive Jesus Christ as your personal Lord and Savior, regardless of your view on the timing of His return. Without Him, you will be subject to His wrath.

There is no need to fear the 70th Week of Daniel. If we are the generation to experience it, we should rejoice and be glad. We may suffer for a while, but it will result in our redemption. As good as this world can be at its very best, it will be nothing compared to the glory to come. We should all long for the appearing of our great God and Savior. While we wait, we must be busy doing His work, striving to be found blameless and remaining faithful—separated, as light and salt.

It is a time for Christians to suit up in the Armor of God and be bold for His name. We need to pray for one another, and we need to pray for Israel. Pray for the persecuted Church, love one another, and show mercy and grace to a fallen world. Bring glory to His name.

Are you ready? These are the last words. You have been warned!

May our Lord and Savior Jesus Christ richly bless you and comfort you in the days and years ahead as you look forward to His coming.

ENDNOTES

Part I: *Setting the Foundation*

Chapter 1 What is eschatology?

[1]Chafer, Lewis Sperry D.D., Litt. D., TH.D. (1980). *Chafer Systematic Theology* (Vol. IV). Dallas, TX: Dallas Seminary Press/ Zondervan.

[2]Rosenthal, Marvin. (1990). *The Pre-Wrath Rapture of the Church*. Nashville, TN: Thomas Nelson Publishers.

[3]*ThePreWrathChart*.com (2008). *Home Page*. Author Allen Hadidian. Used by permission, July 2013.

[4]Rosenthal, Marvin. (1990). *The Pre-Wrath Rapture of the Church*. Nashville, TN: Thomas Nelson Publishers.

Chapter 3 What is systematic theology?

[1]Spencer, Herbert. (1867). *First Principles* (second edition ed.). London: Williams and Norgate.

Part II: *The Plumb Line*

Chapter 4 How do I study God's Word?

[1]ETPS. (2013). *Home Page*. Retrieved March 29, 2013, from The Empire Test Pilots' School: www.ETPS.qinetiq.com

[2]Kipling, Rudyard. (2007). *The Elephant's Child*. London, United Kingdom: Francis Lincoln Limited.

[3]Scofield, C. I. (1909; second edition 1917). *The Scofield Referene Bible*. New York: Oxford University Press.

[4]Newton, Benjamin Wills. (1879). *The Prophecy of the Lord Jesus, as contained in Matthew XXIV and XXV* (third ed.). London: Houlston and Sons.

Part III: *Further Influences on Eschatology*

Chapter 5 What are Biblical Covenants?

[1]Calvin, John. (1559). *Institutes of the Christian Religion*. Geneva: Robert Estienne.

[2]Rubin, Jennifer. (2012, April 16). Washington Post. *P5-Plus-1 Talks with Iran are a Dangerous Charade* , p. 1.

[3]Ibid

Chapter 6 What are Dispensations?

[1]Chafer, Lewis Sperry D.D., Litt.. D., TH.D. (1980). *Chafer Systematic Theology–Biological Sketch and Indexes* (Vol. eight), p. 11, 3.b.

[2]Ibid

[3]Unger, Merrill F. (1980). *Unger's Bible Dictionary*. Chicago: The Moody Bible Institute of Chicago, Thirty-first Printing, p. 356.

Chapter 7 What are the Feasts of Leviticus 23

[1]Edersheim, Alfred. (1984). *Bible History Old Testament, Volume ii* (Vol. ii). Grand Rapids: William B. Erdmans Publishing Company. p. 138-139.

[2]Wilson, William. (1982). *Wilson's Old Testament Word Studies*. McLEAN: MAC DONALD PUBLISHING CO. p. 303-304.

[3]Houghton Miffin Company. (2000). *The American Heritage Dictionary of the English Language Fourth Edition* (Fourth ed.). Boston: Houghton Miffin Company.

Part IV: *Critical Answers and Discovery*

Chapter 8 The "Who, What, When, Where, Why, and How?" of the Rapture

[1]Kipling, Rudyard. (2007). *The Elephant's Child*. London, United Kingdom: Francis Lincoln Limited.

[2]Ibid

Section 1 Who?

[1]Vine, M. A., W. E. (1989). *Vine's Expository Dictionary of New Testament Words–Unabridged Edition* (Unabridged ed.). MC LEAN: MAC DONALD PUBLISHING COMPANY. p. 361.

[2]Ibid

[3]Morris, Henry M. (1983). *The Revelation Record*. Wheaton: Tyndale House Publishers, Inc. and Creation-Life Publishers. p. 88.

[4]Walvoord, John F. (1977, July). Postribulationalsim Today Part XI: The Rapture in Relation to Endtime Events. *Bibliotheca Sacra 134:535* , p. 210.

[5]Vine, M. A., W. E. (1989). *Vine's Expository Dictionary of New Testament Words–Unabridged Edition* (Unabridged ed.). MC LEAN: MAC DONALD PUBLISHING COMPANY. p. 972.

Section 2 What?

[1]Scofield, C. I. (1909; second edition 1917). *The Scofield Referene Bible*. New York: Oxford University Press.

[2]Harrison, Norman. (1941). *The End: Rethinking the Revelation*. Minneapolis: Harrison Service.

[3]Rosenthal, Marvin. (1990). *The Pre-Wrath Rapture of the Church*. Nashville, TN: Thomas Nelson Publishers.

[4]Ibid, xiv

[5]Van Kampen, Robert. (1992). *The Sign*. Wheaton: Crossway Books, a division of Good News Publishers.

[6]Van Kampen, Robert. (1997). *The Rapture Question Answered Plain & Simple*. Grand Rapids: Fleming H. Revell a division of Baker Book House Company.

[7]Newton, Benjamin Wills. (1879). *The Prophecy of the Lord Jesus, as contained in Matthew XXIV and XXV* (third ed.). London: Houlston and Sons.

[8]Ibid (Newton)

[9]Anderson, Sir Robert. (1984). *The Coming Prince* (Vol. 10th edition). Grand Rapids, MI: Kregel Publications.

[10]Cooper, Charles. (2008). *God's Elect and the Great Tribulation, An Interpretration of Matthew 24:1-31 and Daniel*. Bellefonte, PA: Strong Tower Publishing.

[11]Young, LLD, Robert. (1980). *Young's Analytical Concordance to the Bible*. Grand Rapids: William B. Eerdmans Publishing Company. p. 6.

[12]Wilson, William. (1982). *Wilson's Old Testament Word Studies*. McLEAN: MAC DONALD PUBLISHING CO. p. 3.

[13]Wilson, William. (1982). *Wilson's Old Testament Word Studies*. McLEAN: MAC DONALD PUBLISHING CO. p. 118.

[14]Vine, M. A., W. E. (1989). *Vine's Expository Dictionary of New Testament Words–Unabridged Edition* (Unabridged ed.). MC LEAN: MAC DONALD PUBLISHING COMPANY. p. 16.

[15]Young, LLD, Robert. (1980). *Young's Analytical Concordance to the Bible*. Grand Rapids: William B. Eerdmans Publishing Company. p. 249.

[16]Vine, M. A., W. E. (1989). *Vine's Expository Dictionary of New Testament Words–Unabridged Edition* (Unabridged ed.). MC LEAN: MAC DONALD PUBLISHING COMPANY. p. 302.

[17]Vine, M. A., W. E. (1989). *Vine's Expository Dictionary of New Testament Words–Unabridged Edition* (Unabridged ed.). MC LEAN: MAC DONALD PUBLISHING COMPANY. p. 41.

[18]Vine, M. A., W. E. (1989). *Vine's Expository Dictionary of New Testament Words–Unabridged Edition* (Unabridged ed.). MC LEAN: MAC DONALD PUBLISHING COMPANY. p. 210.

Section 3 When?

[1]Vine, M. A., W. E. (1989). *Vine's Expository Dictionary of New Testament Words–Unabridged Edition* (Unabridged ed.). MC LEAN: MAC DONALD PUBLISHING COMPANY. p. 413.

Section 5 Why?

[1]Cooper, Charles. (2012). *Revelation 3:10 A Bombshell*. Winter Garden: PreWrath Resource Institute.

[2]Cooper Dr., David L. (1943). *What Men Must Believe*. Los Angeles: Biblical Research Society. P. 63.

Section 6 How?

[1]Vine, M. A., W. E. (1989). *Vine's Expository Dictionary of New Testament Words–Unabridged Edition* (Unabridged ed.). MC LEAN: MAC DONALD PUBLISHING COMPANY. p. 572.

Part V: *Key Elements and Self-Examination*

Chapter 9 The Day of the Lord's Wrath

[1]Vine, M. A., W. E. (1989). *Vine's Expository Dictionary of New Testament Words–Unabridged Edition* (Unabridged ed.). MC LEAN: MAC DONALD PUBLISHING COMPANY. p. 57-58.

ABOUT THE AUTHOR

R obert L. ("Larry") Pratt is a sinner saved by grace who has a passion for God's Word. He coordinates, teaches, and hosts Bible Seminars for Berean Seminar Ministries. He is one of very few individuals to receive the AWANA® Citation award and complete a dedicated four-year Alpha Kappa Chi Bible course offered by AWANA® youth ministries as an adult.

Larry has taken numerous courses in hermeneutics, and has studied eschatology for over 22 years. He is absolutely passionate about this subject, and has obtained extensive knowledge by completing online short courses, intensive self-study, and extension courses offered at churches he has attended.

Larry's passion and gifts are in the areas of teaching and evangelism. He has served as a volunteer chaplain at two prisons in California, where he ministered with music outreach and Bible lessons. He has served as an AWANA® Commander, lay worship team leader, and musician with a Christian rock band. He has also participated in short-term, overseas mission ministries.

Larry, who is an Eagle Scout, Vietnam Combat Infantry Veteran, and private pilot, recently retired from a very successful career spanning over 26 years with the United States Air Force as both contractor and civilian, where his final position was Director of Operations/ Range Operations Officer with the 412th Range Squadron at Edwards Air Force Test Center in Edwards, California. In this profession, Larry spent many years in the field of Research Development, Test and Evaluation (RDT&E) acquiring a skill set for detailed analysis.

He and his wife, Cindy, host a weekly home Bible study and attend a church in Lancaster, California. They have been blessed with six, grown children and twelve grandchildren.

Larry and Abby

CPSIA information can be obtained at www.ICGtesting.com
Printed in the USA
BVOW09s2003200214

345555BV00001B/93/P